Becoming a Successful
Urban Teacher

Becoming a Successful Urban Teacher

DAVE F. BROWN

Foreword by Eugene Garcia

NMSA

HEINEMANN
Portsmouth, NH

Heinemann
A division of Reed Elsevier Inc.
361 Hanover Street
Portsmouth, NH 03801–3912
www.heinemann.com

National Middle School Association
4151 Executive Parkway
Suite 300
Westerville, OH 43081
www.nmsa.org

Offices and agents throughout the world

Library of Congress Cataloging-in-Publication Data
Brown, Dave F.
Becoming a successful urban teacher / Dave F. Brown.
p. cm.
Includes bibliographical references and index.
ISBN 0-325-00361-0 (alk. paper)
1. Teachers—United States. 2. Education, Urban—United States. 3. Effective teaching.
I. Title.

LB1775.2 .B76 2002
371.1′00973—dc21

2001051721

Editor: Lois Bridges
Production editor: Sonja S. Chapman
Cover design: Jenny Jensen Greenleaf
Manufacturing: Steve Bernier
Typesetter: House of Equations, Inc.

Printed in the United States of America on acid-free paper

08 07 06 05   VP   4 5 6

To Dana,
For sharing the most precious
things in life with me

Contents

Contents

Contents

Foreword

As urban teachers look at the students in their classrooms today, they see a scenario much different from the classrooms of their own childhood. The physical, instructional and curricular resources allocated to this important social enterprise falls seriously short of the need. The schooling experience of their students' parents varies greatly with many of them not having completed a high school education. Yet, all of these same parents have the highest expectations for their children—they want their children to attain the social and economic stability that they often lack. Moreover, one in three of these urban children nationwide is from an ethnic or racial minority group, one in seven speaks a language other than English at home, and one in thirteen was born outside the U.S. In this context of challenges, schools and the educational professionals who inhabit them often spend their time classifying and separating/segregating students as if these students were invisible and became visible only after they are classified as limited English proficient, poor (free lunch/Title I), low performing, immigrant, etc. etc. These urban circumstances generate a remarkably new and expanded set of challenges for teachers who choose to serve these school populations. A recent email from an urban high school teacher says it best:

> Hi . . .
>   Here's the report from the Western Front. Please pass it around.
>   What I initially perceived to be innovative use of year-round scheduling seems to be more mechanization run amok. Although they apparently were able to split the kids into three separate tracks with different vacations with little or no problem, the track system has virtually NO academic benefit,

at least the way it operates here. There are about 600 9th and 10th graders per track and about 200 11th and 12th graders per track. Look at the dropout rate (near 50 percent if not more). And the school just received a 3 year accreditation rather than a 7 year so things are pretty bad.

In short, this school and school district are nightmares.

Reading and writing levels are grotesque. I have only four students who are operating above grade level. That's out of 150 on the rolls.

Teacher support is nil. I still don't have a stapler or even file folders for portfolio writing assessment. The trash is emptied maybe once a week. The floors are filthier than some bars I've been in, and the bathrooms and stairwells stink. There is one computer lab for math, four or five computers in the library and that's about it. The textbooks left for me to use were 1980 copyright 10th-grade lit books, and there were only enough for a classroom set. And, of course, all except one of the short stories was about teenage white (male) characters, and these kids Just Don't Relate to that. Plus, despite this being a major ESL school, no supplementary resources "enrichment" materials exist that I can find that contain black or brown or multi-national short stories or poems.

I have 21 students with perfect attendance and no discipline problems. Half of them turn in work that is perhaps 4th or 5th grade level; the others don't turn in anything at all. I asked other teachers what to do about grades. Well, if they make it every day, pass them with a D even if they don't do anything.

I asked the Union Steward if all the schools in the district were as screwed up as this one. He said that he has taught only here but that he hears it is the same way but the sad thing is that it doesn't have to be that way. Indeed. The English teachers here are cold, intelligent, and superb. But they all tell me to forget everything I know and just do the best you can with what tools you have and forget how it could be. The faculty has rich experience, but I have never seen so many good ideas from attendance to technology disappear into such a black hole.

These kids are sweet. What lives they have led. Its too bad this system here just processes them through.

It is for these reasons that this volume by Dave Brown is so significant. He particularly focuses on the most critical individual that can make a difference in these challenging education contexts. Like others before him that have addressed these set of challenges—Jonathan Kozol, Mike Rose, Jeannie Oakes, Gloria Ladson Billings—

the voices and practices of deeply committed and highly successful teachers are the focus.

Dave Brown's contribution equals those of these esteemed colleagues in a refreshing yet informative voice of his own. He is remarkable in addressing seeming insurmountable barriers that urban teachers face, and gives us a realistic but refreshing view of how one can serve a cohort of students that too often are desperately under served.

Students from linguistically, culturally, socially, economically, and religiously diverse families that populate our urban schools are often defined by the characteristics they share—a lack of educational achievement. But such a definition masks their diversity, and underestimates the challenge facing these schools. Schools serve students who are new immigrants, ignorant of American life beyond what they have seen in movies, as well as African Americans, Mexican Americans, Asian Americans, Native Americans, and European American students whose families have lived here for generations. Students representing dozens of native languages may attend a single school; in some school districts students speak more than 20 languages. These schools more than others face a mobility problem; student turnover is high and the ethnic/linguistic mix can shift radically from year to year.

Yet, these students will change American society. Our society is not the same as it was a century ago, or even a decade ago. The impact of a teacher on the life of young people can hardly be overestimated. For children who lack the educational capital in their homes and communities, education has a tremendous impact; schools are their critical links to society. Without the caring guidance and skills of their teachers, these youth of today will have great difficulty becoming positive contributors to *all* of our social and economic well being.

This volume touches many aspects of how successful urban teachers are meeting these challenges in the educational reform movement of today. There are no easy answers, but this volume provides the in-depth analysis and paints a portrait of the possible. It serves as a forum for dialogue that incorporates teachers' voices so necessary if the expectation of educational success for *all* students is to become a reality.

—Eugene E. Garcia, Ph.D.
University of California, Berkeley

Acknowledgments

I have much to learn about urban education, but I have been adding to my knowledge for the past few years thanks to several people. My personal and professional conversations during my monthly lunch with Anita Nicholson were the impetus for beginning this writing project. She is the ultimate professional educator who has touched the lives of young adolescents in Philadelphia for many years. It is an honor to know Anita and watch her practice the craft of effective teaching. I'd also like to extend my gratitude to the other teachers at Tilden Middle School who are always warm and welcoming when I visit.

The most important words in this book are direct quotes from the thirteen teachers I interviewed from throughout the United States. All of these teachers provided me with an education about how they create effective learning environments for the children and adolescents who attend urban schools. These teachers extended my knowledge of urban education a hundredfold. I cannot thank them enough for sharing their stories and educating me and all those who read this book. Thank you all: Anita, Shanika, Pete, and Colette from Philadelphia; Jackie, formerly from New York City and now Philadelphia; Kathleen and Polly from Chicago; Tim from Minneapolis; Jeff from Wichita; Diane D. and Diane G. (Susan) from San Francisco; and Lisa and Adrienne from Los Angeles. You are all heroes whether you believe it or not!

I would like to thank the teachers, parents, administrators, and students at Upper Darby High School and Bywood Elementary School for their assistance in helping me to complete the book.

Acknowledgments

When I decided to write this book, I knew which editor with whom I wanted to work—Lois Bridges. Every piece of writing bares a part of one's soul, and that can be frightening. Sharing my writing with Lois does not create fear, but instead confidence. Lois is a believer in people, and her positive actions speak even louder than her kind words. Thank you, Lois, for believing in me again and making others believe in me, too!

I enjoy the conversations about diversity with my office mate, Gail Bollin, who has a powerful spirit inside of her watching out for urban children! I am privileged to call Dan Darigan a colleague and personal friend. Dan's energy and enthusiasm for life are unmatched. Our conversations about this profession, the field of literacy, and our role in public education are encouraging and candid with a little bit of humor thrown in for our own sanity. Thanks for sharing the laughter, Dan! It is a pleasure working with Sonja Chapman, the production editor for Heinemann. I thank her for her patience and professionalism.

I always recommend to my education students at the university that, if they choose to marry some day, they marry an educator. I followed my own advice when I met Dana. I have many reasons to thank Dana for her support and encouragement in writing this book. My words aren't going to do justice to how she has helped me; but I'll try. I thank her immensely for putting in hours transcribing tapes, reading text, and providing me with valuable feedback on the book. I sincerely thank Dana for sharing what she knows as she teaches urban students each day. She has taught me much about the education profession as she interacts so confidently and with expertise as a teacher. I am truly fortunate to call Dana a colleague and my wife.

Introduction

The Difference between Surviving and Teaching

Room 253—Jackson Middle School in Philadelphia

It's October 15th in this urban eighth-grade classroom where students are supposed to be learning mathematics. Students who are expected to be in this classroom are scattered around the room—many standing, most talking loudly, and some still running in the hallway. The teacher, Ms. Walters, looks at the clock on the wall and notes that it is 8:25, five minutes past the time that the bell rang to begin this first period of the day. She folds her arms, saunters over to a group of four boys, looks one of them in the eye and says disgustedly in an angry voice, "I think it's time for you all to *sit down*." Two of the boys completely ignore her and continue talking. One of the other two smiles and sarcastically says, "Okay, whatever you want, Ms. Walters." He sits at his desk while the other three boys ignore her request and continue talking to each other. She steps toward the other three and speaks more loudly this time, "I said, 'Sit down!'" They respond by sitting in their desks. As Ms. Walters turns around to speak to other students, one of the four boys says under his breath, "Bitch," and the other three laugh loudly.

Ms. Walters walks to the other side of the room to get the attention of three female students who are having a loud and heated debate. She touches one of them on the arm, and, before she can say anything, the student, Ariel, forcefully pulls her arm away, swings around and stares at her. Ms. Walters recoils fearfully while saying, "I'm sorry, but it's time to begin class." Ariel's response is, "Yeah, so what?"

The look on Ms. Walters face implies she wants to say something, but after repeated head-to-head battles with these three female students, she merely walks away knowing that she can't win this battle either.

As Ms. Walters heads to the front of the room she screams loudly, "Everyone, sit down now! And I mean *now*!" Most students scramble to their desks, two boys run out of the room, and two girls continue their conversation quietly while standing at their desks. Ms. Walters knows the two boys who left are her students, but these two have been uncooperative all fall, and she decides that class will be a little easier to run without them. As she reaches to her desk to get her book and begin class, she can see that maybe seven of the thirty students are prepared for class.

Ms. Walters asks students to get out their homework, exchange papers so that they can grade each other's assignments, and listen for the answers. She allows two minutes for this to happen, but only ten students have their homework. Of the other twenty students, five have failed to bring in a mathematics book, twelve haven't even attempted to do the assignment, and three are inattentive due to their talking to other classmates. Ms. Walters attempts to get through the fifteen problems assigned for homework, but is interrupted at least every six minutes to stop disruptive behavior—including excessive talking, a near fight that breaks out between two boys, a girl who drops her mathematics book out the window, and two girls whom she sends out into the hall for what she describes as "insubordination" when they refuse to open their books. Each of the five periods of mathematics that Ms. Walters teaches is almost an exact replica of this scene from first period.

I witnessed these events recently in an urban school. You might imagine that this is what teaching in an urban school is like:

- uncooperative and threatening students
- demonstrations of students' disrespect for teachers
- students who appear uncaring about learning or academic effort
- an inability by teachers to gain students' cooperation

By the end of the day, I imagine Ms. Walters is utterly exhausted—the kind of exhaustion one feels after moving furniture all day. I know because I felt this frustration and emotional pain in some of my early teaching experiences. I suspect Ms. Walters goes home feeling angry and with a volatile personality. I can picture her walking in the door to her apartment at the end of the school day, slamming the door behind her, throwing her book bag across the floor, sitting on the sofa, placing her hands over her eyes, and crying. Imagine this: there are 135 more days of school left until the year ends! Chances are she won't make it that long. Many teachers who take urban school teaching jobs don't last through the first year, much less for three or more years. Because beginning teachers are given the most challenging assignments, many quit after the first year. Ladson-Billings (2001) reported that the Chicago schools hire one thousand to fifteen hundred new teachers a year while in Los Angeles the number is approximately five thousand new teachers a year.

Urban teachers don't need to experience the frustration that Ms. Walters does each day. Your professional life doesn't have to be like this scenario. There are ways to prevent this frustration, ways to alleviate the fear teachers sometimes feel those first few days and weeks of teaching, and ways to succeed in an urban school.

Room 104—Wayne High School in Philadelphia

It's October 15th in a tenth-grade English class of thirty-three students at this urban school. Only eighteen students are attending class today. The others are missing for some reasons that are valid and many that aren't. Some of the students in this particular class have a reputation for chasing teachers out of the profession. Last year as ninth graders, several of these students created enough havoc to cause two teachers to resign before January. The third teacher hired lasted through the remainder of the year, but at the end of June filed for a voluntary transfer to a school in a different part of Philadelphia.

As this group of students walks in the door of their classroom, their teacher, Ms. Simon, greets each one at the door with a handshake or a high five, and a hug for a couple of the female students. Two boys are running in the hall by her door when she stands in the middle of the hall and stops them. One of the boys, Michael, is six feet two and weighs 200 pounds; a stark contrast to Ms. Simon who is five feet four inches tall at best. It would be easy to be intimidated by Michael's stature. She looks each student in the eye, and they both look down quickly. Ms. Simon asks calmly, "Is there a good reason that you are both running?" Michael answers hurriedly, "We've got to get to the music room before our first period class begins at 8:35!" Ms. Simon replies, "What's in the music room that's so important?" Shaheed adds, "We just wanted to see if we passed the first grading period since Mr. Krebs has posted our grades." Ms. Simon smiles and says sarcastically, "Are you taking bets on whether you passed because I think I could make some money here?" Shaheed and Michael look at each other with expressions of disbelief; then look at Ms. Simon's smile and begin to laugh. "He'll never pass," Shaheed says, jabbing Michael. "You know I'm kidding," Ms. Simon responds with a laugh, "But seriously, you two are like linebackers running through these halls! Somebody's going to get knocked over if you don't slow down. Can you help me out here?" Shaheed answers her, "Sorry, Ms. Simon." "I guess we weren't thinking," adds Michael. "Thank you for considering others. Now walk the rest of the way, please." Ms. Simon smiles at them as she says this, and they smile back and continue down the hall. She calls after them loudly, "Let me know what happens with your grades."

Just as Ms. Simon steps back into the classroom door, the bell rings. All but two of the eighteen students are in their desks with their independent reading books open, and they are reading. Two female students still standing are looking frantically through their book bags for their trade books. They try to stand in the back of the room when they hear the bell ring so Ms. Simon can't see them. As Ms. Simon scans the room, she notices the two students. She walks toward the back of the room and stands next to Shana and Maria, "Did you forget something?" Maria replies first, "I think I left my book at home." What's the policy for not being prepared for class?" Ms. Simon asks. "We have to come see you after school and read for the time that we missed reading in class," Shana quietly answers. Ms. Simon looks out the window and responds in a calm voice, "I'll give you both two minutes to find your books. If you can't find them by then, I expect to see you after school—understand?" "Yes," they both reply.

As Ms. Simon returns to the front of the room, Tonika is standing at the front taking attendance and marking it on the form that she will take to the office. Ben is collecting note cards from students who were assigned to respond to their reading assignment by Ms. Simon. At precisely 8:45, students move their desks together and begin working in pairs to talk about the pages from the novel, *Of Mice and Men* (Steinbeck 1937) they read for homework. Ms. Simon has said nothing to the whole group but instead is working with three boys who have had difficulty reading the material she assigned. She's pretty sure these students are reading at the fourth- or fifth-grade level, despite being in tenth grade.

After ten minutes of students working in pairs, one of the students walks up to Ms. Simon and taps her on the shoulder to remind her that it's time for a whole group discussion. She stands and announces that students are to continue working in pairs to write a scenario with a different ending from the one that they read in the book.

Students begin working but the noise level quickly rises to an uncomfortable chaos. Ms. Simon walks around the room, places her hands on the shoulders of two especially loud students, and says quietly, "Please remember our rule about considering others' needs for learning." They immediately quiet down. One pair of students, Emanuel and Tony, begin arguing. Ms. Simon walks over and asks the two to go into the hall and find an agreeable solution to their dispute in three minutes. If they can't return in three minutes or less, they know they are responsible for meeting after school with Ms. Simon to explain why they felt it necessary to disrupt learning time.

Ms. Simon makes it a point to meet individually with students frequently during each period to discuss their lives outside of school. Students often come in to ask her if they can talk to her about personal problems or just sit in her room to work during their study halls. She's polite to students, and they respond similarly to her. Ms. Simon's class wasn't quite this calm the first few weeks of school, but it remains this way throughout the year with students becoming more and more responsible for their behaviors each week. Ms. Simon's assertive stance on classroom behavior establishes a business atmosphere in her class-room—students know what's expected of them and realize there are consequences for inappropriate behavior.

Although Ms. Simon's classroom atmosphere sounds almost mythi-cal and impossible, it is real. I witnessed these events. There are high school, middle school, and elementary classrooms in urban schools all across America where teachers have created an atmosphere of trust, mutual respect, and a productive learning environment. These are places where students show that they care about the teacher, about their classmates, and about themselves. In these classrooms, school is a place where the serious business of learning occurs everyday.

How can that happen for you? How can you gain the mutual re-spect of students who experience lives that are often fearful, disheart-ening, or poverty stricken. That's what this book is about. It's about finding a comfortable niche in an urban school and creating a profes-sional environment where you look forward to the challenges. I will share with you ideas and stories from teachers who enjoy the impact they have on the lives of children who face unbearable odds each day of their lives. Teaching in an urban community is not for the faint-hearted. It is not for those who have trepidations about trying some-thing new and taking unexpected risks.

Urban teaching is for those who really mean it when they say, "I care about kids, and I want to make a difference in their lives." Urban teaching is for people who clearly understand who they are and with that knowledge discover and adopt alternative strategies to assist and positively influence youth.

Why Read This Book?

Effective urban teachers understand their students' lives and respond to the issues that affect their students: from the poverty they experi-ence to frequent fears associated with living in threatening environ-ments. In this book, I share the stories of how thirteen teachers successfully work with urban youth. I'll explain how they

- negotiate successfully with students to develop a cooperative classroom atmosphere
- respond to the cultural and ethnic needs of students
- listen to students as a critical component of building trust
- alter curricula to match the interests and academic levels of their students
- use instructional strategies that help motivate students
- develop caring relationships with students
- establish reasonable expectations for student learning
- insure some academic success for every student.

I have discovered through my own experiences and by speaking to urban educators that teaching in an urban school is in some ways similar to teaching in the middle of rural Iowa or in the Chicago suburbs. Teachers in nonurban environments can and do have management and discipline problems, deal with students from dysfunctional families, help struggling students attain grade level performance, and argue with parents.

You and I know, however, that the students, parents, and communities surrounding urban schools are worlds apart from suburban environments. This book clarifies how student population differences and their environs affect the way urban teachers interact with students; interactions that are almost always more intense, more laden with risk, and more challenging than the professional lives of rural and suburban teachers. Characterized by a high percentage of students who lead risky lives, urban schools present a series of challenges for teachers that can easily discourage, frustrate, and consume the personal lives of those who lack the knowledge needed to safely navigate these risky waters. I want to help you "see" that with the appropriate knowledge and strategies, teaching in urban environments is promising, exciting, and personally and professionally satisfying.

Reading this book will hopefully lead you to perceive the joys of teaching in urban environments that many teachers experience. One intent for writing this book is to provide you with the attitudes, appropriate philosophy, tools, and strategies needed to succeed in an urban school. I hope as you read that you'll discover new ways of reaching your students that you haven't realized after a year or two of urban teaching. Another intent in writing this book is to provide an inexperienced teacher with opportunities to explore the world of urban teaching; to understand how using appropriate strategies can lead to personally satisfying teaching in urban centers. Reading this provides you with a chance to hear how to create a safe and vibrant place of learning for students *and* teachers and an opportunity to experience success as an educator in an urban environment.

References

LADSON-BILLINGS, G. 2001. *Crossing Over to Canaan: The Journey of New Teachers into Diverse Classrooms*. San Francisco: Jossey-Bass.

STEINBECK, J. 1937. *Of Mice and Men*. New York: Covici, Friede, Inc.

ONE

Why Teach in an Urban School?

The teacher turnover rate in the urban schools is much higher than in the suburban schools. . . . The result is that urban schools, especially those in the inner cities, are often staffed largely by newly hired or uncertified teachers. These teachers, who were trained to teach students from middle class families and who often come from middle class families themselves, now find themselves engulfed by minority students, immigrants, and other students from low income families—students whose values and experiences are very different from their own. The teacher training institutions have not placed sufficient emphasis on preparing new teachers to work in schools that serve minority students.

CROSBY (1999, 302)

The Lives of Urban Teachers

Why would anyone take a job in an urban center when many think it's easier to teach in the suburbs or in a rural district? That was one of the initial questions I asked during the interviews I conducted with thirteen educators who teach in urban environments in New York, Philadelphia, Chicago, Minneapolis, Wichita, Los Angeles, and San Francisco. These are teachers in classrooms from first through twelfth grade who have been in the business of teaching in urban schools from two to thirty-three years. As I share their stories, and their ideas and strategies for successfully teaching urban students, I will also highlight research that supports these teachers' strategies for successful teaching.

High School Teachers

Colette teaches English in a Philadelphia high school where she has been for three years. Colette decided to complete her teaching degree after a twenty-year career as a hairdresser. At forty-two, she didn't need to change professions, but she did. "I'm an immigrant. My parents were immigrants from Northern Ireland. I grew up as a street urchin. I wanted to do some good and help people who were like me—maybe not the same color, but brought up the same way. I'm a very practical teacher. I think that's why I'm suited more for the urban environment because not all of these kids are going to college, but they still need to know basic skills."

Colette didn't have an easy first year: "I started as a substitute in the high school. In my first class a kid said to me, 'F___ you, you white cracker.' As soon as the class ended, I went out to my car. I had a brand new cell phone, and I used up all of my free 90 minutes talking to my husband while I was also crying. I told my husband, 'I can't do this—I'm forty-two years old. I can't deal with this.' He said, 'Get back in there, you'll be fine. You worked all these years for this.' From that day, I realized it was either me or them. By the time the kids got to know me, and I knew them, there was no problem."

Colette talked of her guiding philosophy: "I get the feeling that some teachers don't take it as their responsibility to help these struggling students; they want to put it on the kids. But I believe that these kids are my product—what I produce is a reflection on me. I mean, I feel very responsible." She added, "I believe kids deserve a quality education. I teach them how I would want someone to teach my own kids."

Polly teaches high school students who have been retained at least once in a special program in the Chicago public schools. Polly explains, "I grew up in Chicago. It was all I knew, and so I wanted to teach here." That was twenty-seven years ago, and she's been teaching in the Chicago public school system ever since. Polly has taught both third and fifth grades and now teaches what she describes as "highly at-risk students" in an alternative high school. Polly adds, "Most of these high school students have probation officers, have been arrested and jailed at least once, and some have actually been here under house arrest. Almost every one of them has been retained at least once, and they are not permitted to return to their neighborhood high school until they reach academic success here. Our job is to help them to succeed and actually fit back into the high school near their neighborhood. Our success rate is ninety percent; that is, nine of every ten students we see actually graduate from high school. We're very proud of that. We have the highest success rate in Chicago among the eight or nine high schools designed for this purpose."

Jeff is a third-year English teacher in an urban high school in Wichita, Kansas. The student population in his school is forty percent Hispanic American, thirty percent African American, twenty percent European American, and ten percent primarily Southeast Asian immigrants—a high percentage being Vietnamese. Jeff describes the students: "This is an English-as-a-Second-Language (ESL) school and many of our Hispanic students are quite transitory. Students will leave for extended periods of time, a month or so, to return to Mexico to visit families."

When I asked Jeff if teaching in an urban school was the right job for him, he answered with no hesitation: "Yes! I don't ever see myself doing anything else. I don't want to be a counselor or a principal. I love this school!" Jeff's dedicated attitude is evident when he speaks of his frustration with teachers who don't share his excitement: "It's frustrating to lose kids. Some are borderline dropping out, and we could lose them. It frustrates me that a kid could succeed if just one more person would help him. Some teachers just don't care, and their apathy irritates me."

Pete teaches second language learner (SLL) students in a Philadelphia high school. He has taught in thirteen different schools in the Philadelphia school district at both the middle and high school levels over the past twenty-three years. He grew up in the Boston area and is an immigrant from Greece. Pete did his student teaching in Philadelphia because it was one of the only inner-city practica available during his undergraduate program in education at the University of Massachusetts. Pete explains, "teaching in the city fits my personality and style. I grew up in the city, where I was the minority, so I relate to the ethnic groups that I run across." When Pete first began teaching, he was involved in an innovative program in which he and other teachers spent several hours after school and on weekends with students. As Pete explains, "It was quite an exciting experience for someone just coming out of college. We took students camping, fishing, and brought students to our homes." Teachers have an immense impact on students' lives when they engage in these activities with them.

Adrienne is a high school English teacher in Los Angeles who worked in the corporate world for twenty years before receiving her teaching credentials in California. She is also a teacher trainer providing workshops to teachers on effective literacy strategies. Adrienne has taught at five separate Los Angeles high schools in the past thirteen years. The majority of the students where she currently teaches are African American; however, her first two years were spent in a high school with an eighty percent Hispanic student population. Adrienne explains, "I grew up in a housing project that was multiethnic, so I wanted to have this experience." She describes how her personality and background were a good match for an urban teaching position: "I'm high energy; a former corporate CEO, so I was used to stress—but not this much stress! I started teaching in urban environments thinking, 'I can really make a difference.' I had high expectations, but I had so many kids failing, so I temporarily lowered the standards. By the third year, I put the standards back up. It would be an injustice to these students to keep the standards low."

Middle School Teachers

Anita is an African American teacher in a Philadelphia middle school where she has been teaching for twenty-five years. She talks about her reasons for choosing to teach in this urban environment: "I wanted to teach in Philadelphia because that was home for me. I knew the community, I knew the children, and I felt like I knew what their needs were. I asked, 'Why not go and teach where you know you could make the biggest difference?' I wanted to teach in Philly from the beginning."

Anita describes her philosophy: "I make a real effort to be involved in my children's school lives, and if I have to, to be involved in their home lives by providing some of the things they need. My kids know that I'm willing to help them if they need some help. I don't just look at them as bodies to be educated. I look at them as people that need to be nurtured."

After twenty-five years in this urban environment, Anita indicated her energy for teaching and commitment to her students: "I think all kids deserve to be taught, even those that don't want to be taught. Sometimes you have to battle. Sometimes you get real frustrated with them; but, you have to remember that they don't realize how important this is to them now."

Tim is a music teacher in an urban middle school in Minneapolis. He's in his fourth year of teaching in this building and lives only a mile from the school. "Our students are sixty to seventy percent African American, plus we're an ELL (English-language learners) school, so we have a large percentage of Asian and African immigrants, especially from Somalia. There are thirteen different languages spoken in school, and that fact pretty much reflects the neighborhood population around the school." Tim talks about his connection to the local community: "I do PR in the community. I walk into stores, and people I know will ask me about how the band's coming. I like that connection. I graduated from the Minneapolis public schools, so I knew what it would be like. Plus, my wife went to school in this building. I came into teaching later, so I am older than most new teachers, and I'm not afraid of this environment."

Shanika has three years of teaching experience, two of those in a Philadelphia middle school. Shanika is from Sri Lanka, and explains that her father has always been a strong believer in serving the poor and disadvantaged: "I guess I've set him up as an example for me to follow in the choices I've made in terms of my career. When I first started teaching here [in Philadelphia], I wondered if I'd be able to handle the children." After teaching fifth grade for two years, Shanika has established a comfortable learning environment for students but describes the many frustrations she still experiences: "Last year I beat myself up so much because I thought I was falling short in so many ways." She describes one characteristic many of her students share: "It's not that these kids don't naturally want to learn or that they have bad attitudes about work. I think it's just the environment they're in outside of school that frequently doesn't support their school work or effort."

Elementary Teachers

Jackie taught students in New York City as a first-grade teacher for a few years and currently teaches students from first through eighth grade as a speech therapist in the Philadelphia public schools. Jackie didn't grow up in the city but chooses to teach in urban schools anyway. She initially taught for a couple of years in Philadelphia, then moved to New York City and taught at 168th Street in Harlem in the early 1990s. The community around the school was evenly split between African American students and children from immigrant Dominican Republic families. Jackie explains, "I wanted an urban teaching experience my whole life. I think education is about making a difference. Teachers were very important in my life—they made a difference. Education gave me lots of options in my life. When I look at the world and imagine what kind of difference I want to make, I think education is the most important thing. When I think about how I can be most effective, I think teaching in urban environments is the only way that cities will change and people will change. I think that's where good teachers need to be, and where we can make the most difference."

Diane has taught for thirty-three years in fifth- or sixth-grade classrooms primarily in the Mission District of San Francisco. Many of her students are recent immigrants whose native languages are quite diverse. She and many of her college friends from her undergraduate years chose to student teach in Chicago. When that experience ended, only Diane and one other friend from the larger student teaching group decided to stay in the Chicago schools. They both accepted permanent teaching positions in the primarily African American neighborhood where she lived. Diane was motivated by the opportunities to participate in the civil rights and antiwar movements that were highly active at the time: "I wanted to be in the middle of it [the movements and demonstrations]. It took me three months to discover that I wasn't going to save the world." Diane readily admits that teaching in the city in the beginning was challenging. She describes an incident that occurred her first year of teaching fifth graders: "I got beat up when I went to break up a fight between two boys—I was hit by a board. I decided to go back the second year because I didn't want to escape—if I left [the Chicago public schools] I wanted to leave on my own." Diane left the Chicago public schools after her second year of teaching because she wanted to work with a more diverse set of students. She landed a job in San Francisco and continued to teach in a city environment. Diane describes the joys: "I like working with the families and solving problems for the children. It means a great deal to me to be a part of the community. I didn't want to teach those kids whose parents say, 'Why haven't you taught fractions?'"

Kathleen has taught in elementary schools in the Chicago public school system for eighteen years. Although Kathleen grew up in Chicago, she attended parochial schools as a child. In 1990—her first year back after several years away from the classroom—Kathleen was responsible for teaching thirty-six students in her self-contained third-grade classroom. It wasn't easy, as she describes, "I would be up nights in tears because I couldn't get everything done for all those students." Of the six third-grade classrooms in her building, three are bilingual classes to meet the needs of a high population of Puerto Rican and Mexican American students. Kathleen takes great pride in her teaching and in the role of the Chicago public schools, despite the negative perceptions of many adults about the city schools. Kathleen's decisions about students are made based on her philosophy of teaching: "I ask myself, 'What if it were my child I have to make a decision about,' then, I most likely make the best choice for that child."

Lisa is an elementary teacher in Los Angeles where she has taught for five years. Lisa describes herself as Latina because previous generations of her family are from Mexico. She grew up in San Antonio, Texas, but moved to Los Angeles after graduating from college. In her first year as a teacher in Los Angeles, she taught a class with thirty Spanish-speaking children. Most of her students now are from homes where Spanish is the only language spoken because the families are primarily immigrants. Fortunately, Lisa speaks Spanish fluently. Many of her students experience demoralizing gang activity or have parents who are in gangs. Lisa wanted to be in a bilingual school district so that she could help those students who struggle to adjust as they move into American culture from Mexico.

Susan is an elementary teacher in San Francisco and teaches part-time at a local university. She explains why she chose to teach in the city: "I was born and raised in San Francisco, and I wanted to stay here." The student population in her school is approximately forty percent Japanese American, forty percent European American, and twenty percent is a mix of Asian, Latino, and African American students. She struggled her first couple of years explaining: "The kids were out of control—chaos really! I survived because they liked me—but I cried a lot those first two years." She focuses on helping students by encouraging and expanding their social development. As she describes it: "What I want to give kids are keys. I cannot give them all of the answers. I believe in helping them become readers, problem solvers, and to develop an appreciation of mathematics, literature, and the world."

As I listened to these teachers' stories, it was clear that they did not merely "settle" for a teaching job in the city because they couldn't find positions elsewhere. None of these teachers regrets seeking or obtaining urban teaching positions. It is quite the opposite—they sought these positions with enthusiasm and continue to feel a close connection to urban students. Their philosophies reflect a concern for the children and adolescents in these urban communities. Jackie reflected after almost ten years as an urban teacher: "I'm no longer questioning if this is where I'm supposed to be. I know an urban environment is where I thrive—where I'm meant to be." This commitment to students is what makes teachers effective in any environment, but is especially crucial in urban schools that may appear to offer only unbeatable odds for teacher success.

What Are Urban Communities Like?

The question of whether children in urban classrooms are different from kids elsewhere has been a source of conten-

*tion in educational research and policy for the past hun-
dred years. It's an important issue because the starting
point for our decisions about how we teach should be
judgments of who our students are.*

(WEINER 1999, 50)

What are the students who attend urban schools like? How are
their lives different from your life? What are the communities like, and
how do parents interact with the school? The responses to these questions impact how teachers interact with their students—it defines some
of the differences between how teachers behave in urban environments
and suburban or rural environments. Following are a few stories
from the teachers I interviewed about their students' lives and
neighborhoods.

Pete, the ESOL teacher from a Philadelphia high school, explains
the neighborhood where his students live:

This neighborhood is going through a relatively rapid demographic
change; where the working-class white population, who as the years
have progressed have stopped sending their kids to this high school,
and now send them to the Catholic schools in the area. These white
families have also started to move out. Taking their place are immigrant groups from Cambodia, Liberia, Vietnam, and Ethiopia. The
Asian families are from farming communities in their native lands.
They are more refugees than immigrants; so their education tends
not to be very good. It creates a tremendous divide between these
parents and their children because they're lost. They're lost in a
culture that they are unfamiliar with. Their children acclimate much
more quickly. Many of these students stop coming to school after
middle school or their attendance is sporadic. When students are in
here (this room), we can keep a closer eye on them—they're in a
more protective environment; but as soon as they go out into the
wider world beyond this hallway, these students are dumped on—
the dumpees. When this happens, these high school students opt not
to go here, so they drop out, find an apartment, and hang out. These
students, as they move out of a protective atmosphere, become more
disillusioned and just write everything off. The African students that

9

come in from Liberia and Sierra Leone that were directly caught up in their civil war—their education and childhood are severely limited. I can't imagine what some of them must have witnessed. [As a result of those experiences] you have eighteen-year-olds acting like they're twelve. They have serious psychological regression. I'm not a psychiatrist, but that's my read on them.

Jackie describes the families of the students she taught in a New York City Harlem elementary school in which the population was evenly split between African and Hispanic American students:

Many of the families had immigrated from the Dominican Republic. In the neighborhood, you would see people who would just open up a blanket and sell stuff, like their old plates, their old shoes, or their old clothes. Teachers were very well respected and revered by these Hispanic American families. There was a lot of respect from the kids and the parents as well. These parents would do anything to help their children learn better . . . and these were poor people. One father—his son was having a hard time—went out and bought "Hooked on Phonics," and you know that's not cheap. The father came up to me and said, "I'll pay you, would you please sit with him, and help him do this?" He said to me, "You know my wife and I came to this country, and it's too late for us; but, we want our children to have a chance." They know the value of education.

I noticed a big difference between the African American and Hispanic American parents. I saw more of a sense of hopelessness among the African American parents who don't have that feeling that, "If we work hard enough we'll have choices, we'll be able to do something with our lives."

Anita, who teaches in a Philadelphia middle school, described her students' neighborhood—the place where she grew up:

When I first started at this school twenty-five years ago, it was a much larger white community. It was entirely working class, white, and Catholic. As I ride through the community now, only twenty percent of the community is still white. I didn't see a whole lot of "For Sale" signs up, so my assumption is that a lot of the houses were assumed through "Section Eight" [federal assistance]. So, they weren't really sold, and minorities moved in—not just all black. There is a fairly decent-sized Asian community now in this area, and many more black families.

It makes for some other problems because now you have arguing among the black communities in the area—infighting within the African American community which we never really had before because they all kind of lived in the same area. Once the remaining twenty percent of white people move out of this neighborhood, it will not be whites moving in to these houses—it will primarily be blacks.

Most of these children are from single-parent homes. Some of these families and children put a lot of emphasis on clothing or material things—not necessarily school importance. They don't see the importance of school—it hasn't been indoctrinated into their children. Those [that do value education] are strong families—you can see it.

We have a lot of grandparents raising children and a lot of children who live with their grandmother and mother. Very few are being raised by fathers—in fact, I can't think of any that are. It might be a good twenty-five percent who come from two-parent homes, but the majority are from single-mother families with multiple children—three, four, or five children in the family.

Lisa is the elementary teacher from Los Angeles. She describes the neighborhood and families she works with each day:

This neighborhood was renowned for high gang activity ten years ago—Latino gangs basically. Today it's not as bad. The neighborhood is about ninety percent Latino, and most parents are immigrants and quite poor. The mothers are mostly stay-at-home moms while the dad may work in a local hotel. The children are very respectful—there's a lot of love here. School is academically difficult for them due to the language challenges because all of them speak Spanish at home. I think the parents are naive about what's going on around here because they are from rural neighborhoods in Mexico—they don't understand the dangers of the city.

One of the elementary teachers from San Francisco, Diane, who has taught for over thirty years, talks about the diverse families of the students who attend her school:

> Often there are multiple families living under one roof. Some children sleep on mats or on the floor. Some of these homes have no bedrooms. The families are immigrants from Laos, China, Samoa, Fiji, Cambodia, India, and former Czechoslovakia. All of the children are from poor families. Parents come to me and say, "Thank you for teaching my child. You make America wonderful for us." The Cambodian parents bow as they address me. The kids just love learning, but they don't do well on standardized tests.

Jeff, who teaches high school English in Wichita, describes the community surrounding his school:

> Families are primarily Hispanic with about forty percent of our students being first or second generation immigrants from Mexico and Puerto Rico. Sixty percent of our students are on free or reduced lunch, so poverty is a common characteristic of many of our students' families. Wichita has some White flight happening, but we're not like an inner-city Chicago. Many of the parents don't speak English, but their kids are Americanized—they know the culture and fool their parents often. The school was built in 1929, and there's a lot of community pride in it from those who graduated from here. We recently passed a bond issue to renovate the building, and we're happy about that. The community really pulled together to have this passed and the business community helped as well. Despite all that, we see a lot of lower income kids whose parents are not supportive. These particular students are apprehensive about coming to school.

It may appear to you that urban communities are distressed places —environments where no child should have to grow up. When you think about the word *home*, you probably perceive a series of scenes that have emotional meaning for you; whether your images of home are positive or negative. Your home should be a place of comfort and peace where emotional and physical safety are assured.

Urban cities are home to millions of Americans—places where people create their own emotional and physical security for themselves and their children. For many American children, their dreams begin in these large cities. Their hopes, dreams, and aspirations are as genuine as your own—dreams built by parents, grandparents, and teachers. Despite the obvious challenges that educators choose when they accept a teaching position in urban schools, they hold on to their strong convictions to help students lead comfortable lives and become successful in present and future endeavors. These teachers have high hopes for the children and adolescents with whom they interact. They are just as committed to their roles as educators as are teachers in any environment—perhaps even more so due to the extenuating circumstances their students experience.

References

CROSBY, E. A. 1999. "Urban Schools Forced to Fail." *Phi Delta Kappan* 81, no. 4: 298–303.

WEINER, L. 1999. *Urban Teaching: The Essentials*. New York: Teachers College Press.

Rethinking Your Culture of Education

Few of us . . . would care to admit that the way we teach compromises the learning of members of certain cultural groups. Yet to avoid or remain insensitive to the cultural issues and influences within our teaching situations under the guise, for example, of maintaining academic standards or treating everyone alike is no longer acceptable.

WLODKOWSKI AND GINSBERG (1995, 8)

If teachers pretend not to see students' racial and ethnic differences, they really do not see the students at all and are limited in their ability to meet their educational needs.

LADSON-BILLINGS (1994, 33)

Reflective Activity

Think about your culture. What do people expect of you in your family and in your community? How do people expect you to act? What do others think you should do with your future? How do people around you define success? Does everyone you know have equal opportunities for success? Do you share material items that you own with others frequently? How soon after completing high school are you expected to leave your parents' house? Are there any distinct roles for women only, or men only? Do you believe that competition or collaboration is more important for success in school and future successes? What values do you hold that are consistent with the majority of people with whom you interact?

Culture Influences Educational Views

You may not think that your answers to the preceding questions have any impact on your actions as a teacher; however, your responses reveal your cultural perspectives. Howard (1999) believes that Whites fail to recognize that their beliefs concerning education represent a cultural response because those beliefs appear to be shared by the majority. I specifically mention Whites because eighty-six percent of college students in education programs are white (Ladson-Billings 2001). Our beliefs and the way we act on those beliefs define our culture—whatever our backgrounds. It is a culture that defines how schools work—the way teachers and students relate to each other and the significance and value of those relationships in helping children to grow. Each time we step into a classroom, we bring with us a significantly sized suitcase that describes how we perceive our roles as teachers. That suitcase is filled with our years of experience as family members, friends, students, and as teachers. Here's what most people have in their suitcases:

- beliefs about the role of students in school situations
- theories about how most students learn
- knowledge of the role of homework in American schools
- memories of positive school experiences
- beliefs about parents' roles in their children's school experiences
- perceptions that students will be motivated by the threat of poor grades or the promise of good grades

- a general list of principles students should know as they reach the end of each grade level
- a set of classroom rules that all students will understand and honor
- a picture of how students will respond to requests by teachers
- a belief that competition will inspire greater effort among students
- a belief that it is best for students to work independently to complete school work
- a belief that most students learn information like you do
- the idea that all students are capable of learning everything at the same pace and at the same time
- a belief that if students don't do well academically, it's due to their lack of effort or inadequate academic backgrounds—but not due to any fault of ours as teachers
- the thought that parents are only permitted to become involved in their child's education when they are invited by teachers—usually only when there is a problem.

As you think of your beliefs about school culture, consider the thoughts of Wlodkowski and Ginsberg (1995): "If we teach as we were taught, it is likely that we sanction individual performance, prefer reasoned argumentation, advocate impersonal objectivity, and condone sports-like competition for testing and grading procedures. Such teaching represents a distinct set of cultural norms and values that for many of today's learners are at best culturally unfamiliar and at worst a contradiction to the norms and values of their gender or their racial and ethnic background" (7). Let's examine the influences of our cultural beliefs as they impact our views on schooling.

Reflective Activity

List as many factors as you can think of that influence your beliefs about school (e.g., traditions or motivation to achieve good grades).

16

I suspect your list of influences includes your personal experiences as a successful student—unsuccessful students don't usually make it to college. So, as you examine your beliefs, you may notice a considerable resemblance between your reasons for holding your beliefs about schooling and those of your college-educated colleagues, friends, and family members. To find someone whose ideas differ from yours might be difficult because they are not a part of the college scene. Yet, clearly a minority of high school students attends college in America. It's not appropriate to merely recognize that your views about learning in school are limited to those of primarily academically successful students. *Significant change will occur only when your reflection on these issues helps you to see that what you believe about school culture is a limited view of how schools should operate.* Your general beliefs about schooling can be an enormous roadblock to your ability to successfully teach many students you will encounter in urban schools.

The Traditional Classroom—A Limited Perspective on How to Teach

Picture the typical American suburban high school classroom: Students are sitting in rows and working independently on assignments. Most students behave according to classroom rules developed unilaterally by the teacher. Students spend most class time taking notes, responding to teacher questions, or working on homework individually. Homework is completed diligently and students are anxious to hear what their grades are each week. If students are confused, they may ask questions of the teacher for a few minutes at the end of the period. Curricula are clearly outlined, and variations in either content or the time frame in which the curriculum is completed are not acceptable to teachers, administrators, or parents. All students are given the same assignments and expected to complete them individually. All students are assessed in similar ways with the same tests.

How closely does this scenario resemble your experiences as a student? Think about what your classroom looks like on daily basis. How is your room different? Do expectations for students change? If so, under which circumstances do you alter curricula, instruction, assessment, or standards? What experience will encourage you to think differently? What factors will influence you to alter your strategies for instruction or the way you assess students? Are you willing to change the curriculum to meet students' academic, social, or emotional needs? How often will you assign homework? Will your academic expectations of students be reasonable? How will you insure that every student succeeds regularly?

Educators seldom think about their beliefs in these areas because they have experienced similar traditional models of teaching for so many years as a student. In many classrooms in America, students learn in much the same way as they have for over a century—much like the scenario just presented (Good and Brophy 2000). It's clear why we accept this model of schooling—we have been trained to learn this way since we entered school. It is not likely that four years of university teacher training will alter that (Delpit 1995). It's time to open your suitcase and reveal that your underlying beliefs about how schools should work are as daunting as the contents of Pandora's box. These traditional beliefs are based on an ancient model of learning that generally favors only those well-prepared students from established traditional American Caucasian families. Despite the positive feeling you have about your personal schooling experiences, those experiences are most likely far removed from the experiences of urban students, and your views are not likely to change easily (Pankratius 1997).

You might ask, "Why should I change how I teach when so many people experienced this type of instruction?" Indeed, many future teachers have experienced a traditional educational experience. Ladson-Billings (2001) reports that eighty-eight percent of teachers in America are Caucasian, and many are most likely implementing traditional educational practices based on a narrow cultural perspective. Many are afraid to change because those that aspire to be teachers have experienced a traditional teaching and learning model and have succeeded in that educational environment. Many of us are convinced that the traditional schooling we received is the only way to learn because no one has ever asked us to examine or question this system. There is little in our society and the culture of schooling to alter this distorted view that affects so much of how we act as educators; yet, we continue to fail to meet the needs of so many learners when we refuse to change our instructional perspectives and actions! As

Wlodkowski and Ginsberg (1995) state, "Any educational or training system that ignores the history and perspective of its learners or does not attempt to adjust its teaching practices to benefit all its learners is contributing to inequality of opportunity" (26).

A Brave (Entirely Different) New World

If you believe that traditional views about school will work in urban classrooms today consider the following demographics:

- More than a 1,000 students from foreign countries enter our schools for the first time every day (Rong and Preissle 1998).
- In many large public city school systems, seventy to eighty percent of the students are either Latino or African American (Henry and Kasindorf 2001).
- Forty-two percent of all public school teachers have at least one limited-English proficient (LEP) student in their classrooms (Han and Baker 1997).
- Latinos are the largest minority group in eighteen states and represent twleve point six percent of the population in the United States. The population of Latinos in the United States rose sixty percent between 1990 and 2000 (Jennings 2001).
- Mexican American students, who represent ninety percent of all Hispanic students, are increasing at a rate almost ten times greater than the overall population (Scribner 1999).
- Urban teachers report that over fifty percent of their students have problems that the typical classroom teacher is unable to help them with (Haberman 1995).
- The high school dropout rate is close to twenty-two percent for Hispanic Americans, eighteen percent for African Americans, and eleven percent for European Americans (National Education Association 2001).
- Children who are not native English speakers are the fastest growing population of students in America, having increased by almost forty-four percent to over three million from 1986 to 1994 (Macias and Kelly 1996).

- In three years, the school population of Hispanic Americans is expected to increase by thirty percent, Asian and Pacific Islanders by thirty-nine percent, African Americans by eight percent, and Native Americans by six percent (Crandall et al. 2001).
- The dropout rate among urban youth in large cities is nearly one in every four students (Huston 2000).
- Over 125,000 Hmong live in the United States—most in California—and are among the fastest growing populations of Asian Americans (Walker-Moffat 1995).
- More than one-third of the students needing special instruction because of poor English skills are enrolled in one of the country's forty-seven largest city school districts (Rong and Preissle 1998, 31).

Most of the students and their families you encounter in urban schools may not reflect your own cultural experiences, beliefs, values, or economic privileges. Effective teaching can be partially defined as the ability of a teacher to communicate and relate to the students. Forming meaningful bonds with students begins when you meet them for the first time and continues throughout an entire academic year. If you think your students have much to learn, their needs pale in comparison to what you need to learn about them! You can't teach them until you can reach them—not reach merely their minds—but most importantly you must reach them by touching their hearts!

The Beliefs of Culturally Responsive Teachers

Developing an awareness of other cultures requires identifying your own cultural beliefs. As you think about what you believe about schooling and the roles of teachers, reflect on the questions asked in the previous section and these additional questions: Who are you as a learner? How do you describe the role of a teacher? How do students learn best? What are some other ways that students learn? You may not have answers to these questions—especially as they pertain to the learning profiles of students who are African or Hispanic Americans; however, it's time you knew more about alternative ways of learning that are different—but *not* inferior to the traditional ways with which you are familiar.

Forget the idea of cultural assimilation—the belief that the role of a teacher is to see to it that all students ignore and even forget their cultural, ethnic, and family identities to become more like the nuclear family that dominates much of America. That "melting pot" philosophy is a dated and damaging principle. Weiner (1999) reinforces the absurdity of assimilation beliefs: "I think that American society has shortchanged itself and minorities by insisting that immigrants, African Americans, and Native Americans deny their cultures and languages to become 'real' Americans" (7). People who believe assimilation theory arrogantly and egotistically ignore the lifestyles and beliefs of a large percentage of Americans—especially families living in urban environments. Culturally responsive teaching begins when teachers recognize, demonstrate, and celebrate an equal respect for the backgrounds of all students. Ladson-Billings (1994) further explains that, "Culturally responsive teaching is about questioning (and preparing students to question) the structural inequality, the racism, and the injustice that exists in society" (128).

Recognizing Cultural and Ethnic Differences: Asking the Right Questions

Once you have a clear understanding that the way you learned in school is one specific profile of learning, then you may begin to accept that others from different ethnic and cultural settings have different learning profiles. Keep in mind that my focus is specifically on learning; we must understand how our students best learn if school is to have meaning for them.

What cultural differences affect the classroom learning environment? Consider the following issues:

1. What is the social relationship between students and teachers; that is, how are students expected to respond to you as a teacher? Should they look into your eyes when

21

they speak to you? Are they permitted to challenge your authority? Is laughing with you permitted?

2. What is the role of students during recitations? Students may wonder about the following: Am I supposed to raise my hand when a question is asked? Can I collaborate with others when the teacher asks a question? Am I expected to use my books to respond to questions? Is it acceptable to question another student's answer?

3. What is the most culturally polite way to address students' misbehavior? Is it culturally acceptable to single students out verbally in front of others? Should I ask students to cooperate; that is, invite them or is it better to demand compliance through assertive verbal commands? Should I call parents at home or settle problems myself?

4. What's the best way to help students improve their language so that they speak and write standard and formal English? Should I permit students to speak their language in class and correct them later? Should I correct them every time they use Black English Vernacular or part of their Spanish language in a sentence with mostly English words? How long should I allow them to continue to use Spanish (or other foreign languages) in my room? How should I correct their writing so that they learn to write standard English?

5. How much of my students' culture should I recognize if I want them to succeed economically in America? Can I use part of their background experiences in my curricula, or should I ignore their culture so that they learn enough about American culture? How important is it to use books and other curricular materials that my students recognize as being a part of their cultural experiences?

6. How much homework should I give to students? Should I expect their parents to help them with homework? Should I give students enough time to complete their homework in school? Should I give different homework assignments to students based on their ability levels?

7. Which reading strategies are going to work better for my students: more emphasis on a process approach or a more linear bottom-up skills approach?

8. How quickly should I move through the curriculum? Is it better to cover all the content in the book or move more slowly so that all students learn the principles well before we move to other topics? Can I leave out certain parts of the curriculum if it doesn't interest my students as much as it does me?

9. How much collaborative learning should I permit in my room? Shouldn't I encourage them to work alone most of the time? Wouldn't competition among students motivate them to work harder? Would some of my students learn better if they were allowed to work with a partner or in a group?

10. Should I grade students using the same standard of acceptable work for all of them? Is it better to give an *A* or a *B* to students who are really working hard even though this is their second year in America; or should I just give this student a *D* because she didn't meet the school district or state standards?

11. Which instructional strategies will work best for most of my students? Should I use less lecture? Would discussion groups work better for some of the class activities? Should I use less individualized work and more cooperative learning assignments?

12. Is there a better way to group students during independent activities? Should I group students by ability or allow all ability levels to work together?

13. How do the books that I use in my class influence the views of my students? Do the stories and pictures represent the lives of these children or adolescents? What are other sources of diverse literature and historical books that I can use that will better represent my students' lives?

14. Should I spend any time in class addressing the social and emotional concerns of my students? Is it okay to link their

personal social and emotional problems to some part of the curriculum? How much am I expected to help students with personal problems?

No one expects you to have the answers to all of these questions before you step into a classroom. If you do, then your decisions are based on preconceived notions about your students. Making these kinds of assumptions implies that you possess a set of expected behaviors for both students and teachers that is based on your cultural view of effective teaching—again, a severely limited view. All effective teaching and learning begins with knowing your students; however, we should not generalize. Every class of students differs from the other, and certainly all students who share cultural and ethnic backgrounds are not alike. As Wlodkowski and Ginsberg (1995) state, "There are few hard and fast rules about people, especially those who are culturally different from ourselves" (7). The most important step toward recognizing the cultural needs of different learners is to ask the right questions! A primary goal of culturally responsive teaching is to adjust instruction and curriculum so students from diverse cultural and ethnic backgrounds will have equal opportunities for learning (Ruddell 1999). That won't occur unless you recognize your beliefs and the possibilities that exist for other ways of teaching and learning.

Realizing the Differences: Examples of Culturally Responsive Actions

The teachers interviewed for this study know their students. They take the time to learn about their students using their backgrounds and experiences as the basis for study. Knowing students is the beginning point for developing meaningful relationships, building trust, comprehending their culture, understanding their families, and as a result, developing significant learning experiences. A central belief among all of the teachers I interviewed is that they *can and will* help their students succeed academically. This belief is critical to becoming a successful urban teacher. As Jackie was told by an administrator upon taking her first teaching position in Harlem, "Honey, we need teachers, not missionaries!" Urban teachers aren't there to feel sorry for students or to save them, but instead, to help them develop their strengths and improve their weaknesses. Acting in this way requires a belief that all students are learners and capable of growing.

Respect for African American Students and Families

Polly is the high school administrator/teacher in a Chicago public high school for failing freshman and sophomore students. Most of the students in this school are African American with a high number of Hispanics as well. In her words, as an urban teacher, "You must be willing to learn and respect the students' culture. If you think you're going to change that culture, you can't nor should you! Whatever your cultural background, if you act superior in any way, shape, or form—you're dead meat!" Polly is acutely aware of the gangs that exist within the local neighborhood, and how gang activity affects students in this high school. She describes the school's intervention upon hearing about an impending gang fight: "We helped to negotiate a truce between two rival gangs—the Blackstones and the Gangsta Disciples by inviting the gang leaders into school to talk to one another. The intervention calmed those students who are required to cross over gang lines to attend school each day."

Teachers don't have to be involved in these kinds of threatening interventions. However, the effort alone sends a message to students and families alike that at this school, teachers care enough about students' lives outside of school to become directly involved in resolving neighborhood difficulties. It is a powerful response.

Polly explains that administrators are required to take courses in African and Hispanic American culture as they become principals in Chicago. She also indicates that African history is an important aspect of the curriculum in her school. Hodges (2001) supports Polly's curricular decisions when she writes that effective teaching requires that children be "allowed to have their home and community culture, language, heritage, and experiences acknowledged and incorporated into their schooling" (3).

One aspect of understanding the culture of African American students is to be aware of one of the hurdles that many such students face in their school perspective: a perception and experience of powerlessness in a predominately White world. Due to these overwhelming feelings of hopelessness African American students may perform poorly academically—they believe that their efforts are feckless because their opportunities to attain power and authority through education will be in vain. Teachers who are unaware of or ignore the racial power structure prolong these negative beliefs. Although often unintentionally, they also deny African Americans and students from other cultures opportunities to grow by using traditional teaching philosophies, curricula, and instructional strategies. Howard (1999) describes the problem: "Individuals from the dominate group are usually unaware of their own power and can carry on the daily activities of their lives without any substantial knowledge about, or meaningful interaction with those people who are not part of the dominant group. The luxury of selective forgetting is not afforded those who have suffered the consequences of White dominance. For them, the American dream has often become an unbearable nightmare. We [Whites] have been able to determine the structure and the content of schooling and in this way have institutionalized our ignorance in the name of education" (58–59).

To act on the racial power issue requires knowledge of the beliefs and motivation to respond through daily contact with students, adjustment of curriculum, and use of alternative instructional strategies that are culturally sensitive to the needs of your students. Colette, the high school English teacher in Philadelphia, explains the importance of power with her primarily African American students: "Students have to feel valued and empowered—you have to connect with them and that takes some strong interpersonal skills." She also explains how she connects curriculum to her students' knowledge of social issues and uses their strengths in oral skills to explain literature. "I find that my students aren't generally strong writers when they begin the year; but, they're very intelligent when it comes to answering questions about social issues. When we read a piece of literature, I have them evaluate things by trying to connect it to their backgrounds. I was teaching Julius Caesar while Joey Merlino and the mob were involved in a murder trial in a local federal court; so, I related the Julius Caesar betrayal to members of the mob testifying against one another.

"On another occasion, I asked the question, 'What's your life like?' and the issue came up that some of my students knew people who were in jail—a few thought it was cool. The next day one of my students brought in a chilling cut on a CD about being in jail. As I listened to it, it made the hair stand up on my arms. I could see that listening to the CD was something that my students could use to connect our theme to their lives. Listening to that brought up a long conversation that helped my students use their thinking skills. Some of them didn't want to brag about the idea of going to jail after that discussion."

Colette understands that to create a culturally relevant curriculum for her students, she needs to listen to them and structure the curriculum in a way that touches her students' lives. She clearly recognizes students' strengths and takes advantage of them in planning instruction and curriculum. Ladson-Billings (1994) supports Colette's instructional practices with her comment, "Students' real life experiences are legitimized as they become part of the 'official' curriculum" (117).

To encourage their writing, Colette invites students to submit their poetry to a publication titled, *Pennsylvania Celebrates Young Poets*. Eight of her students had their work published in the book. Colette describes the success of a recent refugee student from Sierra Leone: "This student told me how he buried a three-year-old girl when he was hiding from the rebels in Sierra Leone. He saw bodies and amputations of legs and arms. He doesn't speak English very well, but through his creative writing, he's had three of his poems published in this book. It gives me an opportunity to know them and to help them with their grammar. You know there are a lot of things these students go through that make them mature; but, emotionally and educationally, they're still kids."

Shanika, a second-year Philadelphia middle school teacher, describes her understanding of students: "I'm constantly rethinking how I look at these kids. I think more and more, I'm understanding how different their environment and upbringing are from what I had. I realize I just have to be a lot more sensitive and a lot more aware that this is just a different world." Weiner (1999) explains how Shanika's

27

remark reflects an attribute of effective urban teachers: "I think that the most successful urban teachers regard their students as people from whom they have much to learn as well as much to teach" (59).

Shanika continues describing her own education about her students' lives: "I was reading a book in which a man describes his life growing up in Philadelphia with gangs. He describes how when he went to school he would go from one culture and value system into an entirely different one. He said it was so artificial to be put in a classroom where he would be expected to follow that value system—to be told to 'sit down' or 'it's okay to go to the bathroom, now.' His response was, 'Why are you telling me how to live my life when I have so much control over my life circumstances outside of school? It's completely foreign to how I live my life,' he said."

Shanika continues: "It's like we're expected to instill values, but *our* values don't make any sense!" Empowerment for students requires that teachers understand their students' home lives and respond appropriately in the design of classroom expectations and greater shared responsibilities.

Jackie, whose teaching experiences have been in Harlem and in Philadelphia where most of her students are Hispanic and African American, describes her role as an urban educator: "I believe in a holistic view of teaching where I really try to address the academic, social, and physical needs of students. It's more important to be holistic in an urban environment because students need support in all of these areas." She explains her involvement with her students in Harlem: "One of my students once had the chicken pox so badly that he needed to be in the hospital. I stopped in to see him there. I became the parents' best friend after that and received an invitation to dinner. They were just so thankful that I would show up like that at the hospital." Urban educators who make a difference in the lives of students deliberately visit families to become more acquainted with their students and parents and to begin to understand students' ethnic and cultural backgrounds. Jackie adds: "When you communicate with the students in urban settings, you have to be real. You need to admit to students as I have that, 'I'm not from Harlem in New York

City or Washington Heights in Philadelphia; therefore, your [her students'] life circumstances are not like mine.'"

In becoming acquainted with urban children, Jackie discovered that her students, "Don't deal well with surprises. I let them anticipate what's going to happen next during the day by telling them exactly what we'll be doing during each period that we are together and explain how we'll be learning. They feel comfortable, then."

Many of Adrienne's students in a Los Angeles public high school are African American and live in local housing projects. She explains her feelings about being white in an African American neighborhood and school: "My students are very open about being in brown skin. Teaching here is very humbling to me. I realize that there is a privilege that comes with just being white—even if you're poor and white!" She speaks of her students' endearing qualities: "These students are warm and sunny and they laugh a lot. They're really nice kids, and they'll bond with you when you establish a relationship with them. Kids hang out in my room and ask all types of questions. One recently asked me if I knew an attorney because she and her grandmother were being evicted. Another student was crying in my room when she discovered that her friend had recently died from gunshot wounds." Adrienne's remarks show how aware she is of her students' challenging circumstances. Teachers won't discover the barriers and challenges their students face without developing the interpersonal environment needed to gain students' trust through genuine listening and caring.

Anita is a twenty-five-year veteran teacher who, for all but one year, has taught in the same middle school in Philadelphia. Her students are primarily African Americans to whom she teaches language arts and reading skills. She talks about how she connects with her students: "One of the main things I tell them is that I expect them to come to class prepared. I expect when they don't have things (like pens, pencils, or books), that we can always talk. I journal back and forth with my kids every day. I tell them that if there are concerns, or problems, you can tell me that in your journal. If I read in your journal that you need supplies, I will make sure that you get those—and no one else has to know. There's a real need for young adolescents to connect with adults as they pull away from parents. Teachers need to become that other adult. I know you can't be Mom and Dad all of the time, but I tell my kids, 'I'm your mother here.' " Responsive teachers treat each child as if he or she were theirs; that's the message Anita sends to her students. The interactions with students must be genuine, though. Kind words by themselves are not enough to convince students that you genuinely care about them—the old adage, "Actions speak louder than words," rings so true in developing meaningful relationships with any child!

Effective urban teachers must accept that if they want to do what's best for all students, using different instructional strategies based on the cultural orientations of African Americans is *not* racial discrimination; instead, it is a sign of effective teaching that insures student academic success (Gay 2000).

Understanding Immigrant Students

Developing a healthy cultural and ethnic identity is challenging for African American students for many reasons; however, the challenges may be multiplied for students from other countries who arrive on American soil speaking another language and may not have received much formal schooling in their native countries. Often Americans make generalizations about certain immigrant students that demonstrate ignorance; for instance, "All Asian students are good at mathematics," or "Latino students prefer cooperative learning." These sweeping generalizations harm rather than assist students. When we speak of immigrant students in America, consider all of the possibilities: Asian immigrants could be from Cambodia, Laos, Vietnam, Taiwan, China, Japan, Korea, or many other Asian countries. Pacific Islanders are often identified as Asian students although their cultures are clearly different. Pacific Islanders may include students from Fiji, the Philippines, Indonesia, and other island nations. African immigrants could be from Sierra Leone, South Africa, Ethiopia, Liberia, and other African countries. Many Hispanic immigrants are from Mexico, but others are arriving from Central and South American countries as well as the islands of Cuba, Puerto Rico, Haiti, the Dominican Republic, and other islands off the Atlantic coast. Eastern European students bring a distinct culture and a variety of languages to America.

Making generalizations that all Asian or all native Spanish-speaking students have the same academic, social, and emotional learning needs is entirely inappropriate! Naturally, their cultures differ from one another. Responding appropriately to their cultural identities requires you to gain information from your students and their parents through personal discussions and visits into their communities. All of the teachers I interviewed teach immigrant students. Here are descriptions of their understanding of their students' lives.

Pete teaches high school SSL [second language learner] students in Philadelphia. Most of his students are recent immigrants or refugees from places like Sierra Leone, Cambodia, Vietnam, Ethiopia, and Liberia. He describes the challenges his students frequently experience: "A lot of these students stop coming to school after middle school. As these immigrant students become more adept at the language and move out of a protective atmosphere, they become more disillusioned. Some of the African American students resent the Asians because they perceive the Asians as getting things. The Asians move in and the government gives them $20,000 to start a business. The African American students tease the African immigrants about the way they dress. There are a lot of physical exchanges, fights, and intimidation. " Rong and Preissle (1998) explain how many Asian immigrant students experience social problems: "Despite the academic success of some, many Asian students continue to experience feelings of inferiority, alienation, and social isolation in school. Psychologists and sociologists have reported severe problems in development of ethnic identity and ethnic attitude among Asian youth" (146).

Immigrant students are doubly cursed by their lack of language and good organizational skills. Some of the students went from refugee school to refugee school and don't know the techniques of organizing materials or how to get prepared for class. Pete counters this view to explain that some immigrants are well schooled prior to entering America, particularly students he has encountered from Bangladesh. "All of these students have a tremendous need for attention and contact. They're very sensitive to what's going on around them and want to fit in. I have tried to develop a safe place for the ESOL students—creating a place of security and belonging has been my focus above the academic stuff. The academic stuff can't happen unless students feel safe, valued, and secure."

A natural tendency for some immigrant students when adapting to a new language and environment is to sit quietly in class and listen in an attempt to learn the language. Many may feel too embarrassed to speak because they don't know all of the words they want to use or because they have an accent (Rong and Preissle 1998). Pete recognized this: "When I first started teaching at this high school, there was a tendency by other teachers to give passing grades to students who were quiet. I sent out a letter asking teachers not to do that. I feel it is a disservice to students to give credit when they couldn't speak the language. Before I started doing that, we were graduating students who couldn't speak English well enough to pass. When we implemented the new policy, some students became motivated to work harder and some dropped out." Scribner (1999) informs us that, "When teacher expectations are low, students become vulnerable. They lose interest, develop negative reactions, and perform poorly. The vulnerability of SLL children is further compounded due to the inadequate supply of professionals who share cultural identity with these students" (2–3).

When Pete demanded that teachers hold higher standards for the immigrant students, another dilemma was created: "Some of the teachers and administrators wanted the immigrant students to graduate with all of the same requirements as native students. You can't possibly expect that. So, the question becomes, 'Are there going to be accommodations made for all of these students?'"

Without appropriate accommodations, immigrant students whose background educational experiences are limited are likely to fail, drop out, and struggle to achieve some sense of quality of life that education should provide them. Equality in education implies that all students will receive the instructional assistance they need to reach academic success. Students with special needs have at least been provided with the legal means to receive the appropriate accommodations that are needed for them to receive support from schooling experiences.

Many of this country's urban poor, African, Hispanic, and Asian American, and other immigrant children, however, have consistently been denied cultural recognition and a level of support needed to achieve academic equality or success.

Lisa, who teaches primarily Latino students in a Los Angeles public elementary school, describes how she helps her Spanish-speaking students learn English while getting to know them: "I think my forte is getting students to talk to me. I have a constant conversation about words and rules. I expect them to talk all the time because I know this is how they will learn English." In her attempts to recognize their cultural heritage, Lisa adds, "I try to respect where they come from. I always find some way to cultivate strengths in students. One of my students can't read English, so I encourage her to write. I'm trying to find a way inside her head, but I'm not there yet. I must find an 'in' for low achievers—a way to help them succeed." Lisa's views represent a culturally relevant response as she accepts responsibility for helping students grow despite the barriers they may face. Weiner (1999) describes how some teachers refuse to accept responsibility for their inadequacies: "Rather than saying, 'I can't help this kid,' they say, 'This kid can't/won't learn.' It's almost never so clear that a child can't learn, and in putting responsibility for academic failure on the student, teachers absolve themselves of any obligation to change their own practices" (22).

Jeff, the Wichita high school English teacher, describes the troubling attitudes of some of his colleagues, "Some teachers will say, 'If I could just teach different kids, I'd do so many different things.' My response is, 'Well, these are our students—teach them!'" It means a great deal to Jeff to see students succeed—especially the ones who haven't in the past. Jeff states that success is measured in many ways. He describes some of the ways he attempts to create success for his students: "I give out my home phone number and encourage them to call. If they didn't do their homework because they didn't understand it, I explain that I can't accept their excuse because they could have called me, and they didn't. I have been picking a few students up in the morning to bring them to school—sometimes their being here is in itself a success. My wife and I have had students over for dinner and

33

taken some to football games. Some of these students seem to have the attitude, 'I'm only here until I get kicked out'; or 'I'll leave soon because I'll flunk too many classes.' I try to get kids out of bad personal situations and turn them around—that's success. I want my students to know that something else is possible in their lives—like graduating for some." Weiner's (1999) comment supports Jeff's efforts of becoming familiar with students as a valuable strategy: "The more information you can tap about students' lives outside of school, the more efficient you'll become in developing hypotheses and solutions in your teaching" (53).

Diane describes a strategy she used to become acquainted with her elementary students in San Francisco, many who are recent immigrants and second language learners: "One year we made baseball cards of ourselves so we could share our lives with each other. The students provided wonderful descriptions of themselves on these cards. I really learned a great deal about them this way." There are numerous strategies for gaining information about your students' cultures. Wagstaff and Fusarelli (1999) describe how one school's faculty began to learn about their students: "Teachers at this school made home visits at the beginning of the year to get to know parents better. Every teacher also rode student buses during the first week of school to get to know where students lived and the problems and issues they faced and had to resolve" (30).

Assessing Your Cultural Expectations

Reflective Activity

Think about your responses to these questions: How academically capable are urban students? Do limitations exist for academic development of African American and immigrant students? What is the role of a teacher in helping urban students? What percentage of your students will you try to help?

Teachers' expectations of students' academic ability and growth potential greatly impact their effectiveness (Ladson-Billings 1994).

Winfield (1986) categorized teachers' beliefs about inner-city students along four dimensions: seeking improvement as opposed to maintaining the status quo; and, assuming responsibility as opposed to shifting responsibility. Four possible teacher beliefs and accompanying actions derive from this viewpoint:

1. *Tutors* believe the potential exists for students to improve and that they can help.
2. *General contractors* believe that improvement is possible but not with their assistance; instead other school personnel are responsible for helping students (e.g., teacher aides).
3. *Custodians* have little faith in students improving.
4. *Referral agents* don't believe that students are capable of improving and place the responsibility for maintaining the status quo on special education teachers or school counselors.

Ladson-Billings (1994) stresses that there is a more culturally responsive role for teachers: "Rather than aiming for slight improvement or maintenance, culturally relevant teaching aims at another level—excellence—and transforms shifting responsibility into *sharing* responsibility. As they strive for excellence, such teachers function as *conductors* or *coaches*. *Conductors* believe that students are capable of excellence and they assume responsibility for ensuring that their students achieve that excellence" (23). Weiner (1999) adds, "When teachers say that certain kinds of children are uneducable, they are expressing frustration and anger at their inability to teach successfully" (22).

Tim, the music teacher from a Minneapolis urban middle school speaks of the vision he has for his African American students: "I have an expectation that students will work when they're here. I expect students to be striving for their best achievement. We have posters around the school with that phrase, 'Strive for your best achievement.'

"When I arrived here four years ago, I was the fifth band director in four years. A student asked me that first day if things were going to be different this year. I told him, 'I'm here to build a band program.' I have kept that focus, and every concert over the past four years has been better than the last. I was so excited by one student's comment her third year with me when she proclaimed, 'We really sound like a band.'" Tim's pride was pervasive throughout our conversation as he spoke of the students. Tim is a genuine band conductor, and his attitude about helping his students reach excellence reflects Ladson-Billings' description of a "conductor" for urban students.

Ladson-Billings (1994) further describes culturally responsive teachers: "They see their teaching as an art rather than as a technical skill. They see themselves as part of the community, and they see teaching as giving back to the community. They demonstrate a connectedness with all of their students and encourage that same connectedness between the students" (25).

Wlodkowski and Ginsberg (1995) describe the attitudes such as "The Blame Cycle" that ineffective teachers frequently adopt when they fail to respond to students' needs (71). The stages of the blame cycle are as follows:

> *First stage:* "What the teacher normally does to help student is ineffective."
> *Second stage—student response:* "Student appears unappreciative, frustrated, and/or withdrawn."
> *Third stage:* "Teacher's further efforts seem to increase mutual feelings of incompetence, frustration, and helplessness."
> *Fourth stage:* "Teacher and/or student begin to feel blameful and start to lower expectations."
> *Fifth stage:* "Self-fulfilling prophecies begin to emerge with tendencies."
> *Sixth stage:* "Student and/or teacher withdraw or become hostile."
> *Seventh stage:* "Teacher and/or student generate stereotypes" (71).

Teachers and students could easily adopt these positions when teachers refuse to respond to the social, emotional, and academic needs of students in a culturally responsive manner. Success needs to be measured one student at a time and with a different measuring stick for each student. It is critical to establish realistic expectations, remembering that each student is capable of progressing.

Culturally Responsive Strategies

Effective teaching in a classroom of diverse learners requires a multitude of strategies to insure student success. The teachers interviewed described a number of activities and beliefs that demonstrate their concern for the growth of all their students. Some of the strategies for developing a culturally responsive environment include the following:

- Create a classroom and school climate that promotes a community of learners.
- Demonstrate how students can accomplish their best academic work and apply that expectation to all students.
- Establish a caring environment by developing personal connections to all your students (Scribner 1999).
- Demonstrate "an open and accommodating sensitivity to the learner's knowledge, experience, values, and tastes" (Wlodkowski and Ginsberg 1995, 119).
- "Acknowledge the legitimacy of the cultural heritages of different ethnic groups . . . as they affect students' dispositions, attitudes, and approaches to learning" (Gay 2000, 29).
- Actively "facilitate student and family involvement in school life" (Reed-Victor and Stronge 2001, 14).
- Eliminate competition as a means of classroom discourse to enable all learners to be successful at their level of academic ability. (Ladson-Billings 1994).
- Accommodate students' learning needs by altering instruction and choosing alternative texts, novels, and other reading materials.
- Choose alternative discussion formats that encourage more student engagement through accepting students' native discourse patterns.
- Reflect on your beliefs about students' abilities with colleagues, to insure positive expectations for all students.

- Help students to develop pride in their ethnic and cultural backgrounds.
- Build the confidence levels of students by providing academic challenges that are realistic and attainable for each.
- Demonstrate value for students' native speech patterns and, in time, model appropriate uses of standard English.
- Use individual and alternative assessment practices that permit students to demonstrate their knowledge in developmentally appropriate ways.

Reading these suggestions is not enough to become an effective urban educator—you must implement them to help urban students. These suggestions represent an initial list of strategies for considering and ultimately meeting the social, emotional, and learning needs of all students. I provided some examples of how these urban teachers use culturally responsive teaching components. More detailed information on effective instructional strategies, appropriate curricular focus, and meaningful assessment activities are provided in later chapters of the book (see Chapters 5, 6, 7, and 8). Adopting a philosophy and implementing culturally responsive teaching is not always popular or supported by administrators, parents, or fellow teachers. However, adopting and implementing culturally responsive actions is a critical step in helping students develop personally satisfying lives—now and in the future.

Some teachers may be unable to actually understand or implement culturally responsive teaching due to a cultural handicap; that is a misguided belief they are incapable of transcending. Weiner (1993) explains this barrier, which was defined in a study of 700 teachers by the National Center for Research on Teacher Learning: "Despite course work in multicultural education, teachers could not move beyond two contradictory moral imperatives: all children should be treated equally, and teachers should individualize to accommodate students' needs" (111). Teachers who comprehend the importance of meeting each student's needs recognize that all students cannot and should not be treated equally. Try to understand that in an educational realm, *equality* means "each student gets what he/she needs" (Lavoie 1989). That translates into establishing a separate set of expectations for each student, utilizing different instructional strategies, offering different curricula, and developing alternative ways of assessing individual students. If you are able to make one outcome a priority of school—to help each and every student grow to an extent that represents her or his cognitive capabilities—then perhaps you will begin to comprehend the meaning and value of culturally responsive teaching.

References

CRANDALL, J., A. JARAMILLO, L. OLSEN, AND J. KREEFT PEYTON. 2001. "Diverse Teaching Strategies for Immigrant Children." In *More Strategies for Educating Everybody's Children*, edited by R. W. Cole. Alexandria, VA: Association for Supervision and Curriculum Development. 33–71.

DELPIT, L. 1996. *Other Peoples' Children: Cultural Conflict in the Classroom.* New York: New Press.

GAY, G. 2000. *Culturally Responsive Teaching: Theory, Practice, and Research.* New York: Teachers College Press.

GOOD, T. L., AND J. E. BROPHY. 2000. *Looking in Classrooms*, 8th ed. Reading, MA: Addison Wesley Longman.

HABERMAN, M. 1995. *Star Teachers of Children in Poverty.* Lafayette, IN: Kappa Delta Pi.

HAN, M., AND D. BAKER. 1997. "A Profile of Policies and Practices for Limited English Proficient Students: Screening Methods, Program Support, and Teacher Training." SASS 1993–1994 (NCES 97–472). Washington, DC: National Center for Education Statistics.

HENRY, T., AND M. KASINDORF. 2001. "Testing Could be *the* Test for Bush Plan." *USA Today*, February 27, 2A.

HODGES, H. 2001. "Overcoming a Pedagogy of Poverty." In *More Strategies for Educating Everybody's Children*, edited by R. W. Cole. Alexandria, VA: Association for Supervision and Curriculum Development. 1–9.

HOWARD, G. R. 1999. *We Can't Teach What We Don't Know: White Teachers, Multiracial Schools.* New York: Teachers College Press.

HUSTON, B. 2000. "A School with a Mission to Care." In *Caring As Tenacity: Stories of Urban School Survival*, edited by M. A. Pittman, and D. Zorn. Creskill, NJ: Hampton Press. 107–115.

JENNINGS, P. 2001, March 7. *World News Tonight*. New York: American Broadcast Company.

LADSON-BILLINGS, G. 1994. *The Dreamkeepers: Successful Teachers of African American Children*. San Francisco: Jossey-Bass.

———. 2001. *Crossing Over to Canaan: The Journey of New Teachers in Diverse Classrooms*. San Francisco: Jossey-Bass.

LAVOIE, R. 1989. *Frustration, Anxiety, and Tension: How Difficult Can This Be? Understanding Learning Disabilities: The F. A. T. City Video*. Arlington, VA: WETA.

MACIAS, R. F., AND C. KELLY. 1996. *Summary Report of the Survey of the States' Limited English Proficient Students and Available Educational Programs and Services, 1994–1995*. Washington, DC: National Clearinghouse for Bilingual Education.

NATIONAL EDUCATION ASSOCIATION. 2001. "The Bottom Line." *National Education Association Today*, March, 19.

PANKRATIUS, W. J. 1997. "Preservice Teachers Construct a View on Teaching and Learning Styles." *Action in Teacher Education* 18, no. 4: 68–76.

REED-VICTOR, E., AND J. H. STRONGE. 2001. "Diverse Teaching Strategies for Homeless Children." In *More Strategies for Educating Everybody's Children*, edited by R. W. Cole. Alexandria, VA: Association for Supervision and Curriculum Development. 10–32.

RONG, X. L., AND J. PREISSLE. 1998. *Educating Immigrant Students*. Thousand Oaks, CA: Corwin Press.

RUDDELL, R. B. 1999. *Teaching Children to Read and Write: Becoming an Influential Teacher*. 2nd ed. Needham Heights, MA: Allyn & Bacon.

SCRIBNER, A. P. 1999. "High Performing Hispanic Schools: An Introduction." In *Lessons from High Performing Hispanic Schools*, edited by P. Reyes, J. D. Scribner, and A. P. Scribner. New York: Teachers College Press. 1–18.

WAGSTAFF, L. H., AND L. D. FUSARELLI. 1999. "Establishing Collaborative Governance and Leadership." In *Lessons from High Performing Hispanic*

Schools, edited by P. Reyes, J. D. Scribner, and A. P. Scribner. New York: Teachers College Press. 19–35.

WALKER-MOFFAT, W. 1995. *The Other Side of the Asian American Success Story.* San Francisco: Jossey-Bass.

WEINER. L. 1993. *Preparing Teachers for Urban Schools.* New York: Teachers College Press.

———. 1999. *Urban Teaching: The Essentials.* New York: Teachers College Press.

WINFIELD, L. 1986. "Teacher Beliefs Toward Academically At-Risk Students in Inner City Schools." *The Urban Review* 18, no. 4: 253–267.

WLODKOWSKI, R. J., AND M. B. GINSBERG. 1995. *Diversity and Motivation Culturally Responsive Teaching.* San Francisco: Jossey-Bass.

THREE

The First Year of Urban Teaching

This has got to be the only profession that eats its young.

ADRIENNE, LOS ANGELES HIGH SCHOOL TEACHER

I didn't think I could make it through the year. It was so many things—including a new culture. I wondered what I was doing there; I wondered if I was making a difference; and, I wondered if this was good for me.

JACKIE, HARLEM ELEMENTARY TEACHER

What a shock I had my first semester as a city teacher! Much of my knowledge of teaching seemed irrelevant, and I had trouble connecting with my students as people. I felt a lack of success and saw myself becoming antagonistic to my students, acting like teachers I had vowed never to become.

WEINER (1999, 2)

First-Year Challenges

I feel a sense of pride in knowing that some of my former undergraduate students attained a teaching position. My bubble of enthusiasm, however, is slightly burst as they explain, "You know, you never really taught us how to be prepared for this first year of teaching." Ladson-Billings (2001) reports, "More than half of the new teachers feel their teacher education program focused too much on theory and not enough on the practical aspects of teaching" (8). Perhaps that belief rings true more so for teachers who enter urban schools. Schwartz (1996) reports that approximately one-fifth of new teachers will leave the New York City public schools following their first year of teaching and one of three will leave after their third year of teaching. Kronowitz (1999) predicts that among all teachers, fifty percent will leave the profession within five years and eighty percent will leave after ten years. Kronowitz cites several reasons for this high percentage of departures:

- unrealistic expectations
- lack of physical and mental conditioning
- isolation from other teachers
- psychological fatigue
- discrepancy between beliefs about teaching and reality of daily challenges (3).

Some of these factors are uncontrollable primarily because the culture of teaching entails

- high student-to-teacher ratios
- few opportunities to collaborate with colleagues
- self-contained classroom design of schools
- minimal professional development opportunities
- little, if any support for novice teachers.

As you begin teaching in an urban environment, you obviously want to be well prepared. Possessing content and pedagogical knowledge are certainly critical pieces of the puzzle. Those skills alone, however, will not ensure your success or satisfactory performance as a first-year teacher. When the school year begins, you are immediately responsible for many organizational components: establishing daily routines, policies, rules, consequences, and procedures; choosing curricula and materials; planning instruction; handling a wide range of students' academic, social, and emotional needs; and, meeting professional responsibilities outside of the classroom. It is unlikely that anyone can ever be effectively prepared for all of these roles. Prioritizing responsibilities seems impossible.

Understanding and relating to your students, particularly if their backgrounds are different from yours, are two primary responsibilities for educators that are crucial for successful teaching. The National Center for Educational Statistics (1999) in a study conducted with over four thousand teachers reported that eighty percent of those surveyed believe they are not prepared for working with students from diverse backgrounds. DePaul (1998) noted that the greatest challenge novice teachers face is coping with diversity of student achievement and ability levels.

As you read the stories of these thirteen teachers, try to imagine how you feel as you prepare for, or experienced, your first year or two of urban teaching. You will read about their mistakes and also hear how these teachers improved as they gained more experience. Keep in mind these words of advice from Kevin Ryan (1992): "The first year is not a good sample of what a teaching career is like; it is not a good basis upon which to make an important professional decision," such as choosing to leave the profession (v). First-year teachers thrive on a modus operandi of trial and error. Many of the decisions and actions novice teachers take during their first year are inappropriate despite their good intentions and adequate pedagogical knowledge. I hope to convince you that the first year can be productive despite the mistakes that you will make.

Beginner Mistakes

Many novice teachers become obsessed with managing students. The challenge of gaining students' cooperation and designing and delivering meaningful instruction can be overwhelming. The word *management* generally implies the ability to organize and conduct meaningful learning activities that engage students and encourage cooperation. Novice teachers at all grade levels and in all community settings fre-

44

quently identify management issues as one, if not the greatest area in which they need assistance (Kent 2000; Maxson, Wright, and Wilson-Houck 2000; Veenman 1984). These rookie mistakes are caused partially by inexperience and inadequate knowledge of and reactions to learner needs (Fogarty, Wang, and Creek 1982). Knowledge of students' academic, social, emotional, and cultural learning needs is as significant in gaining students' cooperation as are content and pedagogical knowledge. When asked about their first year of teaching, each of the teachers I interviewed frequently spoke of the challenges of handling students.

Jeff, the high school English teacher from Wichita, speaks of the challenges he faced his first year in a teaching position that should have entitled him to authority: "I started teaching here when I was twenty-one years old. My students' brothers and sisters were older than I was. When I wasn't sure what I wanted to do, they [my students] would tell me. I had a hard time establishing authority. I also didn't know how to get the kids motivated." Ladson-Billings (2001) reported that in-service teachers who were placed in urban environments experienced similar problems: "In their attempt to be democratic and nonhierarchical they allowed the children to make decisions they were unprepared to make. The prospective teachers' democracies were turning into anarchy, and their understanding of a teacher's power and authority was distorted" (139). When anarchy begins, teachers quickly become frustrated and angry. Irritated by their inability to gain students' cooperation, teachers blame students instead of reacting in a way that alters their practice to improve student-teacher relationships.

Jackie, who was teaching elementary students in Harlem, had difficulties establishing a reasonable learning environment in her primary classroom: "That first year, I would lose my temper and scream—screaming doesn't work—no matter what students experience at home. Another mistake is that I used to allow too much time for individualized work. I just wasn't prepared enough for students that finished early." A lack of effective and comprehensive planning is also a common novice's mistake that often leads to student misbehavior (Roskos 1996).

Shanika, who moved from a first-grade position in the suburbs into a Philadelphia middle school, struggled with management issues that first year in Philadelphia: "I started off very softly with my management techniques. I didn't set any limits, and so I had a hard time the rest of the year."

Diane began teaching fifth grade in inner-city Chicago immediately following college graduation. She wanted to make a difference with urban students but didn't always know how to do that. "There were two doorways in my first classroom in Chicago. I put my desk in front of one door and stood in front of the other to prevent students from leaving without permission. There really wasn't much support from administrators, parents, or other teachers."

Establishing a caring and supportive learning atmosphere while upholding classroom rules and policies is a fine line to navigate; a line that is challenged daily by students as they ascertain their limits of power in your classroom through their constant interactions with you and each other. Equipped with an understanding of, and the ability to create, a safe and cooperative learning environment, first-year teachers can progress professionally to the stage of addressing more critical components of effective teaching: meeting the instructional and curricular needs of urban students.

Help from Colleagues?

Ladson-Billings (2001) describes the typical plight of first-year urban teachers: "Once hired, few teachers in urban schools (serving large numbers of students who are poor, or various racial and ethnic backgrounds, and who speak a first language other than English) receive adequate induction into the profession" (22). The number of new teachers in urban schools is an issue that confuses administrators, frustrates parents, and disappoints students. A more serious concern is the lack of educators interested in teaching in urban schools. Among those who do show an interest, many are not certified to teach. Wong (2000) reported that instead of certified teachers, teachers' aides were teaching many students in Title I schools. Mandates to reduce class size in California have a considerable effect on staffing in urban schools, where as many as one out of every four teachers may have emergency teaching certificates (Maxson, Wright, and Wilson-Houck 2000). Archer (2000) reported that as many as sixty percent of urban districts permit uncertified individuals to teach with emergency licenses. Those who enter the profession without knowledge of pedagogical theory and practice, child and adolescent developmental characteristics, or prior field experience are immensely unprepared for the realities of urban classrooms. These teachers may be more susceptible to leaving their positions than those who are certified.

Leaving students does have an impact on their lives. Haberman (1995) describes the significance of effective urban teachers: "For the children and youth in poverty from diverse cultural backgrounds who attend urban schools, having effective teachers is a matter of life and death. These children have no life options for achieving decent lives other than by experiencing success in school" (1). One study described the feelings of urban middle school students who had been taught by eight different mathematics teachers from September until February of the same academic year (Brown 1999). These students were hurt that teachers abandoned them. These feelings of disappointment became personalized to the extent that students began to question their merit and value when teachers chose to leave them.

Tim, a music teacher from Minneapolis, explained that there were thirty new teachers hired in the middle school his first year. He further explains, "The new teachers couldn't handle the students or the curriculum. I was so frustrated. I'd say to my wife, 'I sure wish I was teaching at the high school.'"

The reception for new teachers by seasoned faculty in urban schools is seldom pleasant, as Lisa describes in her comments about her initial year as a first-grade teacher in Los Angeles: "Other teachers treat you like shit that first year because you haven't been where they've been. They want you to suffer like they have." This negative response may explain why some teachers are so discouraged their first year.

Kathleen, a Chicago elementary school teacher, frequently experienced an uneasy anxiousness her first year of teaching: "Every Sunday night my stomach was in knots thinking about my responsibilities the next day. I had no support from administrators or other teachers. The only advice I received was, 'Be friendly, fair, and firm.' I had no supplies and so many students with special needs. I was left on my own."

Adrienne, who teaches high school English in Los Angeles, was appalled at the lack of professionalism in teaching when she entered the field. "It was a shock when I moved to education from my corporate position. I think I was most surprised that decisions made in schools are not made in the best interest of students. We only give lip service to students. The poor way that teachers are treated surprised me. The community doesn't treat you well; the administrators don't treat you well; and, teachers are not very respectful of one another."

Jackie, whose professional experiences include elementary teaching in Harlem and Philadelphia, explained her first year: "Initially there was *no* support because the faculty there was terrible. There was a lot of backbiting. I discovered that I needed to stay out of the faculty room at school—that way you can bypass the crap! Urban schools have not been very nurturing or supportive in any of the cities I've been in. I think one of the worst parts for me was competing. I had a grade partner my first year, and I wanted to finish the reading book before she did. Now . . . it doesn't matter. That kind of stuff used to bring me down."

First-year elementary teachers in one survey reported emotional support as one of the top three needs for assistance (Odell 1986). Many first-year teachers need support from colleagues to avoid what Lidstone and Hollingsworth (1992) describe as, "excessive self-criticism" (cited in Kronowitz 1999, 4). A characteristic of effective educators is the ability to frequently reflect on their practice, but this micro-analysis can lead to unrealistic expectations that may be difficult to reach. A focus on personal blame without realizing teacher limitations can be devastating to your morale as a first-year educator.

Colette, the Philadelphia high school English teacher, shares her frustration from her first few days: "I had a choice of which school I could go to once I was offered a job by the district. I showed up at that school three weeks before I was supposed to start because I thought I was going to get the curriculum. I called them [administrators] to say I was coming, but they had nothing to give me when I got here."

Philadelphia middle school teacher, Shanika, explained her frustration with the organization of orientation sessions: "I was excited about the job offer; however, I was afraid later. Teacher orientation was very disorganized. I thought, 'If this is the way it is now, I wonder how it will be when the kids show up.'"

As if teaching isn't challenging enough, it would seem that the least you could expect is support from fellow faculty members. Of the thirteen teachers I interviewed, however, only two mentioned receiving ample support from colleagues their first year of teaching. You must find someone in the building to confide in when problems arise—someone you can trust. This person should be experienced enough to understand how the system works at your school and empathetic enough to listen well and provide practical advice when needed. I suggest establishing daily meetings with your colleague to create opportunities for dialogue about every aspect of urban teaching from how to handle students, parents, and administrators to how to secure supplies for projects. Although frequent talks with family members are also advised, only a fellow teacher in the same building with you can provide the care and understanding that you need to find solutions to many of the contextual problems inherent only to your school. Developing the following philosophy and accompanying action plan may help save you unnecessary distress: "Asking for and obtaining help from my fellow teachers is *not* a sign of weakness; but instead, a strategy for insuring my survival and success as an urban educator!"

Enjoying the First Year

I realize that after you have read the first part of this chapter, it appears that no one could possibly *enjoy* the first year of teaching in an urban school. Success, however, occurs for many teachers during the first year and the years after. The question is, "How did they survive the first year?" The answer is simple for those who entered teaching for the right reason: "It's the students!"

Positve Student Interactions

Many elementary preservice teachers explain that their reason for entering teaching is their love of children. I know that teaching is much more than demonstrating your love for youth. However, despite my intent to downplay the power of interactions with students, many of us have witnessed teachers who despise children and adolescents and are ineffective due to their attitudes toward youth. I am always curious how those teachers continue to drive to school for 180 days year after year when they cannot stomach interactions with youth.

Jackie explains what effective teachers learn quite quickly: "During your initial years of teaching, you'll learn more from your students than you'll ever teach them. You'll need to be okay with that."

Pete, a high school teacher in Philadelphia, speaks of his delight in working with challenging students: "My favorite students have always been the troublemakers. Many times they're the bright ones. These students are bored, they feel disenfranchised by what you're teaching them—it's bullshit and not useful to them in any shape or form. These students have a tremendous need for attention, and if they can't get it by being reasonable, then they'll be off the wall. Some students are very organized, very methodical, and have pride in what they do. You have to find a balance in helping all students."

Colette describes her students: "They're certainly very bright. They have native intelligence that can be developed, but it has to be harnessed and focused. Kids have to be challenged. I think that's a big problem—some of these kids are very bright, and they're bored."

Diane, a thirty-three-year veteran elementary school teacher, describes her first years in San Francisco: "This elementary school was a haven in the middle of ugliness. There were always a lot of homeless men and hookers standing around the school. As a whole, as teachers, we loved being in the building. I brought in volunteers; we got computers; we wrote grants for free books; and we went camping at least once a month with the students. We made it a wonderful place for our students."

These teachers exhibit the common characteristic of recognizing that the appropriate focus in classrooms needs to be on students' lives.

In developing these kinds of relationships with students, teachers help students enjoy school through the creation of meaningful learning experiences based on students' interests. An ethic of caring for students is a dynamic that teachers exhibit, which positively influences teacher-student relationships.

Shanika describes her favorite moments: "I like seeing the children's pride in presenting their projects. They had really taken ownership of their work, and they were eager to show the class how hard they worked on it. Seeing the way they cared was really inspiring to me. I just like that look on their faces when a lightbulb goes on in their heads. It's also great to see their imaginations emerge when you give them a project. To see them figure something out without me having to tell them, is great!"

Diane echoes a similar excitement for student learning: "I like the lower-ability students who haven't had the chain pulled on their lightbulbs. When I first started teaching, I took Spanish to get my certificate to teach second language learners. If I had some time, I would study during the school day, and my students would come over and help me. They enjoyed that role reversal of helping me."

As I think about their comments, I clearly recognize that these teachers don't hold biases about their students' learning capabilities. Their beliefs are that children and adolescents are at school to satisfy their curiosity; that as educators they are excited about helping students develop socially, emotionally, and academically. These basic tenets about students are demonstrated in every way that teachers interact with their students. Influential teachers don't need to say they care about their students—it shows in their faces, their voices, and in the instructional strategies they use.

Support from Colleagues and Administrators

We have already established that you will need to find an advocate in your building. That first year, it may be more appropriate to refer to your trusted colleague down the hall as your *surrogate parent*. Whatever name you give this person, contacts with her or him should be daily and lengthy when you have the need. I suggest exchanging telephone numbers and email addresses for those evenings when you desperately need to speak to someone who genuinely understands the cultural dimensions of students and teachers at your school. It may take some time before you discover which person on the faculty really cares and has your best interests in mind. Begin your search early so that your support system is in place early in the year. Be proactive about finding a colleague who can help you. If you aren't speaking to others about the challenges you experience, then no one will think that you need help.

Diane provides sound advice for faculty in urban schools: "The days of closing our doors in education are out! We [teachers] have to open our doors and collaborate, share ideas, and take responsibility for each other. If you see someone in trouble, open your door and help that teacher." Similarly, when you need help, let others know!

I value forming friendly relationships with all the teachers in the building. Situations will arise that require information and assistance from many of the other teachers at some point in your career. Kronowitz (1999) suggests staying clear of, ". . . whiners, complainers, and gossips" (139). If you are influenced easily by others, don't spend much time with pessimistic colleagues. As I walk through urban schools, the stories I often hear from pessimistic teachers are about how bad the students are in their building. Negative teachers are like students who have an external locus of control—the problems in the building are always someone else's fault, not theirs. This strategy of blaming students, parents, or administrators does nothing to improve the climate for student learning.

You won't learn about the school's culture without making regular, astute observations and asking many questions of those colleagues you trust. Many policies are unwritten. You will flounder needlessly if you don't seek answers to questions you have—particularly those that affect timelines, official reports, and other paperwork. Being involved in the professional adult culture of your school is almost like accepting an additional job while you simultaneously attempt to focus on your students' lives. Learning about the school's culture is a continual process that requires daily attention. The more you know, though, the easier your professional life will be that first year.

Is the Principal Really Your Pal?

Principals can and should be allies. Teachers frequently are reluctant to go to immediate supervisors for help, for fear of appearing incompetent. Jeff describes how he felt: "I didn't know where to start that first year. I mean, whom can you look to for help—not knowing whom to trust? How do you know if you're doing a good job? I was afraid to ask for help so I wouldn't look weak." Most teachers adopt a similar view for dealing with the principal. Principals who know how to assist first-year teachers will be there to help because they understand that need for support. As a caution, however, don't count on having a principal that will take the time to help you on a regular basis. Urban schools are frequently overcrowded and have large enrollments, so principals have much to do with students and may expect you to survive on your own.

Kronowitz (1999) provides some sound advice for novice teachers regarding principal-teacher relationships: "You are at least 50 percent responsible for establishing a productive relationship with your principal, and you are 100 percent responsible for meeting the expectations that your principal has for you" (135). Discovering a principal's expectations requires that you examine the culture of faculty-administrator dynamics through quiet observation and active listening to colleagues about the unwritten mores that exist between administrators and teachers. It is also your responsibility to communicate with the principal on a regular basis. Many of these interchanges should be about the positive actions occurring in your classroom. Do not limit your contacts with the principal to the negative situations that occur over time.

Keep in mind that you will not be praised by the principal for constantly sending students to the office. That practice is rarely valued by principals and also has the potential to deteriorate the relationships you must build with your students. As you progress through your first year, you will recognize that some student behaviors are too extreme to handle alone. In those situations, the principal expects to be called on to help resolve the problem. Anytime an incident is emotionally charged and requires parental intervention, it is wise to inform the principal of your intentions to contact parents. If you anticipate a call or a visit from a parent to the principal due to your actions, I encourage you to inform the principal before the parents do. This may help to alleviate any misunderstandings before the situation escalates. You don't want your principal to hear of a serious problem from someone else before she or he gets the facts from you!

Changing for the Better after the First Year

Reflection on your daily teaching experiences is a key to personal and professional growth. Teachers will not improve as a result of the feedback received after a few visits from the principal each year. Teachers improve as they become adept at evaluating their interactions with students. You must become aware of the effect you have on students during lessons and in your conversations with them. Grant and Zeichner (1984) describe three components of a reflective educator:

1. open-mindedness, a willingness to consider and even admit that you are wrong;
2. responsibility, a willingness to look at the consequences of your actions; and,
3. wholeheartedness, a willingness to accept all students and to practice what you preach (cited in Kronowitz 1999, 168).

Changes in your teaching behavior will occur when you are able to spend time thinking about how your actions affect students' personal interests, motivation, and ability to grow. Listening to students and watching them are the primary means for discovering the value of your teaching strategies. Recognizing how your actions influence students and seeking alternatives requires a willingness to seek more information when strategies fail to help you reach your desired outcomes. Use as many resources as possible to discover alternative strategies to better meet students' needs: discussions with colleagues, reading of professional journals, taking additional course work, and of course, asking your students about their needs. Based on advice from colleagues and through their own reflections, the interviewees made changes that improved their relationships with their students. They discussed some of these changes with me.

Susan from San Francisco describes the changes she initiated in her development from novice educator to a more successful teacher: "I always explored options for improving my teaching with colleagues. I did manage to engage my students through improving and altering the curriculum. I also developed my inner teacher's voice. I improved my management problems by following the philosophy of a woman, Gilda Bloom, who urges us to, 'find your inner bitch.' It means you mean business—and it's got to come from your toes!" Bloom's unforgettable phrase has significant meaning for developing assertiveness when communicating and enforcing your expectations of students. I'll address the issue of assertiveness and its place in effectively communicating with students in Chapter 4.

Lisa from Los Angeles indicated her growth as a professional with these comments: "I have faith in what I am doing and what I'm supposed to do. I'm helping them [my students] to be what they can be— to find that happy space. I provide something intellectual in their lives with quiet time to read and think. Outside of school, there's frequently too much chaos in their lives. I really get to know these kids well. They really learn, and you can see it in first grade."

Tim, a Minneapolis middle school teacher, explains how he has changed: "My management issues have changed. I have better strategies, and I've learned more about kids. I'm really happy to be a part of their lives at what is a crossroads for many of them."

These stories all have a common theme: teachers becoming more acquainted with the lives of their students. Success in any school needs to be measured one student and one period at a time. Celebrate the small things that occur each hour, and let the students know about your excitement of their accomplishments.

How to Keep Your Sanity and Want to Stay a Second Year

Every first-year teacher sets high expectations, struggles regularly, falls often, makes numerous mistakes, has moments of brilliance, and probably asks at least once, "What am I doing here?" Moir (1991) provides five common phases of the development of novice teachers:

1. *Anticipation phase:* Preservice teachers romanticize teaching, believing that they will make a difference in the lives of all students. New teachers believe this for the first few weeks of teaching.
2. *Survival phase:* After the first few weeks, teachers realize that the responsibilities are enormous and time-consuming.
3. *Disillusionment phase:* Following six to eight weeks of teaching, teachers are overwhelmed by the stress associated with responsibilities, such as parent-teacher conferences and preparing report cards. Some teachers succumb to illness, and many question their decision to become a teacher or their ability to succeed.
4. *Rejuvenation phase:* Winter break arrives and teachers have time to rest, enjoy their families, and get better organized.
5. *Reflection phase:* Near the end of the year, novice teachers reflect on their successes and mistakes and plan to improve next year.

This brings them back to the *anticipation phase.*

As I read these phases and reflect on my own experiences as a first-year teacher, it occurs to me that teaching doesn't sound particularly rewarding during the first year. There are many reasons for that. To begin with, teaching is a stressful business. Picture it as one lone adult striving to remain afloat in a sea of youth. Every classroom contains a mix of students who are experiencing a multitude of emotions and are all living in their own separate world of dreams and fears. Perhaps the most common stressor we experience as educators is believing that we have the power to change the lives of every one of our students; then realizing that the task as we envision it may be beyond our capabilities. Approximately forty percent of teachers leave the field within the first five years due to stressful conditions brought on by their own disillusionment (Wilkins-Canter, Edwards, and Young 2000).

Reasonable expectations are key to successful interactions with students; but most first-year teachers establish a set of expectations that demonstrate unreasonable standards. The pain associated with setting unreasonable outcomes can pollute your view of an appropriate role for teachers and cause you to blame others instead of dealing with your students in a reasonable manner.

Instead of focusing on your students' deficits, enjoy the journey of discovering each child's strengths. Accept that there may be circumstances that you cannot control such as,

- your students' past educational experiences, developmental stages, and personalities
- vast differences in students' developmental and academic levels
- fellow teachers' poor attitudes
- the general public's negative views of urban schools
- low general funding levels for your district
- a crumbling school building.

Understanding your limitations is an important step toward focusing on the issues you are responsible for and can alter. Focus on your students—every child and adolescent has a personality that you should become familiar with as soon as possible. Find the joy that each child or adolescent brings into your room every day. Set realistic expectations for each student and focus on the progress each child makes toward those expectations.

Greet students every day as they walk into your room, and act confidently even in the face of your own uncertainty about the specific questions and events that arise each day. The adage, "Never let them see you sweat," is sound advice for every teacher. You will certainly have questions about the way you handle many situations; but handle them with confidence so students see you are capable of handling the role of teacher.

Teaching is a social business, or at least it needs to be for educators! Yee (1986) indicated that teachers prioritize *collegiality* as what they most enjoy about the profession. But finding time to socialize with colleagues can be difficult when classroom doors are closed and everyone teaches in a self-contained room. Find time to develop meaningful friendships with some of your colleagues, and use those relationships to get you through the year's hardships.

Be diligent in your preparation for school, but remember to relax frequently also. Enjoy your time away from school by engaging in regular exercise, hobbies, listening to music, and reading books that have nothing to do with education. The strength that you bring to a classroom is your own personal journey through life. Your personal life shouldn't end after you become a teacher. If it does end, then you will lose the energy that brought you into the profession. Maintain your enthusiasm for life through living loudly outside of school. Haberman (1995) called effective teachers of children of poverty "stars" and described them as, ". . . lifelong learners of various subjects, skills, and fields of study" (18).

Your students are social animals also—of course, I mean that in a positive way. Laugh with your students. Share your interests, your dreams, and your fears with students so that you come to see them as your family as well as your students. You will make plenty of mistakes throughout your teaching career—probably more your first few years though. Learn to laugh at yourself at those times and point out some of those minor mistakes to your students so they understand that you are human, too.

Always remember an important distinction for teachers: you are not friends with your students—you are friendly and businesslike when it comes to accomplishing your objectives. If you seek to learn much about your students, you will become well acquainted with their learning needs. They will value you because you have demonstrated your care and concern for their lives; however, it is not important for you to find a way to get all students to like you. Pleasing every student is impossible and is not a goal of teaching. Don't be surprised or disappointed that some students don't like you. Helping students learn is your primary role, and their liking you isn't necessarily a prerequisite for learning to occur.

First-year teachers often share their stories about being sick regularly. I have noticed that many of my former university students look

58

quite ill during their first year of teaching. I humorously recommend that they maintain a greater distance between themselves and the students. You and I know that creating physical or social distance between teachers and students is impossible and not appropriate either. On especially frustrating days during my public school teaching experiences, I used to draw a circle on the floor with chalk around my desk and announce to the students that no one was allowed into the circle. Honoring my request seemed impossible for some students who desperately needed to maintain close proximity to me during the day. Elementary and middle school students who know you care about them stand close to you and often stand on your feet when they share stories with you or need your help. You will suffer the consequences of these encounters by catching every germ that enters the room. Physical survival requires getting adequate rest and exercise—make time for both during your first year as a teacher.

Teachers who thrive in urban schools are comfortable with uncertainty. Those of you who expect predictability will become frustrated by the reality of adolescents' and children's characteristics, behaviors, and developmental abilities. Children and adolescents are not identical plastic parts that can be easily molded when the right amount of pressure is applied. They are emotional, social, physical, and cognitive beings who, despite their proximity in age, are more different from one another than alike. One of the most appealing aspects of teaching for me has always been the unpredictability of student behavior. Learn to accept or ignore those behaviors that are not disruptive or threatening to you or other students.

When unacceptable student behavior or academic performance becomes chronic and you feel helpless in resolving the problem, contact the appropriate support personnel. Initiate discussions with school counselors, psychologists, resource teachers, and reading specialists to assure proper assessments are conducted and accommodations made. Seek the advice of previous year's teachers for those students who create the greatest challenges for you. Contact parents early and often when problems emerge with their children. Early interventions may help you to establish a pattern of success with students. Be persistent in your efforts to help those students who need additional attention or services.

As important as effective planning is to the success of lessons, flexibility is just as crucial to successful lesson design and delivery. Often the best lessons and interactions occur with a spontaneous reaction to the events that unfold during the day. It is a strength to be able to adjust to the uncertainty that will be a part of every day of your teaching career. While you may adopt an understanding of the value of being flexible, novice teachers commonly note that having adequate time for planning and preparation is a problem (Kent 2000). Poor planning is one of the most frequent causes of student misbehavior. Plan well— better yet, overplan. Every experienced teacher will tell you how important it is to have more planned for students than you can possibly accomplish in one time period. That's wise advice for insuring student engagement for the time they are in your room.

Teaching is a rewarding experience for many, but it is not a job for everyone. Many of us know friends and family members who would be horrible teachers. I don't want you to merely survive your first year of teaching. I hope that you will experience many joys and in the process discover your own inner strength and value as a teacher. The teachers I interviewed realize that urban teaching is the best job for them. They have managed to escape the negativity that too many people erroneously associate with urban schools. These teachers realize that children and adolescents growing up in America's urban centers need to be nurtured and supported to gain access to the world. Gordon and Maxey (2000) report that many of the teachers who leave after the first year were some of the most promising. May you realize the value, significance, and power of your efforts to succeed as a teacher in urban schools, despite the challenges you experience the first year.

References

ARCHER, J. 2000. "Teacher Recruitment Harder in Urban Areas Report Says." *Education Week* 19, no. 20: 26 January.

BROWN, D. F. 1999. "The Value of Advisory Sessions: Perceptions of Young

Adolescents at an Urban Middle School." *Research in Middle Level Education Quarterly* 22, no. 4: 41–58.

DePaul, A. 1998. "What to Expect Your First Year of Teaching." Washington, DC: United States Department of Education, Office of Educational Research and Improvement.

Fogarty, J., M. Wang, and R. Creek. 1982, March. "A Descriptive Study of Experienced and Novice Teachers' Interactive Instructional Decision Processes." Paper presented at the annual meeting of the American Educational Research Association, New York (ERIC Document Reproduction Service No. ED 216007).

Gordon, S. P., and S. Maxey. 2000. *How to Help Beginning Teachers Succeed.* 2nd ed. Alexandria, VA: Association for Supervision and Curriculum Development.

Grant, C., and K. Zeichner. 1984. "On Becoming a Reflective Teacher." In *Preparing for Reflective Teaching*, edited by C. Grant. Boston: Allyn & Bacon. 1–8.

Haberman, M. 1995. *Star Teachers of Children of Poverty.* West Lafayette, IN: Kappa Delta Pi.

Kent, S. I. 2000. "Problems of Beginning Teachers: Comparing Graduates of Bachelor's and Master's Level Teacher Preparation Programs." *The Teacher Educator* 35, no. 4: 83–96.

Kronowitz, E. L. 1999. *Your First Year of Teaching and Beyond.* 3rd ed. Reading, MA: Longman.

Ladson-Billings, G. 2001. *Crossing Over to Canaan: The Journey of New Teachers in Diverse Classrooms.* San Francisco: Jossey-Bass.

Lidstone, M., and S. Hollingsworth. 1992. "A Longitudinal Study of Cognitive Change of Beginning Teachers: Two Patterns of Learning to Teach." *Teacher Education Quarterly* 19, no. 4: 39–57.

Maxson, S., C. R. Wright, and J. Wilson-Houck. 2000. "Urban Teachers' Views on Areas of Need for K–12/University Collaboration." *Action in Teacher Education* 22, no. 2: 39–53.

Moir, E. 1991. "Phases of New Teacher Growth." In *A Guide to Prepare Support Providers for Work with Beginning Teachers: Training Module.* Sacramento, CA: California Department of Education. 25–26.

NATIONAL CENTER FOR EDUCATIONAL STATISTICS. 1999. "Teacher Quality: A Report of the Preparation and Qualifications of Public School Teachers." Washington, DC: United States Department of Education.

ODELL, S. J. 1986. "Induction of New Teachers: A Functional Approach." *Journal of Teacher Education* 37, no. 1: 26–29.

ROSKOS, K. A. 1996. "When Two Heads Are Better Than One: Beginning Teachers' Planning Processes in an Integrated Instruction Planning Process." *Journal of Teacher Education* 47, no. 2: 120–129.

RYAN, K., ED. 1992. "Preface." In *The Roller Coaster Year: Essays by and for Beginning Teachers.* New York: Harper Collins. v.

SCHWARTZ, F. 1996. "Why Many New Teachers Are Unprepared to Teach in Most New York City Schools." *Phi Delta Kappan* 78, no. 1: 82–84.

VEENMAN, S. 1984. "Perceived Problems of Beginning Teachers." *Review of Educational Research* 54, no. 2: 143–178.

WEINER, L. 1999. *Urban Teaching: The Essentials.* New York: Teachers College Press.

WILKINS-CANTER, E. A., A. T. EDWARDS, AND A. L. YOUNG. 2000. "Preparing Novice Teachers to Handle Stress." *Kappa Delta Pi Record* 36, no. 3: 128–130.

WONG, E. 2000. "Poorest Schools Lack Teachers and Computers." *The New York Times*, 13 August, 16.

YEE, S. L. 1986. *Careers in the Classroom: When Teaching Is More Than a Job.* New York: Teachers College Press.

FOUR

Creating a Positive and Productive Learning Environment

The best urban teachers show warmth and affection to their students and give priority to the development of their relationships with students as an avenue to student growth.

GORDON (1999, 305)

. . . [A] national study that compared violent and safe schools demonstrated that safe schools were characterized by leadership that instilled a sense of fairness, belongingness, and empowerment to effect change. It was not the strict, authoritarian, rule-bound schools that were the safest.

HYMAN AND SNOOK (2000, 492)

The Challenges Urban Teachers Face

"Don't smile until Thanksgiving." "Be tough on them the first nine weeks and you'll be fine." "Make them respect you." "Let them know who's boss!" "You'll never get him to do any work, so just send him down for in-school suspension everyday!" I could fill two pages of text with phrases that teachers have disseminated through the years concerning how to manage a class of students. These friends and colleagues all mean well; however, most of the time they're passing on pieces of school lore that have little empirical support. Plus, these words of advice are not indicative of the philosophies or strategies that effective teachers use to establish a safe culture for learning in their classrooms.

The task of creating a classroom atmosphere in which students are cooperative and respectful presents the single most challenging responsibility for teachers—experienced or novice. Creating a respectful learning environment should be the first order of business for all classrooms—from the class of thirty-eight students in a New York City school to the one-room school in the hills of Montana. It can be a daunting task, especially if teachers have no compass to lead them in the right direction. I find it amusing that legislators and state departments of education often establish mandates for teacher candidates to take more content courses at the universities to better prepare them for teaching. More courses in history, literature, or biology will not cure the ills associated with the development of poor relationships between teachers and their students. The strength of teachers' academic backgrounds is not the primary reason that they struggle with students or choose to leave the profession. The failure to establish a classroom atmosphere of mutual respect is the number one reason that teachers leave the profession after their first or second year (Cangelosi 2000).

Regardless of where you choose to teach, no excuses are permitted for failing to establish a comfortable place to learn. Haberman (1995) explains, "Whatever the reasons for children's behavior—whether poverty, personality, a handicapping condition, a dysfunctional home, or an abusive environment—classroom teachers are responsible for managing children, seeing that they work together in a confined space for long periods, and ensuring that they learn" (22). Many novice teachers experience fear when they think of managing a class of urban students due to inaccurate beliefs about how to gain their cooperation. Beyond the advice from colleagues and friends are a philosophy and a set of strategies to guide teachers to successful teaching and learning with students in urban schools. Even more powerful than a set of beliefs and strategies is the power of your heart to touch the emotions of your students. Our classrooms must be a place of comfort for students: a place of physical safety as well as emotional calm. How do teachers create this kind of peacefulness in their rooms—especially when some students are not familiar with a trusting environment?

Some of you know the challenges of urban teaching, but if you're unaware of what you may experience, these statistics may reveal some of the realities of urban environments. Students' school behavior may be affected by poor diet, relationships with family, a history of poor academic achievement, negative relationships with peers, and challenges in adapting to a different culture or community (Gibbs, Huang, and Associates 1998). Haynes and Comer (1990) point out, "Children who are hungry, who feel unsafe, or who lack a sense of belonging are most concerned about getting their hunger, safety, and belonging needs satisfied. They are least concerned about deriving self-esteem or self-actualization through high academic achievement" (104).

Crosby (1999) reports that, "The new wave of immigrants of the past 25 years from Hispanic countries, from the Middle East, and from Asian countries has washed over the urban schools like a tidal wave, bringing with it additional challenges, this time cultural and linguistic" (300). Urban teachers are more recently experiencing an increase in the population of African and Southeast Asian refugees and immigrants. Many of these immigrant and refugee students experience language problems that cause increased stress. These students must also cope with adjusting to a new culture along with the loss of their previous culture (Gong-Guy, Craveks, and Patterson 1991). Gibbs and associates (1998) report that, "In adolescents, school phobia or truancy may actually represent fear of a violent or chaotic school environment or fear of social rejection due to some cultural, racial, or economic difference from the majority of the student body" (17). School should be a place of comfort, but for many high school and middle level students the social milieu creates even greater challenges than those experienced in their communities. Often African, Hispanic, Asian, and Native American and immigrant students struggle with the dichotomy of two competing sets of values that forces them to choose one set of behaviors for family settings and another for school.

As inclusion becomes a prevalent practice in public schools, students with special needs continue to enter urban classrooms in schools deeply understaffed in the area of special education. Students in urban environments who need individualized educational programs are seldom diagnosed or misdiagnosed, and as a result, fail to receive the assistance they need to succeed academically (Crosby 1999).

Additional stressors are frequently a part of urban students' lives. Dryfoos (1998) revealed that the incidence of school violence, substance abuse, and gang activity is much higher in urban schools than suburban schools. She added that urban schools, ". . . often have low expectations for students, oppressive environments, high suspension and expulsion rates, and discouraged teachers who produce students who 'act out' more frequently" (38). Adolescent nonwhites also experience identity development challenges as they struggle to understand if or how they should fit into a Eurocentric culture (Ladson-Billings 1994; Wlodkowski and Ginsberg 1995). Simply stated, students in urban environments are more likely to display disruptive behaviors in school, causing more disciplinary problems for teachers who have an inadequate number of support systems available to handle the challenges (Gibbs, Huang, and Associates 1998).

Even without knowledge of these trends, many of us realize the breadth of challenges involved in teaching in urban schools. How can teachers create a place of learning despite these challenges? The intent of this chapter is to provide information to assist you in developing a classroom atmosphere that leads to meaningful relationships with students and encourages cooperative behavior.

Developing Trusting and Caring Relationships

In extensive interviews for three years with over 150 middle school students in six Philadelphia urban schools, Wilson and Corbett (2001) discovered a common need identified by students: "Essentially the students naturally zeroed in on a phenomenon central to effective urban education that researchers have labored to depict for years—the quality of the relationship between inner-city students and their teachers"

(88). Developing a classroom atmosphere of learning begins with showing students that you care about them. Caring teachers recognize students' social and emotional needs and respond to those needs when necessary. Students' safety concerns are frequently related to emotional and social issues rather than physical issues. When Gloria Ladson-Billings (1994) studied the classrooms of effective teachers of African American students, she described an essential component: "Psychological safety is a hallmark of each of these classrooms. The students feel comfortable and supported" (73). Students will depend on you to support them through their personal struggles at school with fellow students and teachers. Without understanding your responsibility to your students' personal lives, you risk the chance of never completely connecting with your students—never really educating them.

Anita, from a Philadelphia middle school, shares her philosophy about creating a caring classroom: "Kids feel that if you really don't care about them, then they're not going to care about you. If you're in education you have to have that caring spirit. You can't just come in, teach them, and walk away. These kids have so many other needs." Anita added that getting to know students individually is one strategy for showing you care about them: "I think you have to deal with children this age in a humanistic way. They like the one-on-one touch. They like for you to be a person with them—not just this body." Showing these humanistic qualities to your students is critical to gaining their trust and cooperation. Colette, a Philadelphia high school English teacher, emphasizes the value of connecting with students: "I really believe you have to make that social and emotional connection with kids in order to get inside their heads. You have to get their heart before you get their head. The fact that you care makes them see you differently."

Building a classroom atmosphere in which trust is the foundation takes time; but it begins with learning about each student's life—by genuinely knowing students. High school teachers are just as responsible for playing this vital role for their students as are elementary and middle school teachers. Learning is an emotional as well as cognitive process, and knowing students well can establish a positive social and emotional bond. Effective urban educators capitalize on personal information they know about students to create a comfortable emotional space. Dryfoos (1998) summarized the research on the value of developing positive personal relationships with students: "The best-documented fact in the extensive U. S. literature on youth is the importance of social bonding between a young person and an adult" (39).

Pete, a high school ESOL teacher, describes the relationship he develops with his students and how his demeanor and attitude affect the class. "Academic stuff can't happen unless people feel safe, valued, and secure. My classes are a mirror of me. Whenever I've walked into a class happy, positive, and upbeat, I've never had a problem. But, I've never walked into a class ready to go toe-to-toe with someone and *not* had a problem. And how quickly they [students] pick up on it is amazing." Although there are many components to managing a classroom successfully, Pete places the caring piece into perspective: "It doesn't matter what good content you have, or what good curriculum you have, or what exciting lessons you have; if you don't care about students and they know that, you don't have a chance to get to them."

How Do You Get to Know Students?

Knowing students begins with carving time out of the academic schedule at the beginning of the year to purposely develop close ties with students. During the first few weeks of school students should be provided opportunities to:

- share stories orally about their families
- design personal shields that reflect their interests
- develop a collage with pictures that represents who they are
- write a letter that describes their goals for the year and future aspirations
- talk to classmates to find those who have common interests, experiences, and families
- describe their heroes.

Although these are primarily student activities, teachers must also become involved in them. Developing meaningful relationships with students involves sharing parts of your personal life so students can see your human side. Students begin to appreciate and understand why you choose to be with them when they see that you too have personal interests, family stories, and heroes. Students want teachers who are genuine; as Pete describes it: "Everyone can tell who's [teachers] being real and who's just putting on a show." Jeff, from Wichita, talked about how he attempts to become engaged in his high school students' lives: "I try to get to know as many kids as possible on a personal level—a one-on-one level, so when I see them in the halls, I can ask about their families. I try to see them in other settings outside of school, too."

Activities designed to become familiar with students can be connected to curricula. They don't have to be done in isolation from what students are already studying. A discussion about heroes can be connected to pertinent historical events and related literature students are reading. Personal shields can be linked to the characterization of a story.

Some urban students lack meaningful relationships in their lives. They may be missing the kind of caring that is needed to develop trust with significant family members, friends, or neighbors. Anita provides her view of a teacher's responsibilities: "We don't expect you to be their social worker or their parent; but, sometimes you better step out of that, 'I am the teacher' box." Understand that gaining the trust of every student takes time; it may be February or March before you completely unlock the mysteries of establishing a mutual respectful relationship with some students. Pete spoke of the years he faced those challenges: "There were some middle schools where I taught [in Philadelphia] that I almost gave up; however, after six months in those classrooms, I was fine. If students believe that you have their best interests at heart, they can be very tolerant of your shortcomings."

It may sound like all a teacher has to do to establish a smoothly operating classroom is begin to bridge the interpersonal gaps that can naturally exist between teachers and students; but, it's much more than that. A critical issue to consider is the distance teachers must also preserve between themselves and students. You are not a close personal friend to students. Effective educators know how to establish a comfortable social and emotional space between themselves and students to uphold an adult leadership role they must play for students and to maintain a businesslike atmosphere to insure productive learning. Some other critical pieces to developing a cooperative learning environment include

- communicating effectively with students
- establishing a set of democratic principles to maintain mutual respect
- developing and enforcing expectations
- acting assertively to protect students' right to learn
- applying consequences to students who refuse to cooperate
- choosing and delivering a meaningful curriculum
- designing learning experiences that promote student motivation.

None of these areas can be neglected if you expect students to become a part of the learning community you want to establish. Make no mistake, however; if teachers fail to develop personal connections with every student in class, attempts to gain students' cooperation will fail.

Communicating Effectively with Students

Part of caring is listening. Teachers must make a commitment to listen to students—not merely in the course of a lesson, but to stories about their personal lives. Elementary teachers will tell you that if they permitted it, their students would spend the entire day taking turns telling stories about their lives. The morning scene in the classroom is of students crowded around the desk jockeying for position to be closest to the teacher to share their stories. This scenario won't occur, though, unless students see you as interested in their lives. Developing a listening ear is a necessary part of building trust with students.

As I was waiting to interview Colette in a Philadelphia high school, several students came into the room and Colette caught them at the door to tell them that she needed to speak to me during her planning period this particular day. That meant they couldn't spend time in her room. Students frequently come into her room during their study halls and lunch periods to chat with her. Colette explains, "I talk to them, I'll listen to them. A kid told me, 'I can tell you anything.' I don't have any boys [children of her own], and they want to talk to me about personal stuff. Why are they telling me? Don't they have anybody at home to talk to about this? I think it's just an indicator that they feel comfortable. I think they know that I care about them."

Your role is to find the time during various parts of the day to talk to your students. There are many situations when you can listen to students:

- during a specifically planned part of your lesson
- between periods when students are passing in the halls
- during the first five to seven minutes of class
- in the final five to seven minutes of class
- at lunch—invite students to eat with you
- as a part of after-school detentions in which the main intent is to get to know a student who is particularly disruptive
- at students' after-school athletic, musical, or theatre activities.

These small but significant gestures can be the difference between merely playing a traditional teacher role and providing a personal support system to students.

It is common for caring teachers to recognize and become involved in students' sensitive and dangerous personal situations. Teachers have a legal and moral responsibility to respond to and report serious issues such as parental child abuse, students' misuse of alcohol and drug products, and possession of dangerous weapons when personal safety is threatened. Often the decision to report incidents to proper authorities places teachers in a dilemma with a student who has come to trust and confide in them. Although the decision to contact authorities may cause confusion, responding professionally by being honest with students is most frequently the best course of action. A wise strategy is to inform students in the beginning of the year of your interest in helping them and discussing problems when they arise. I would add in your comments to students at that point, a cautionary note: "If any controversial issues arise that I believe require contacting other professionals; such as counselors, administrators, police, or your parents/caregivers, I will do that to protect you or others who are involved in dangerous issues."

Most of the problems that students experience are not life threatening or severe enough to warrant a great deal of attention. Many of these problems can seem trivial to us as adults due to our age and life experiences. However, when we actively listen to students and provide supportive responses, they can begin to see how much we care about them. Ladson-Billings (1994) revealed the responses of eighth-grade students from one urban school when she asked what they liked about their teacher:

She listens to us!
She respects us!
She let's us express our opinions!
She looks us in the eye when she talks to us!
She smiles at us!
She speaks to us when she sees us in the hall or in the cafeteria!
    (68).

You may notice from these responses that students recognize our *nonverbal* language more so than our verbal responses to their behaviors and comments. It is of primary importance that teachers demonstrate active listening through appropriate body language. Simple actions like, facing students, maintaining eye contact, and lightly touching students on the shoulder during conversations are ways to demonstrate genuine concern. Keep in mind though that the way in which many upper- and middle-class families communicate with each other and expect others to communicate with them may be entirely different from the expectations in many urban students' lives. Additionally, second language learners may not understand your nonverbal cues. You may need to explain significant nonverbal actions to immigrant students.

Verbal Interaction Styles

I frequently ask my four-year-old daughter to do certain tasks. The words I use are not direct, yet she knows what is expected by the way I say those words: "Shouldn't you brush your teeth now?" "It's about time for bed," or "Are you ready to eat lunch?" Each of these statements is a request for action on her part, and she knows it by the way I act when I make these requests. But Delpit (1995) informs us that many urban children are used to much more direct commands. Delpit cited Snow et al. (1976) in explaining "working-class mothers use more directives to their children than do middle- and upper-class" (34). In other words, their requests sound this way, "Get to bed now," "Go in and wash your hands this minute," or for teachers "Get out your papers and place them face down on your desk." Heath (1983) indicated that children from working-class families had difficulty following the indirect requests that many teachers use because they didn't sound like rules or explicit directives to them (cited in Delpit 1995). A concisely worded directive may sound rude to you, but for many urban children, this style of discourse is necessary for them to comply with your requests. The words and tone of your voice should indicate that you're not asking for their cooperation at the moment; but instead, demanding it. These directives don't have to be yelled; but the tone of your voice should be authoritative if you expect cooperation from students. Your requests would be more appropriately worded as, "Get to class, now," "Show me your paper immediately," and "Take your hands off of Robert."

Delpit further explained that when urban students ignore commands that sound more like questions than directives, teachers may perceive students as uncooperative and insubordinate; whereas, students innocently fail to understand what's expected and why they are being disciplined. In Delpit's words, "Black children expect an authority figure to act with authority" (35).

Differences in communication styles can also affect the quality of relationships between teachers and African, Hispanic, and Native American and immigrant students. Geneva Gay (2000) explained that African Americans have a social interaction style referred to as "call-response" (91) in which students may frequently speak while the teacher is speaking as a response to their feelings about a teacher's comments. These are not meant as rude disruptions but rather as an acknowledgment of agreement or perhaps concern about teachers' comments, lectures, or explanations. Gay added, "African Americans 'gain the floor' or get participatory entry into conversations through personal assertiveness, the strength of the impulse to be involved, and the persuasive power of the point they wish to make, rather than waiting for an 'authority' to grant permission" (91). The Eurocentric tradition of taking turns is not an instructional strategy that would be beneficial for many African American students. Adrienne describes her African American high school students from Los Angeles: "Conversation is their primary priority. It's so unconscious. They are from very verbal environments. I find that they can handle side discussions and engage in the main discussion at the same time. They're not talking to be disruptive."

Among some Asian students, smiling and laughing are reactions to their confusion with and misunderstanding of language or principles being taught (Gay 2000). Gay indicated that this behavior is common among Japanese, Chinese, Korean, Taiwanese, and Cambodians who "explain that 'ritualized laughter' is a means of maintaining harmonious relationships and avoiding challenging the authority or disrespecting the status of the teacher" (103). I can see how some teachers may interpret this laughter as being disrespectful despite students' intent for it to show respect. Many cultural factors affect classroom discourse styles of all students. Gay mentions that Asians are affected by ". . . traditional values and socialization that emphasize collectivism, saving face, maintaining harmony, filial piety, interdependence, modesty in self-preservation, and restraint in taking oppositional points of view" (105).

Many immigrant students may be quite mute during lessons because of the challenges they experience learning English. Learning another language requires listening and processing much information prior to speaking it, which explains the silent behavior of many urban students. Do not confuse this silence with inability to learn or a poor attitude about learning.

It is not appropriate to generalize about a student's cultural beliefs or behavior based on identification of general background, such as assuming that all Asian students will laugh when they don't understand something. As Wlodkowski and Ginsberg (1995) stated, "There are few hard and fast rules about people, especially those who are culturally different from ourselves" (7). The power of a student's cultural identity is unleashed and celebrated when teachers initiate ways of learning more about their students' lives.

The best teachers specifically schedule individual conferences with students to establish a relationship that demonstrates a commitment to each student's success. Communicating effectively may appear to be a simple task to succeed at with students; but it requires constant attention to detail and a commitment of time to listen.

Creating a Cooperative Community

An essential aspect of effective communication is the development of a classroom community. Classrooms should be safe havens for students where their rights and property are protected. It may be more challenging establishing and maintaining a community spirit in elementary grades due to the nature of self-contained classrooms. Imagine the challenges of maintaining cooperation among thirty to thirty-five students who have been together up to six hours a day for 180 days a year. Middle and high school students present challenges also, due to the social and emotional growth that occurs between the ages of eleven to eighteen. Your classroom can be a place where students treat each other with respect and value others' property. It won't happen naturally, though. A teacher's role is to explicitly state what it means to maintain a cooperative spirit and how each student will contribute to maintaining a friendly, family atmosphere. Remember, the reason that you must create a place of comfort and safety is due to the challenges and fears that many urban students experience outside of school. You can create a comfort zone by

- establishing and enforcing a classroom policy preventing students from ridiculing or bullying other students

- demonstrating support for academic risk taking
- creating cooperative learning base groups to handle issues such as assisting students who have missed assignments due to absences
- designing many assignments that require student collaboration
- initiating peer tutoring teams to assist those students who may be considerably below grade level in reading
- encouraging students to share stories about family culture.

These are a few actions that can help teachers begin to establish a learning community. Teachers who create a community of learners enforce the attitude and belief that, "When we're all in this room, we're here to help one another; any behavior that threatens this value will be addressed." One of teachers who Ladson-Billings (1994) interviewed, "[I]nsists that her students form a viable social community before they can become a viable learning community" (40). Colette, a Philadelphia high school teacher, describes one of her community-building activities: "We play this game at the beginning of the year. Each person introduces himself (or herself), and then states something he has done that he thinks no one in the class has done. I always tell them to keep it clean! I tell them about myself first, just to get them talking. I try to get them to laugh, because when you laugh, you're more receptive. I try to create an atmosphere of trust."

Learning is a highly emotional process, and teachers and other students are frequently responsible for how a student feels emotionally and socially. Establishing a safe community may be perceived as off-task instructional behavior; however, these actions actually lead to a productive learning environment. Diane, who teaches fifth graders in San Francisco, explains, "I'm a toucher; I use proximity as I get to know kids. I welcome them when they arrive at my door in the morning. You have to have a relationship with each child. Students feel safe and nurtured here." Wilson and Corbett (2001) placed the value of focusing on the learning environments in perspective: "These classroom environment differences had little to do with gradations of individuals' acquisition of knowledge or with nuances in the content covered;

instead, environmental characteristics determined whether the majority of students learned anything at all" (42).

Creating a caring learning environment while maintaining a businesslike atmosphere is a major accomplishment in effective classroom management. Developing the appropriate balance between these two is a like walking a tightrope everyday. Let's look at the business side of effective management.

Establishing Behavioral Expectations

Although most American students attend school for thirteen years, every year teachers must explicitly inform students of classroom policies and procedures on topics such as how to respect others, consequences for not completing homework, rules for cooperative learning activities, punishments for excessive talking, and other general behavioral expectations. Teaching appropriate behavior is another curricular responsibility for educators—a responsibility that requires some prior planning and daily review for the students. Establishing a businesslike atmosphere in which students clearly understand expected behaviors, know they are responsible for their behavior, and cooperate with you requires persistence.

Developing a Student Bill of Rights

Facing a classroom of unknown students on that first day creates anxiety for teachers. Students are just as anxious. For students, they are sizing up the teacher, quietly asking, then finding answers to questions such as,

- Will I like her/him?
- Will she/he like me?
- How much work will I have to do?
- How will my needs be met? Needs such as,
  How can I get water when I need it?
  When will I be able to use the restroom?
  When will I be allowed to talk to my friends?

Will I be able to get away with showing up late?
Can I get out of my desk when I want to walk
    around?
- How can I get her/his attention?
- Will she/he help me when I'm confused?
- Will she/he embarrass me when I make a mistake?

The dance begins—students and teachers negotiating—each for their personal needs; deciding when to challenge and when to cooperate. What occurs in the first week has much to do with the comfort that students and teachers experience for the remainder of the year. Teachers set the tone for the year. Teachers have an amazing influence on students' decisions to cooperate. Yet, when teachers fail to develop a plan or publicize it as formal policy, students don't understand what's expected. Their confusion plays out in negative ways as teachers struggle to maintain a sense of order in a classroom. Students from all communities want order in their classrooms. They want to be treated with respect and provided an opportunity to grow. You won't hear many students say this, but the need is there. Adrienne, the Los Angeles high school teacher, has on occasion dismissed students from her room. She builds a businesslike attitude in her room when it's time for learning, and her students often support it: "One student said to me, 'Can't we get rid of this student? She's bothering me.'"

Designing a classroom in which students are respectful begins with the development of a student bill of rights. The expectations for student behavior should be stated in positive terms. All students from second grade through high school should participate in developing these expectations with the teacher. It may take several days to develop a list, but students' suggestions for expected behaviors and permissible actions are solicited and noted by the teacher. The list is shortened after many suggestions are collected, and the final list should be approved by all students. For approval, I suggest that students are provided with a written copy of the list of expected behaviors and be required to sign it as an indication of their intent to abide by these expectations. This signed document becomes their bill of rights—rights

to engage in learning activities without interference from others. I suggest that the contract for behavior or bill of rights may look like this:
As a student in Ms. Orland's class, I intend to:

- show respect for others and their property
- act responsibly (that means I'll have materials and homework ready when required)
- be safe
- demonstrate politeness
- cooperate with teachers and fellow students
- engage in learning activities
- ask questions when I don't understand how my behavior affects others.

Teachers also have promises to make and keep. A teacher's signed statement of expected behavior may look like this:

> As your teacher, I intend to uphold your rights to learn in a high-quality, educational environment within my classroom by enforcing these expected behaviors. I will address those students who disrespect other classmates or choose to ignore class expectations. I also intend to develop and design learning activities that meet your needs and challenge you as a learner. I promise to respect and uphold your right to ask questions about how you are treated in this classroom so that you better understand the need for a learning atmosphere. I'll respond in a fair manner to conflicts that arise between us and provide a forum for discussing disagreements between us.

This signed contract explains your role: enforcing the contract that students sign and dealing fairly and openly with those students who don't cooperate. Teachers who fail to follow through with these promises create their own management and behavior problems. Students need assurances that teachers will respond to reasonable queries concerning how situations are handled and be open to listening to their concerns. Teachers must demonstrate their sincerity to be fair and accepting of extenuating circumstances that arise.

Polly, who teaches ninth and tenth graders who have failed to do passing work prior to entering her high school in Chicago, describes her management style: "Tough love—I use it with students and teachers. I tell students, 'I'm here to help you. I'm not going to let you slide! You're not going to get away with acting the wrong way or not doing the work.' We use very structured routines here. Students know what to expect down to every little detail." Many of Polly's students have police records from gang activity and other illegal actions that may explain the structured environment that exists in her school. Despite the policies in this Chicago high school, many urban students have a need for a voice in the development of classroom policies due to their responsibilities outside of home.

Recently, some school districts have implemented a *zero tolerance* policy for certain unacceptable student actions. This policy usually results in automatic suspensions for fighting, carrying weapons, personal threats, or having any type of medication or drugs in school. These severe punishments without concern for the circumstances that create these events fail to recognize that some students do not have control over all events that occur in their lives; or, that students have a justified need for acting in ways that appear to be in direct conflict with school policy. Effective veteran teachers develop close ties with students who have reputations for disruptive behavior by renegotiating policies and behavioral expectations to better meet these students' needs without disturbing the learning process. This flexibility demonstrates your willingness to act in a fair and sympathetic manner when special circumstances require it. Teachers, however, don't permit these compromises to endanger a respectful classroom environment or disrupt the smooth flow of a cooperative classroom.

Implementing Democratic Ideals

The development of a cooperative classroom environment should be supported by a philosophy of democratic roles and responsibilities for students. If we expect students to participate in the larger democratic ideals following graduation from high school, it is imperative that we engage students in those processes in our classrooms. Establishing democratic ideals in a classroom begins with students' involvement in determining classroom expectations and policies. Teachers further encourage student participation in class decision making by having students develop a personal list of goals that they are interested in achieving throughout the year, both academic and behavioral. The teacher must take the time within the first two weeks of the year to meet individually with each student to communicate her expectations for student academic progress and listen to the intended goals of students. The goal-setting process places responsibility for learning and growth in the hands of the student—yet another action to assure that students internalize their expected responsibilities throughout the year.

Class meetings as proposed by Nelsen, Lott, and Glenn (1997) are instituted as a method of addressing problems that arise between teachers and students. The class meeting is another component of democratic principles applied to troubling classroom situations. The primary purpose of these meetings is to provide an open forum for discussion among students and with the teacher. Either teachers or students may request a class meeting to discuss a pertinent problem and develop solutions to problems that exist within a class. Teachers again reinforce the idea that students are responsible for maintaining appropriate classroom decorum through the use of class meetings, thereby increasing the chance that students will internalize their behavior. Internalization occurs when students demonstrate an awareness of how their behavior affects others and a willingness to control unruly behavior.

Many urban youth lead challenging lives outside of school. They may be responsible for raising siblings, work to make money for the family several hours a week, or be raising their own families. Despite all of these responsibilities, some teachers are reluctant to permit students to make simple decisions about their behaviors, what they study, or how they learn best. Urban students with these kinds of responsibilities outside of school resent being treated like preschoolers when decision-making opportunities arise. Shanika, a middle school teacher in Philadelphia, describes the life of one of her fifth graders:

One of my students was in court last week. She's on probation for shoplifting. She has a hard time accepting authority. The school psychologist informed me that she is basically the mother figure for the family. Her own mother relies on her to take care of all of the other children—including a baby the mother has now. So, when this student comes to school and someone tells her she can't go to the bathroom, she gives you a look that says, "What are you talking about? I take care of everyone at home!" I think it's like that for a lot of kids. I'm starting to feel that they are not badly behaved or they don't respect authority, but they are given a lot authority at home. They can fend for themselves. It's unrealistic now for them to come in and be expected to respect someone else's rules.

When these conditions do exist, particularly for middle and high school students, it's imperative that teachers use this information to determine the level of student involvement in classroom decision making.

Many students are ready to take control over circumstances of their learning. School is an appropriate forum for these democratic processes to be shared. Hyman and Snook (2000) emphasized this idea: "By using democratic processes in parenting and teaching, we help children develop internal controls based on the social contracts negotiated among parents, teachers, and peers. Teachers in democratic classrooms emphasize cooperation, mutual goal setting, and shared responsibility. Students behave because it is the right thing to do and because they respect the rights of others" (495).

Being Assertive

Most teachers are kind, considerate, respectful, sympathetic, and empathetic to the needs of others, particularly their students. It is common for preservice teachers to proclaim, "I really love children, that's why I'd like to be a teacher." These valued qualities are crucial to developing a teaching style that meets the needs of students. However, these same qualities are often accompanied by a lack of assertiveness at times when an authoritative stance is required. Novice teachers expect a return of kindness and cooperation from their students for their caring behavior. Teachers might reason, "If I act in a nice way to my students and respect them, they will treat me nicely as well."

But every student doesn't react in a positive way to our kindness. Many urban students expect teachers to maintain order and effectively neutralize students who disrupt others' learning. A serious mistake at any grade level is acting afraid of students. Many teachers enter urban classrooms with a fearful attitude that further isolates and frustrates students. Weiner (1999) warned,

> When teachers are intimidated by their students, they're unable to address behavior straightforwardly because their fear is paralyzing. In my experience in working with new teachers who are afraid of their students but unwilling to admit it, the strategy most adopt is to ignore the misconduct. Children know when teachers fear them and resent it because the fear is demeaning in its reversal of appropriate adult-child relations. The misbehaving child is not receiving suitable guidance from the adult in authority, and he or she realizes it perhaps more quickly than the adult (76).

Fearful teachers create more stress for children and adolescents who may already be experiencing seemingly impossible circumstances outside of school.

Novice teachers develop more expert skills when they finally act assertively. Assertive teachers

- uphold student-established rules
- address and correct students who violate behavioral expectations
- respond immediately to disruptive student behavior
- discourage students from hurting each other—physically or emotionally
- establish and apply a set of consequences to misbehaving students
- protect students' rights to learn
- explain to misbehaving students why their behavior is inappropriate
- involve parents and administrators when student behavior is chronic or dangerous.

Colette, the high school English teacher, provides advice for novice urban teachers: "I think somebody that really wants to be an urban teacher has to have heart; but they have to have hutspa, too. You can't come in here all soft voiced and meek and mild. They're [students] going to eat you up and spit you out. And those kids can sense whether you're afraid of them or not. I said in a joking manner, while I was wearing a Burger King crown one day, 'I am the queen in here.' They have to know that you expect things of them because sometimes these kids don't have anything expected of them at home."

Delpit (1995) speaks of the expectations of many African American students: "Black people often view issues of power and authority differently than people from mainstream middle-class backgrounds. Many people of color expect authority to be earned by personal efforts and exhibited by personal characteristics. In other words, 'the authoritative person gets to be a teacher because she is authoritative.' Some members of middle-class cultures, by contrast, expect one to achieve authority by the acquisition of an authoritative role. That is, 'the teacher is the authority because she is the teacher'" (35). Delpit describes how to establish authority in a classroom. "The authoritative teacher can control the class through exhibition of personal power; establishes meaningful interpersonal relationships that garner student respect; exhibits a strong belief that all students can learn; establishes a standard of achievement and 'pushes' the students to achieve that standard; and holds the attention of the students by incorporating interactional features of black communicative style in his or her teaching" (36).

Avoiding Power Struggles

Cangelosi (2000) distinguished between assertive, passive, and hostile responses to students. Teachers are likely to become hostile when they don't respond immediately to disruptive students, fail to establish a comfortable learning atmosphere, and are lax in enforcing class policies and expectations. Teachers act hostile because they expect students to behave appropriately but do nothing to encourage them to do so. Hostile feelings can emerge when teachers believe they have lost control of running a smooth class and are too passive with students.

Typically teachers become more assertive after their first year or two of teaching—which may be too late in an urban environment!

Shanika, who is in her second year of teaching in a Philadelphia middle school, describes how she fell into power struggles with students: "Some kids acting out just want power. Then, when you give them attention, they're taking the power away from you. I definitely fall into that with certain students. They just push my buttons. Then I sometimes say something to embarrass them in front of the class. That's cruel, and it's engaging in a power struggle that really wastes everyone's time. That's something I really want to work on—how to communicate with students when they're really in their thing. I really don't want to kick students out." Shanika's reflection on this problem is an indication of her interest in finding another strategy rather than giving up on students. Many first-year teachers, however, fail to establish an authoritative role with urban students when that's how students expect teachers to act.

Some teachers never really develop mutual respect with students because they believe that students aren't entitled to respect. Cangelosi (2000) described these hostile teachers as those who "[S]eem to view students as adversaries" (85). Teachers with this philosophy treat students like they might treat pets. They *refuse* to

- engage in personal conversation with students
- respond to individual needs
- consider students' social or physical needs
- learn about students' personal lives
- adjust curriculum to meet student needs
- respond to students who need additional assistance.

Students naturally recognize this negative teacher attitude. The resultant reaction is either a complete disregard for learning due to a lack of an emotional attachment to the teacher, or an attempt by students to gain respect by initiating power struggles with the teacher.

Power struggles between teachers and students often result in hostility and a complete lack of respect between the two. Teachers must avoid power struggles initiated by students. As students enter middle school and advance to high school their power base increases as they attempt to impress peers and other classmates by initiating arguments with teachers. Effective educators recognize students' power and defuse it by ignoring a student's attempt to engage in an argument, or providing the student with an escape route to save face in front of peers. Escape routes include defusing arguments by dropping out of a debate and turning to another topic; dismissing the class so that other students aren't an audience to a disagreement with a student; or, agreeing with an upset student when possible to demonstrate concern for difficult circumstances. Colette shares her view of handling power issues with students: "I don't get into any pissing contests with any kid. I learned that early on. I just think to myself, 'This situation has more power than my arguing about it will.'" Often merely listening to a frustrated student defuses a possible power struggle. Never enter the battle when you discover that a student needs power. Find a plausible way for the student to maintain dignity without hurting you or other students.

What Students Want

Based on interviews with Philadelphia middle school students who were primarily African American, Wilson and Corbett (2001) compiled a list of characteristics of effective teachers: "They [the students] wanted to spend their time in the company of adults who were eager to help students without playing favorites, who were strict but nice and respectful, and who took the time to explain work clearly without becoming tediously repetitive" (32). These authors further explained that students distinguished the meaning of *strict*: "[B]eing strict really had two components: maintaining order in the classroom and pushing students to complete their schoolwork" (32). These young adolescents were adamant in their explanation of the role of teachers to continuously push students to complete homework despite the amount of resistance they may offer. Teachers also need to be persistent in their efforts to help students, even in the face of numerous excuses students devise. Wilson and Corbett (2001) described their views: "Essentially, we interpreted students to be saying that the effective teachers adhered to a '*no excuses*' policy. That is, there were no acceptable reasons why every student eventually could not complete his or her work, and there were no acceptable reasons why a teacher would give up on a child. The premise was that every child should complete every assignment and that was the teacher's job to ensure that this happened" (64).

Adopting these teacher roles implies that students have a semi-external locus of control; that is, they are not completely responsible for their behavior, but instead teachers are responsible for influencing their attitudes and behaviors. By adopting this view, you are more responsible for insuring student success than is normally expected in nonurban teaching communities. This may not be a comfortable role for you if you believe students are primarily "on their own" in academic endeavors, yet, as you can see, many urban students expect and need this kind of personal prodding and support from you. The students Wilson and Corbett interviewed described the actions of one particularly effective teacher: "Teacher #1A relied on a variety of means by which he cajoled, nudged, and commanded the students to complete their assignments. These included his taking a keen interest even in the unmotivated students, always providing words of encouragement, giving students the opportunity to make up work, inviting students to come in for after-school tutoring, going over work until everyone understood it, making the work relevant to students' lives, and engaging students in the work of hands-on activities" (66). These influential teacher behaviors affect student motivation, interest, and cooperation and include components from personal relationships to instructional and curricular actions.

Inviting Cooperation

Novice teachers often believe that they can *control* student behavior and make students act appropriately. *Nothing could be further from reality.* The only way to make students do anything is to physically move them to take whatever action it is you want them to take. Physically moving students is usually not wise, not recommended, and not necessary. It is crucial to understand that when students act appropriately, *they are agreeing to cooperate with teachers.* At any time students could choose to throw chairs, push each other, talk loudly, walk out of the room, or argue with us. They don't have to act cooperatively; yet, most choose to do so. Let's focus on *why* they choose to cooperate.

Think about cooperation in your own life. Why do you cooperate with colleagues, friends, and family members? For me, the decision to cooperate is based on my interest in helping someone who has gained my respect and perhaps my admiration. The respect between us is based on the feelings associated with shared experiences. Positive feelings may have developed because this person listened to me when I was upset, showed concern when I had a minor problem, provided help when I struggled, laughed with me during an embarrassing moment, or encouraged me when I wasn't sure I was going to succeed. Remember that respect has to be earned—you are not entitled to it merely due to your position as a teacher (Delpit 1995). These are simple acts of caring between adults; the same simple acts are required between students and teachers. When students experience your caring words and efforts to assist them, the result is the development of an environment in which students see that they are valued.

Part of creating a classroom of mutual respect is how you react to disruptive students. Teachers are constant role models; and, as such, need to recognize how they react to students is a public forum in which every student is watching. In the normal course of a day, teachers may have thousands of social interactions (verbal and nonverbal) with students. Each separate communication with students is an opportunity to encourage them or perhaps destroy their self-efficacy. Actions such as kind words, soft touches, and positive nonverbal signals all affect how students perceive you.

It takes assertive behavior to also gain a level of respect among students. Effective teachers act calmly, but firmly, when they address disruptive behavior. Being direct in the way you communicate with students sends a message that you are determined to gain students' cooperation and will definitely take the necessary steps to protect other students' rights and your own during frustrating moments. To protect students, teachers react to infractions of established expectations in ways that send the message that inappropriate behaviors are not acceptable; and, that these behaviors will be addressed immediately and

in a logical manner. Acting this way requires consistency on your part;
meaning you'll consistently

- treat students with dignity even when they violate policy
- permit students to explain the reasons for acting inappropriately
- involve students in determining how they will change their behavior
- explain how disruptive students affect other students' learning.

Adrienne describes the management style in her high school class
in Los Angeles: "My students know that I really want what's best for
them. I give a lot of praise, and they know it's real. I'll say to students,
'If you're in my class, you've made a decision.' They have an external
locus of control, and I try to help them take control of those factors
they can affect. I say to them, 'If your behavior affects someone else's
learning, you're out of here.' I also send students out when they're not
ready for class." Adrienne creates the learning environment that students described to Wilson and Corbett (2001) and that Delpit (1995)
promotes in which expectations are clearly stated, no excuses are permitted, and inappropriate behaviors are dealt with immediately.

Teachers with whom students experience positive interactions develop relationships that encourage student cooperation. Students value
the relationship with the teacher in these environments and choose
to help maintain a positive learning environment. Every student will
not immediately become compliant with you because you show concern and respect for them; however, most students will cooperate.

Being Fair Means "Different Strokes for Different Folks"

Naturally, it's those two or three students in every class who are chronically disruptive with whom you need to know how to negotiate. Acting consistently as described in the previous steps sends a message to
students that you are willing to uphold the expectations for learning
that the class developed collaboratively. Some educators insist that

teacher consistency also extend to how consequences are applied. I disagree with this belief.

Most teachers readily accept and acknowledge the fact that each student is at a different place cognitively—that each brings a set of skills, strategies, and a base of knowledge that is distinct from every other student. Intellectual difference is where many teachers, however, draw the line in their recognition of and reaction to students' varying personal characteristics. What's missing is a clear understanding and reaction to the fact that every student has a distinct social, emotional, and physical makeup that requires individualized treatment. After the first two weeks of school, every teacher knows which students become upset by simple disapproval and which ones feel no embarrassment for acting absurdly inappropriately. Knowing from whom to expect the worst behavior, effective teachers begin to react to inappropriate behavior with different sets of responses: a response as punitive as out of school suspension and others as simple as a tap on the shoulder and a scowl to denote disapproval. These two reactions may even be applied to the same misbehavior. Are teachers justified in individualizing their application of consequences?

If you believe that students are indeed diverse socially, emotionally, and physically, then you have good reason for reacting differently to similar behavioral infractions. For example, Tessa shows up late to your first-period class every day. You become concerned after four days of this. The late notes that you gave her that she was required to take to the office didn't seem to have the impact of altering her behavior. You ask her to speak to you after class so that you can gain her perspective on the problem. You discover in your conversation that she is responsible for walking her five-year-old younger brother to her aunt's house located several blocks away from the school every morning. This causes her to be late. Her parents speak little English, and you're certain they won't be able to alter these circumstances for her. You have many options to deal with her actions; but the ones available will do nothing to change Tessa's behavior—and you're certain that she understands her school responsibilities. An in-school suspension will not improve Tessa's lateness. So, you ignore school policy (remember zero tolerance policies) and explain to Tessa that she should sit close to her classmate when she comes in late so that Maria can help her catch up with the rest of the class without disrupting other students. No penalties are attached to this—just the expectation that Tessa will act responsibly to keep up with the class.

Jim, who's in the same class as Tessa, shows up late almost as frequently as Tessa. When you address this by speaking to Jim after class, he explains defensively, "I don't have to be on time, and you can't really make me show up on time!" Your response, given calmly, is, "Jim, I become upset when you choose to miss the first part of my class because I believe that you need this information. If you have a valid reason for coming in late, I'm willing to listen to it. For now, I'm going to require that you see me after school for a conference to discuss what we can do about this to prevent it from occurring again." Jim knows that Tessa is coming in even later than he is some days, so he blurts out, "Tessa is always later than me, and nothing happens to her! That's really not fair!" A possible response is, "Tessa needs to come in later because of family responsibilities that you may not have to deal with in your life. She gets treated differently because she has different needs than you."

That's a simple case to resolve, and students may be more likely to understand family responsibilities than why some students are permitted to stand during class when they aren't. But the response for the student that isn't permitted to stand when another is allowed is the same as it is for Jim: "She needs to stand due to her physical energy level during this class time—however; you don't have the same physical energy level; and therefore, not the same need to stand." This explanation of *fair* may be needed when some students need to eat in class, others need more time to complete assignments, or someone has permission to draw during teacher-directed instruction.

Effective educators are able to explain these differences to their students in ways that clarify a more accurate and advanced meaning of the word *fair*. Parents will need to hear your version of *fair* also. You shouldn't apologize for treating students differently based on their physical, social, or emotional needs; especially when we think nothing of placing students into different classes or require they read at different levels to match their appropriate reading abilities. Lavoie

(1989) defined *fair* as, "Each student getting what he or she needs." Those needs are not the same for each student—even when we're talking about how we choose to enforce expectations and apply consequences. Students at first may not understand that they will be treated differently. I suggest adding the principle of *fair* to the list of values that teachers are responsible for passing on to their students to assure a sense of civility and respect in schools.

Alternatives to Punishment and Appropriate Consequences

Nothing gets as challenging as finding a consequence for misbehavior that actually has the impact of altering students' behaviors. Altering behavior is the specific purpose and part of the definition of *punishment*. Redl and Wattenberg (cited in Charles 1999) defined punishment as, "Planned, unpleasant consequences, not physical, the purpose of which is to change behavior in positive directions" (300). As an experienced teacher, the key phrase in this definition is, "the purpose of which is to change behavior." Think of all the circumstances in which teachers punish but students' behaviors seldom change. The same children are kept in for recess for days on end. Is their behavior changing—apparently not! Day after day, the same high school students are placed into in-school suspension. To what extent does their behavior change? I believe that if teachers considered whether their punitive actions might actually alter a student's behavior, they would choose to treat students differently when misbehavior occurs.

Students won't actually change behavior until they take time to internalize their actions. Students internalize when they think about how their behaviors affect others, then choose to act differently based on a personal reflection or "internal voice" (Covaleskie 1992, 176). Teachers must encourage misbehaving students to reflect on the effects of their behaviors, and invite them to think of alternative ways of acting. Of course, one of the problems for chronically misbehaving students is their inability to consider or care about how their behaviors affect others. Helping students to understand how their behaviors affect others takes time—particularly with children and adolescents from distressed environments. Brendtro and Long (1995) described why many children act violently: "[C]hronically violent behaviors may result from broken social bonds, stress and conflict, a culture of violence, and unhealthy brains" (53). Developing close social bonds with teachers is a way for children and adolescents to want to self-manage behavior as they begin to trust adults. However, many teachers aren't willing to take the time to pass through this stage of unrest with students to develop the trusting relationships required to gain students' cooperation. As Brendtro and Long stated, "Although understanding teachers could offer surrogate bonds, these children's behavior drives most adults away" (53).

It takes a serious commitment of time and the patience of a saint for teachers to establish a level of trust needed to gain cooperation from some children and adolescents; especially students who lack meaningful relationships with other adults in their lives. Establishing these bonds may take months, and many teachers are too impatient to permit these personal relationships to unfold. Teachers will encourage student internalization while establishing social bonds if they

- establish and uphold a classroom atmosphere of mutual respect
- involve students in making decisions about classroom expectations
- establish a congruent communication pattern with students
- set realistic expectations of behavior for students; especially those who have a history of chronic disruptive behavior
- use punishment as a last resort
- connect punishment to the inappropriate behavior
- help students to discover their own emotional, social, and cognitive needs
- establish short-term behavioral contracts with chronic disruptive students with clearly determined consequences.

Anytime teachers choose to enforce their expected behaviors, they must find strategies to encourage students to think about their behavior so that they will be discouraged from acting inappropriately again. Punishment is seldom the best course of action. Punitive teachers actually have a higher percentage of student misbehavior than teachers who use alternative strategies to gain students' cooperation (Cangelosi 2000). There are other dangers associated with using excessive and extreme punishment in urban schools. As Brendtro and Long (1995) stated, "[S]chool discipline rooted in punishment or exclusion only further estranges these [socially at-risk] students" (53). Yet, I often hear preservice teachers say, "You have to really punish these [urban] students and yell at them because that's all they respond to." It doesn't take much yelling at students before they completely shut down and ignore teachers.

Students are more likely to cooperate if teachers help them discover their own emotional needs. Marshall Shelton (2000) spoke of how teachers can help students to perceive their emotional needs by helping them focus on three areas:

1. *self-awareness:* recognizing one's feelings, temperament, and style
2. *self-management:* impulse control, organization, and outlook
3. *relationships:* social skills and team mindedness (30).

In this model, the teacher makes the usual observations of students in the course of the day based on these three components. Students are then asked to personally assess how they respond to learning situations in all three areas: self-awareness, self-management, and relationships with others. After students identify their skills in these areas, teachers meet individually with each student to discuss their observations and students' conclusions. During this conference, the teacher and student develop a set of skills that the student needs to work on and sign a contract that establishes a tentative timeline for improvement (Shelton 2000).

Teachers are responsible for applying consequences that have the chance of altering behavior when students persist in acting inappropriately. The most effective means of assuring that students will cooperate is establishing a classroom in which students want to be engaged in learning with you and other students. This chapter began with a section on creating trusting and caring relationships because developing that foundation with students is the start of creating a place where students want to be each day. Therefore, if students want to be in your classroom, and they know you want to be with them, then a logical consequence for misbehaving is removal from your room. Let me explain *removal*. I am not referring to permanent banishment from your room—as in suspension or in-school suspension. Removal simply means that if students don't choose to cooperate, then effective, assertive educators ask students to leave so that fellow students may learn, and teachers may teach in a calm and orderly environment.

Students have hundreds of reasons for not being ready to cooperate with teachers, interact with classmates, or engage in learning activities on any given day. Effective managers don't take disruptive students' behaviors personally; they simply uphold the class expectations by removing students from a situation that apparently doesn't match their level of attention or control. Asking students to leave is done with a calm voice and gentle manner. In these instances of student misbehavior, teachers maintain emotional control, speak calmly, and treat students with dignity. Remember that mutual respect is a need for you and your students—regardless of their actions. So, removal from class is treated more like a cooling off period—a chance for students to reflect on their behavior and choose whether they want to return and cooperate for the day, or meet you at a later time to make up for missed learning. In posing this question, students are given the responsibility and decision-making authority to choose how they will handle their emotional and social needs at the moment. Teachers must constantly remind and demonstrate to students that they are responsible for and in control of their behavior. The alternative is for students to blame teachers for their problems, an easy response for students looking for excuses to act inappropriately.

Students don't go into hallways when they are asked to leave; they go into another teacher's room—a colleague of yours with whom you have an agreement to exchange and harbor students who are having a challenging day. The removal period can last for the remainder of the time that students are expected to be in your room or for just a few minutes. Removal is not intended to be punitive; but instead, used an intervention that sends the message that a student is not ready for class at this point and therefore, is not allowed to disrupt the learning of others. The most critical question to ask is, "Will removing a student alter behavior?" That question cannot be answered immediately. The response is based on the student's desire to be with you as a teacher or involved in learning with classmates. The answer may not be determined for several days because it takes many interventions to actually alter a student's behavior. That's where most teachers fail in choosing strategies to alter behavior—they refuse to try an intervention for a long enough period of time to note its impact. If you want to discover whether a strategy you use actually works, keep records of disruptive students' behavior in a daily journal to see if your interventions over extended periods of time have an impact. Patience is again imperative to seeing your efforts as successful interventions.

There are other strategies and consequences for encouraging students to cooperate that are not as punitive as traditional ones. The focus in disciplining students should be to send a message that you want them in class, and that they are responsible for displaying cooperative behavior. These overriding views should be considered whenever teachers choose a consequence for students' misbehavior.

I believe that after-school detentions are necessary; but not in a punitive sense. The way that they are handled determines how effectively they alter future behavior. If teachers, for instance, use detentions to develop a closer relationship with a student, then the time spent after school leads to more productive behavior. Detentions should involve a chance for the teacher to investigate a number of student characteristics. I suggest teachers engage in conversation with the student about topics such as

- a student's home life—siblings, parent relationships, after-school routines
- social relationships with peers
- relationships with other teachers and academic status in other classes
- student's perceived strengths
- student's perceived areas of need

96

- discovering the student's perspective on how you can help her or him
- developing a set of goals for future behavior control
- drafting a contract to encourage appropriate behavior
- negotiating different expectations for cooperative behavior
- choosing a classmate as a partner to help improve behavioral and academic performance.

These are a few of the possible topics that should become components of the discussion that occurs between teachers and students in after-school detentions. After you get to know the student better, other activities may be necessary. Perhaps detentions will be needed so that you can assist the student in completing assignments or so two students can work through a conflict. The philosophy for detentions is that they provide needed one-on-one time between teacher and student when disruptive behavior occurs. Although you may think this sounds like a reward instead of a punishment, please recall that the purpose of these interventions is to alter future behavior. Building levels of trust through getting to know students is the most salient route to gaining their cooperation. Remember that trusting relationships, particularly with adults, is one of the greatest needs of many urban youth.

Keeping Students in Class

Students won't get the help they need if they are removed from your class daily. Time after time, urban teachers mention to me that many students have difficulty working independently. Several reasons for this exist: the academic work is too difficult; students aren't comfortable taking the risks needed to accomplish a task due to previous failures; some students can't focus for long periods of time; some students need constant reassurance that they are on the right track with assignments; and others simply refuse to engage in academic work because they have gotten away with avoiding it for so many years. Many urban classrooms are filled with too many students—student-teacher ratios of one to thirty-three and even one to thirty-eight students are common. It is an impossibility for you to get to all students and provide the assistance they need with these crowded conditions. The result of teacher inattention and students' inability to work independently is behavior problems. It is certainly unreasonable to remove three to ten students from class every day! Yet, you need help getting to every student; and, if you don't, disruptions will most certainly occur.

Wise teachers avert potential disruptions by pairing students together early in the year so that they can use each other for assistance when they work on assignments. Choosing appropriate pairs takes time. You want to be certain that students are capable of developing a cooperative relationship—one that is productive and symbiotic. Paired students should be in close proximity academically and also be capable of helping one another succeed with challenging assignments. It is imperative to model effective interactions for paired students by initially role playing situations so that students have a clear idea of how to work collaboratively. Early student evaluations of their paired activity also provide feedback to you and the students about the effectiveness of their collaboration and strategies for changing their interactions. I know that pairing students isn't a solution for every disruptive behavior problem teachers encounter; however, this type of intervention is preventative. Effective teachers think of how they can prevent students from being disruptive before problems arise.

A strategy that some elementary and middle school teachers find to be effective is having students themselves keep records of their behavior patterns. In this scenario, chronic disruptive students are required to keep a five-by-eight card taped to their desk. Whenever the teacher notes inappropriate behavior, she or he signals to the student to record a mark on the card. Within a week, the student is encouraged to make her or his own marks. The teacher and student review the marks each week and decide on a course of action to alter future behavior. This self-evaluation increases the likelihood that students will internalize their behavior and consider alternative behaviors.

These are a few strategies that urban teachers have found beneficial in gaining students' cooperation. This list isn't meant to be inclusive of every strategy that could influence an urban child's behavior. The focus of management in effective classrooms is on gaining cooperation; and whatever interventions are used, cooperative behavior is the intended goal. However, structuring learning activities around the needs and interests of students is even more effective in encouraging student cooperation than punitive actions.

How Do Curriculum and Instruction Affect Management?

Students may need several reasons to agree to cooperate with teachers. Establishing a mutually respectful class, showing concern for students' personal lives, and using congruent communication are all critical components of gaining students' cooperation; but there's more. Because teachers are responsible for students' academic growth— despite the lack of skills and background knowledge some urban students may bring to school—teachers must use materials, instructional strategies, and curricula that are meaningful to urban youth.

Many urban teachers readily admit that a high percentage of their students are reading below grade level. Using traditional grade level textbooks, therefore, will not meet the needs of many urban students. The alternative is to choose reading material that matches the needs of students. Urban teachers need to collect trade books, picture books, and novels for students that address the themes and topics that students need to learn at a level that they can comprehend. Trade books may be used in every subject area from reading to social studies to mathematics. The teaching of essential skills and strategies is not abandoned. Students receive the same information but through a medium that better matches their learning needs. Remember that teachers must find ways for students to succeed in school in order to maintain a cooperative classroom. Students are unlikely to be motivated by or succeed with instructional materials that ignore their academic abilities.

Students need to believe that they can succeed. Choosing the appropriate reading level materials provides students with the opportunities for success. This may involve spending your own money on some books. A better plan is to seek to use textbook funds from the district for alternative books. Whatever resources are used, teachers are responsible for discovering the abilities of their students and providing appropriate materials to match their needs.

Curriculum guidelines are generally communicated and directed to teachers quite bureaucratically. The idea of standardization seems plausible to administrators and school boards of large urban districts. This philosophy, however, that one curriculum fits all students is ludicrous! Students, especially at-risk students, will not become engaged with curricula that fail to address their personal lives. However, no teacher will be able to maintain the interests of students without purposely designing curricula with the needs of students in mind. When students find meaning in the topics that are studied, their engagement with learning is increased and the chance for continual behavior problems is diminished. National Middle School Association (1995) suggests that schools offer "curriculum that is challenging, integrative, and exploratory" (20). Teachers who choose curricular topics that are relevant to the lives of students create a solid foundation of learning that cements the cooperation of students.

Many teachers believe they have more control over how the curriculum is taught than what is taught (Brown 1990). The joys of teaching are derived from the successes teachers gain from the creative design and delivery of lessons that actively engage students in learning. Lesson design is the artist's canvas for teachers—an opportunity to provide experiences for students that make the trip to school a meaningful and lasting event. Effective teachers design powerful lessons by gauging the needs of their students, considering the level of their abilities, providing diverse ways for students to interact with materials, and monitoring student learning during the course of a lesson to adjust their plans for student success. These minute calculations and alterations during the course of a lesson are the tricks of the trade and have an impact of insuring that all students are engaged in learning.

When teachers attend to the details of lesson planning and delivery, student behavior can be positively affected. Chapters 6 and 7 provide more information on how teachers can design and deliver lessons that positively impact urban students. Effective teachers understand how critical lesson planning and delivery are to their students' behaviors. Teachers must be mindful of how students will act if specific instructional strategies are chosen—from cooperative learning activities, to independent seatwork, to planning individual conferences in the course of a daily lesson. Understanding and predicting how students will act during a lesson are crucial details that cannot be overlooked when planning.

Limits of Responsibility

Many circumstances in the lives of urban students are beyond the control and power of classroom teachers. Teachers should not believe that they can solve every problem that arises in their classroom. The lives of urban youth are shaped by experiences and circumstances that we frequently cannot directly affect despite how much we care. Wise educators listen to students and send the message that they are there to help, but also realize when more appropriate interventions are necessary. Schools are responsible for providing counseling and nursing services, and often a teacher's best course of action is to refer students for counseling or medical assistance. Often a teacher's job is to involve an administrator or call a child's caregivers to choose an appropriate intervention. Special services are sometimes necessary for students.

Sometimes practical advice for handling a student problem can come from students' former teachers, administrators, or from students' caregivers. Asking for assistance in times of trouble is an appropriate action to take and provides a net for you to fall into when you have exhausted all possible options within your control. When a student of yours is teetering on the edge of danger, you can't always be the lifeguard. Inquire about the services available to you as you begin your teaching career in an urban school and use those services when needed.

Timing can be critical to assisting a student that needs additional services. You will notice within the first few weeks of school that some students who struggle both academically and emotionally need additional help as soon as possible. Each school district has a policy for recommending students for additional services. That process begins with you! If you hope to help students receive services they need within the same school year that you teach them, then the process begins with you recording information about a student immediately upon noticing his or her difficulties. The information you collect depends on the problem, but your role in providing appropriate interventions begins with keeping a daily journal in which you record specific student actions. The comments you write may be academic problems, such as noticing that a student isn't able to identify letter sounds or hasn't learned multiplication tables up to ten despite being in sixth grade. Perhaps the problems are emotionally related, such as an adolescent starting fights regularly, a student showing signs of severe depression, or a student who never speaks in class. After speaking to teachers who have known the student from previous years, you may be ready to make a formal request for assistance.

The first comment you'll probably hear from an administrator, a learning support teacher, a psychologist, a social worker, or a member of the school's instructional support team is, "What have you done already to alleviate the problem?" If your response is, "I've just done the first thing; I told you there's a problem," then you will be required to attempt some specific strategies and note how successful the interventions are for the student. In many schools, an instructional support team or IST exists. The IST may be composed of the following personnel:

- school principal
- reading specialist
- social worker
- district school psychologist
- learning support teachers.

Parents and caregivers are also invited to participate in the initial meeting with these personnel to listen and provide pertinent data about previous interventions and behavior at home. The IST group meets, discusses the student's behaviors and academic abilities, and suggests interventions to help this student succeed. You are expected to apply these suggested interventions and keep accurate records on their effectiveness.

After a period of at least thirty to sixty days from the first meeting, you report back to parents and the IST on the effectiveness of the interventions. At this second meeting, more strategies and interventions are suggested if the original ideas failed. Following another thirty- to sixty-day trial-and-error period with the newly suggested interventions, another meeting may be called to request that specific tests be initiated to determine if more strenuous interventions are needed. Additional tests such as achievement tests, I.Q. tests, or psychological assessments typically require parental permission before they can be initiated. The value of working with parents and caregivers from the beginning is sometimes rewarded when they approve of specific interventions and testing that may be necessary to assist a child or adolescent. It is imperative to persist in your attempts to provide additional assistance for students who need it despite the barriers you may experience in urban school districts.

Classroom teacher interactions are usually the most powerful and often the only interventions that will be implemented during an academic year with students who have special needs. Urban schools frequently lack the infrastructure, especially support personnel, to provide additional services for many students—particularly students who need minor interventions or accommodations to succeed. The bottom line becomes, "Handle it the best you can within your room."

While you're attempting to handle every situation and crisis effectively, remember to demonstrate your sense of humor—that may be your most effective tool for gaining the respect and trust of your students and the best strategy for keeping your head above water when the crises seem insurmountable. Despite the advice and research provided here, gaining trust and respect from urban students is an unpredictable venture involving many instances of trial and error and risks. Reaching students emotionally and socially is necessary to form the meaningful connections required for genuine learning to occur.

Lois Weiner (1999) explained that urban teachers need "moral authority" to be successful: "Urban teachers' primary source of control is their 'moral authority,' which rests on the perception of students and parents that the teacher is knowledgeable about the subject matter, competent in pedagogy, and committed to helping all students succeed, in school and life. When you make instruction engaging and worthwhile and when you establish a classroom environment that is based on mutual respect, you establish your moral authority, which gives you more control and authority than the threat or use of punishment" (77–78). Creating meaningful learning environments for urban students involves more than establishing personal bonds with students—it also requires developing and delivering engaging curricula and instruction.

References

BRENDTRO, L., AND N. LONG. 1995. "Breaking the Cycle of Conflict." *Educational Leadership* 52, no. 5: 52–56.

BROWN, D. F. 1990. "The Effects of State Mandated Testing on Elementary Classroom Instruction." Diss. University of Tennessee.

CANGELOSI, J. S. 2000. *Classroom Management Strategies: Gaining and Maintaining Students' Cooperation.* 4th ed. New York: John Wiley.

CHARLES, C. M. 1999. *Building Classroom Discipline.* 6th ed. New York: Addison Wesley Longman.

COVALESKIE, J. F. 1992. "Discipline and Morality: Beyond Rules and Consequences." *The Educational Forum* 56, no. 2: 172–183.

CROSBY, E. A. 1999. "Urban Schools Forced to Fail." *Phi Delta Kappan* 81, no. 4: 298–303.

DELPIT, L. 1995. *Other People's Children: Cultural Conflict in the Classroom.* New York: New Press.

DRYFOOS, J. 1998. *Safe Passage: Making It Through Adolescence in a Risky Society: What Parents, Schools, and Communities Can Do.* New York: Oxford University Press.

GAY, G. 2000. *Culturally Responsive Teaching: Theory, Research, and Practice.* New York: Teachers College Press.

GIBBS, J. T., L. N. HUANG, AND ASSOCIATES. 1998. *Children of Color: Psychological Interventions with Culturally Diverse Youth.* Updated edition. San Francisco: Jossey-Bass.

GONG-GUY, E., R. CRAVEKS, AND T. PATTERSON. 1991. "Clinical Issues in Mental Health Service Delivery to Refugees." *American Psychologist* 46, no. 6: 642–648.

GORDON, G. L. 1999. "Teacher Talent and Urban Schools." *Phi Delta Kappan* 81, no. 4: 304–307.

HABERMAN, M. 1995. *Star Teachers of Children in Poverty.* West Lafayette, IN: Kappa Delta Pi.

HAYNES, N. M., AND J. P. COMER 1990. "Helping Black Children Succeed: The Significance of Some Social Factors." In *Going to School: The African-American Experience*, edited by K. Lomotey, 103–112. Albany, NY: State University of New York Press.

HEATH, S. B. 1983. *Ways with Words.* Cambridge: Cambridge University Press.

HYMAN, I. A., AND P. A. SNOOK 2000. "Dangerous Schools and What You Can Do About Them." *Phi Delta Kappan* 81, no. 7: 488–501.

LADSON-BILLINGS, G. 1994. *The Dreamkeepers: Successful Teachers of African American Children.* San Francisco: Jossey-Bass.

LAVOIE, R. D. 1989. *How Difficult Can This Be? Frustration, Anxiety, and Tension Understanding Learning Disabilities: The F.A.T. City Video.* Arlington, VA: WETA.

NATIONAL MIDDLE SCHOOL ASSOCIATION. 1995. *This We Believe: Developmentally Responsive Middle Level Schools.* Columbus, OH: Author.

NELSEN, J., L. LOTT, AND H. S. GLENN. 1997. *Positive Discipline in the Classroom.* Rocklin, CA: Prima.

SHELTON, C. M. 2000. "Portraits in Emotional Awareness." *Educational Leadership* 58, no. 1: 30–32.

SNOW, C. E., A. ARLMAN-RUP, Y. HASSING, J. JOSBE, J. JOOSTEN, AND J.

VORSTER. 1976. "Mother's Speech in Three Social Classes." *Journal of Psycholinguistic Research* 5: 1–20.

WEINER, L. 1999. *Urban Teaching: The Essentials.* New York: Teachers College Press.

WILSON, B. L., AND H. D. CORBETT. 2001. *Listening to Urban Kids: School Reform and the Teachers They Want.* Albany, NY: State University of New York Press.

WLODKOWSKI, R. J., AND M. B. GINSBERG. 1995. *Diversity and Motivation: Culturally Responsive Teaching.* San Francisco: Jossey-Bass.

FIVE

Choosing Appropriate Curricula

I think curriculum guides are non-thinking, closed-ended, and just for rote. That's not what I consider learning.

SUSAN, SAN FRANCISCO TEACHER

That's what school should be about: Teachers and curriculum being flexible enough to meet the needs of each student, not shoving every kid through some distant committee's phantasmic pipe dream of a necessary curriculum for tomorrow's workforce

SUSAN OHANIAN (1999, 2)

For SLL [second language learners] students, even those with moderately strong literacy skills, few things are as daunting or as potentially demoralizing as an inch-and-a-half thick textbook, designed for native English speakers, dense with print, bursting with facts and questions, and lousy with new vocabulary.

STEPHEN CARY (2000, 56)

The Real Meaning of Curriculum

Curriculum is an encompassing term that has many different connotations for the stakeholders in education: parents, teachers, children, administrators, school board members, and legislators. Constant debate and rhetoric about what students should learn continue as each interest group touts its priorities—and it seems every decade teachers hear more voices pleading their case for a specific curricular focus! Helping students become Americanized through the "melting pot" analogy became the role of urban schools, for many years during the late 1880s and again in the early 1900s as large populations of immigrants entered the United States. As a result, curricula were designed for that purpose. This emphasis has become a tradition, and curricula continue to reflect a Eurocentric perspective to insure that all children and adolescents learn a prioritized and predetermined set of facts. Curricula in many school districts are designed to be teacher proof to insure that a standardized scope and sequence of facts are taught from year to year without the threat of teacher influence. When teachers accept these premises for delivering curricula, their role becomes one of covering as much of the curriculum as is possible in a year. In an effort to cover so much content in a short time period, anything that is learned is easily forgotten and seldom holds significant meaning for students (Caine and Caine 1994).

As a result of this push to deliver ever-more content, students' cognitive and social needs as well as their backgrounds and abilities are ignored. Real learning, the kind of growth that leads to the development of better minds, is seldom associated with the act of accumulating isolated facts in short time periods. Yet, standardized curricula delivered in short time periods through isolated disciplines continue to influence teaching and learning (or lack there of) in classrooms.

Researchers in the late 1980s and throughout the 1990s provided an alternative curricular focus based on newfound information on learning or brain-based theories and the need to promote thinking processes (Caine and Caine 1994; Costa 1991; Ennis 1985; Jensen 1998; Perkins 1992; Wolfe and Brandt 1998). Following the dissemination of the research on brain-based learning and teaching for thinking, a few schools began to adopt a different view of curricula. In alternative approaches to curricular foci, students are involved in indepth investigations and integration of content through the study of broad themes that reflect *their* interests (Beane 1993)—not the interests of a few dead white Anglo males who recommended what everyone should know over 100 years ago.

The influence of research in early childhood education during the 1980s managed to arrest the practice of pushing complex and abstract content from the upper grades into preschool and primary-age classrooms. Appropriate age-level activities and curricula called developmentally appropriate practices (DAP) were adopted in preschool and primary classrooms through the influence of organizations like the National Association of the Education of Young Children (NAEYC) (NAEYC 1988; Elkind 1987). In developmentally appropriate curricula, activities are designed to meet the cognitive needs of children rather than the desires of overzealous parents and legislators. Unfortunately, high school and middle school curricula were unchanged by DAP theory. The idea that learning materials should match the cognitive ability levels of students didn't catch on at the secondary level. The thinking skills emphasis and an understanding of brain-based learning have also minimally altered the delivery of standardized curricula. So-called "rigorous" standards continue as urban secondary school students especially suffer through the malaise of poorly designed curricula.

The American Heritage Dictionary (2000) defines *curriculum* as, "All the courses of study offered by an educational institution"; however, it is much more than merely "courses of study" (446). Many teachers believe that curricula are those concepts and principles covered in textbooks. Other educators believe that the curricula they are expected to teach are clearly outlined in district guides that are usually redesigned and distributed once every three to five years. Knowles and Brown (2000) provide a broader focus in defining curricula: "Curriculum is

- the total experience of students at school
- a plan that involves students in learning
- a construct that enables students to access, process, interpret, and make connections to information" (73).

109

Teachers Decide What Students Learn

Regardless of the beliefs of the public, educational researchers, or school administrators, curriculum is ultimately determined by what occurs in each classroom. Teachers decide what students will learn in their rooms. Curricula, therefore, are determined by teachers, or as Ohanian (1999) put it, "We are the curriculum" (9). Curricula are not merely the materials or the concepts and principles we all hope students will learn. Curricula include our behaviors as teachers: such as the way we speak and listen to students; the respect we show them; recognition of their culture and families; identification of and responses to their differences and stages of development; plus, the strategies we use to engage students in the learning process. Despite mandates, textbook adoptions, the influence of achievement test scores, and district guidelines, each teacher is responsible for the learning that occurs in their classroom. Every action taken is a demonstration of what each teacher intends for students to learn. Some call the unwritten principles that students learn the "hidden curriculum," that is, those ideas that are not explicitly stated in the district guidelines. The hidden curriculum is more obvious than that, however, and every student you encounter will clearly understand your agenda by your actions. There's nothing hidden about the way teachers act in classrooms! How can you, then, positively influence learning in your classroom through the curricular decisions you make?

A definitive way to decide what to teach is to ask the question, "What should students know and be able to do as a result of being in your classroom for a year?" Experienced educators know something that I wish every legislator and administrator could accept: each student has a different set of curricular needs based on her or his personal interests, academic and social backgrounds, and developmental characteristics. Based on the fact that classrooms are usually comprised of a student-to-teacher ratio of approximately thirty-to-one, it seems highly unlikely teachers will be able to individualize instruction and curriculum for so many students. Forced into this arrangement, teachers generally choose to deliver a standardized curriculum to all students despite obvious differences in abilities, interests, and developmental characteristics. That's not acceptable: not to me and not to other parents and caregivers of children in America. By delivering a standardized curriculum, you demonstrate a belief that every student is the same. Nothing is further from reality!

Every urban teacher realizes shortly into the academic year that the standard curriculum is not personally meaningful or motivating for many students. Urban school student populations have particularly diverse ability levels at each grade level (many achieving at below grade level standards) and many second language learners. Teachers in urban schools know that standardized, planned, and sequenced curricula fail to meet the learning needs of most students. Additionally, a focus on western philosophy, history, and geography makes it difficult for students to identify or relate the content to their own experiences, further reducing the credibility of most curricula. The result of persisting to deliver such ineffective curricula is the development of unmotivated students that fail to reach the elusive performance standards arbitrarily selected and mandated by local, state, and federal legislators and administrators. When such ignorance is displayed by noneducators, teachers realize that their effectiveness is judged by student scores on curriculum-based standardized tests, and, thus feel forced to deliver a standardized curriculum. Students also fail because they are not able to successfully understand or connect to curricula. Students voluntarily drop out of school because they are frequently not challenged by a standard curriculum. Jeff, a high school English teacher, spoke about the absurdity of the curriculum for his students: "They're required to study about Puritans! Yes, I alter the curriculum. I focus on themes, such as war, conflict, and a unit on heroes." It strikes me as quite odd that primarily African and Hispanic American students are spending time studying the Puritans in literature. Although I value learning some American history topics, studying the Puritans demonstrates disregard for urban students' learning needs, especially for building on second language learners' background schemata. So many more pertinent examples and models of immigration and culture exist that relate to the lives of immigrants of the twenty-first century.

Asking the Right Questions to Choose Appropriate Curricula

You must answer several questions to effectively choose appropriate curricula for students:

- What are the cognitive abilities of each of my students (e.g., levels of basic skills, English proficiency, and background knowledge)?
- What are the profiles of each student; that is, how can I address each student's learning styles? For example, are students visual, auditory, or kinesthetic learners; are they field dependent/independent? What are other possible learning preferences?
- Who are these students; that is, what do I know about their personal lives, their histories, and their families?
- What are students' baseline data in content and skill areas; that is, what do they already know, and what can they do?
- What are some strategies and skills students might *begin* to learn at this grade level (notice I said, "begin," *not* "know")?
- What will I choose to teach in my classroom that excites the interests and touches the background schemata of these specific students who share life with me for 180 days of the year?

When you understand that these questions must be asked and that you must answer them, you can begin to develop curricula that may make a difference in the cognitive growth of your students. Curricula based on the responses to these questions are not predetermined. Instead, these curricula are developed in a fluid manner, with change occurring frequently throughout the academic year. Curricula need to be based on students' needs. Let's examine the specific needs of many urban students.

Delivering Student and Culturally Responsive Curricula

Most Anglos fail to recognize that curricular guidelines, textbooks, and standardized tests reflect Eurocentric history, values, and culture. As

Gay (2000) informed us, "Most textbooks used in schools are controlled by the dominant group (European Americans) and confirm its status, culture and contributions" (113). Textbooks control the curricular decisions in most American classrooms (Apple 1985; Wade 1993). European Americans fail to realize this because they live this culture. It's like fish not being able to recognize the need for water until taken out of it. Whites are too close and familiar with the culture to understand its influence on our conscience. This egocentric ignorance leads to the failure of many urban students. I use the word *our* to denote the responsibility that all adults have for the education of all children.

What is culturally responsive curriculum? Geneva Gay (2000) provides the basis for culturally responsive teaching: "The fundamental aim of culturally responsive pedagogy is to *empower* ethnically diverse students through academic success, cultural affiliation, and personal efficacy. Knowledge in the form of curriculum content is central to this empowerment. To be effective, this knowledge must be accessible to students and connected to their lives and experiences outside of school" (111). Culturally responsive curricula are

- materials and resources that reflect students' cultural values, history, and beliefs
- derived from students' interests and curiosities
- classroom experiences designed to encourage a connection between students' lives and the principles they study
- reading resources that match students' developmental levels—particularly the levels of second language learners
- "[T]ool[s] to help students assert and accentuate their present and future powers, capabilities, attitudes, and experiences" (Gay 2000, 111)
- teacher behaviors that demonstrate respect and understanding for students' cultural and ethnic backgrounds and socioeconomic conditions
- teacher recognition and support for differentiated learning
- selection of curricular materials that encourages the development of thinking processes, particularly research skills, analytical thinking, and problem solving.

Your responsibility as a teacher is to choose or help students choose appropriate materials that match their distinct learning needs, regardless of which grade level you teach. Imagine if the curricula of most California schools, where European Americans are the minority, reflected the values and ethnicities of the communities. Students would probably not be studying Puritans; the history of the Southwest part of the United States would be told from a Mexican perspective instead of the European perspective; second language learners would receive much greater support; and the events at Pearl Harbor might also be described from a Japanese perspective. Imagine how different class discussions might be under these circumstances!

Selecting Appropriate Materials

Because textbooks have a major influence on teachers' curricular decision making, finding the appropriate materials for students to read is a critical beginning point for developing a culturally responsive curriculum. Teachers are responsible for learning about and finding textbooks, trade books, magazines, literature, and music that reflect students' interests and help them to make connections between their experiences and the themes they study. Gay (2000) informed us that, "Textbooks continue to be flawed with respect to their treatment of ethnic and cultural diversity" (114).

You should be cognizant of how textbook content realistically addresses the following issues before you choose to teach from it or choose a text for your students:

- the lives of all groups of people
- relationships among people from diverse cultures, particularly how groups have interacted with European Americans
- gender equity and social-class differences
- accurate depictions and descriptions of all groups
- pictures, drawings, and diagrams that equally reflect different cultures' contributions to society (Gay 2000).

You, in essence, become a professional censor for the sake of your students and their families in choosing materials with which students can positively identify to create high interest.

114

Middle and high school teachers may be able to receive help from their students in locating appropriate materials. Gay suggests that students can help you evaluate certain materials as you collaboratively create rubrics that can be used to identify the cultural characteristics of books. Collaborative evaluation of reading materials is a valuable way to encourage reflection on diverse cultural perspectives and critical thinking among students. Tharp (1992) indicated that, "[T]eaching and learning are more effective when they are contextualized in the experiences, skills, and values of the community and when learning is a joint productive activity involving both peers and teachers" (cited in Saravia-Shore and Garcia 1995, 57).

If you believe that students won't notice whether the curriculum reflects their cultural heritage, think again! Rodriguez (1992) discovered in interviews conducted with high school students that, "they feel left out when the curriculum of the school contains nothing that relates to their own culture" (Saravia-Shore and Garcia 1995, 56). High school students also "[F]eel that both they and their culture are valued when their culture is included in the curriculum" (56).

Critiquing how the media addresses different cultural groups is also an important activity for children from fourth to twelfth grades. Television watching is certainly a significant pastime of American children. Media images leave a lasting impression on children's self-perceptions and the expectations that other cultures have for families of a different ethnicity. A survey of 1,200 adolescents between the ages of ten and seventeen from several ethnic groups revealed that adolescents

1. are not always encouraged by the ethnic images they see on television;
2. perceive that Latinos and African Americans are depicted more negatively than European and Asian Americans;
3. are aware of media stereotypes at an early age; and
4. understand the power of television to shape opinions (Gay 2000, 127).

Teachers should initiate frank discussions about the content of television shows and news reports. Such discussions should focus on how accurately these shows present the cultures that are represented in the class. These discussions serve as opportunities for establishing realistic portraits of each ethnic group rather than reinforcing negative stereotypes and can be integrated with literature or social studies lessons.

Personal hands-on experiences have the greatest impact on students' learning. Activities such as field trips, experiments, videos, re-enactments, and simulations directly influence learners in a powerful way. Colette, who teaches high school English in Philadelphia, speaks of a project she designed to respond to the cultural needs of her primarily African American students: "I wrote a grant and got $2,500 from the Michael Jordan Foundation to study the Harlem Renaissance. I took the students on a trip to Harlem and visited a couple of sites like the Apollo Center and a tour of other historic areas. We had already read Langston Hughes and studied Frederick Douglass, so the students were able to make some connections." Colette finds that for her students to make connections, it is imperative for her to select culturally responsive curricula and design meaningful learning experiences to accompany the material her students read.

Gay (2000) suggested that teachers use the *Multicultural Review* to find recommended lists of books, films, and videotapes that depict a variety of ethnic groups including Hmong, Native Americans, Jewish Americans, and Caribbean Americans to name a few. Robert Ruddell (1999) provided lists of African, Hispanic, Native, and Asian American children's books with reading levels identified for use in elementary classrooms. Ruddell also provides a list of general reference books for multicultural literature resources. Darigan, Tunnell, and Jacobs (2002) provide the most recent and comprehensive list of multicultural children's literature in their book and accompanying database. Finding appropriate materials involves regular searches to insure that your students have access to appropriate and recently produced materials. Using culturally relevant materials provides an opportunity for each ethnic group to establish a healthy and mutual respect for other groups as well as their own families.

Do these materials actually make a difference in the interests, motivation, and performance of urban students? Gay (2000) provides evidence from studies that support the value of using culturally relevant materials. The Multicultural Literacy Program (MLP) (Diamond and Moore 1995) included multiethnic literature, a whole-language approach, and the use of ". . . [A] socioculturally sensitive learning environment" (cited in Gay 2000, 131). Use of the MLP yielded the following results among a diverse population of students from kindergarten through eighth grade:

- more interest and enjoyment in reading multicultural books
- more positive attitudes toward reading and writing in general
- expanded vocabularies, sentence patterns, and decoding abilities
- better reading comprehension and writing performance
- enhanced reading rate and fluency
- improved self-confidence and self-esteem (cited in Gay 2000, 132).

Other researchers discovered that students provided with reading materials that contained "[C]haracters, settings, and events similar to their lived experiences" (132) showed improved academic, social, and personal growth (Bishop 1992; Mason and Au 1991). Dick, Estell, and McCarty (1994) discovered that Navajo students made significant gains in achievement when more time was spent with curricular materials designed and written by students and teachers within the community than with commercially published materials.

An example of integrating specific aspects of African American culture into a literacy program might include the introduction of literature through "short stories and personal narratives written in conversational styles; oral language interpretations; storytelling, script reading, and play writing; call-response and dramatic performance; [and] language variation" as demonstrated in literary works (Gay 2000, 133). When these materials and processes were used in a Missouri writing program, students demonstrated improvements in several areas of their writing.

Don't wait for an administrator to show up at your classroom door to tell you about how to choose and deliver culturally responsive curricula—that's not likely to occur. Instead, dive into the field of materials on your own or with a colleague who has similar interests or a wealth of knowledge to help you.

Choosing Developmentally Appropriate Materials

Developmentally appropriate materials are also required if you expect students to succeed. Because many urban students face the challenge of being a second language learner, grade level textbooks are often inappropriate for helping them to learn. You will need to spend the first few weeks of school assessing the academic abilities of your students as you search for appropriate materials that are at students' independent or instructional reading levels. We all know what happens when we choose to read a selection or book that contains unfamiliar vocabulary—we become frustrated and quit. I get that feeling every April as I begin to decipher the federal tax forms prior to the April 15 deadline.

Materials for Second Language Learners

Second language learners (SLL) have an entirely different set of reading challenges from our native students. Their level of English proficiency may not reflect their potential to read. You might misinterpret a child's silence as an inability to understand directions, or a sign of low levels of reading, speaking, or listening vocabulary. Perhaps you believe that immigrant students don't understand some of the principles you teach but it may merely be the language barrier that prevents them from communicating what they know.

Try to imagine your own development in speaking, reading, and writing another language. Remember that your inability to communicate well in that language does not necessarily indicate a lack of potential, desire, understanding, or intelligence on your part. Perhaps you pronounce Spanish words well and can read the language fluently but have no idea what those words mean; or, you can't really understand the spoken language or write it. Those deficits don't prevent you from communicating in Spanish. Perhaps you would do well reading Spanish if the content were accompanied by elaborate pictures or diagrams. Maybe as you sit in your Spanish science class, you can understand a

118

complex science principle due to a quality demonstration but have no idea which words to use to explain it to your classmates. As Teemant et al. (2000) explained, "[SLL] [S]tudents can grasp concepts that far exceed their ability to express themselves in English" (32).

Most materials you expect many SLL students to comprehend must be accompanied by both visual and verbal explanations to encourage the development of a reading and speaking vocabulary. Stephen Cary (2000) provides realistic answers to many questions about teaching second language learners in his book, *Working with Second Language Learners: Answers to Teachers' Top Ten Questions*. Cary's examples are genuine, and his suggestions will help you as you seek success with SLL students.

Selecting Appropriate Reading Level Materials
Finding developmentally appropriate reading materials for students is another curricular step for teachers at all grade levels. Teaching new concepts and principles in each subject area requires a careful examination of content. Your students may be able recognize and pronounce words they are required to read, but not be able to understand them based on the principles being discussed. For instance, in the text of a typical sixth-grade science book, I see the words, "rods, "fuel," "spent," and "cake." Students know these words in the contexts of typical conversations; however, not when associated with how a nuclear power plant works. Reading comprehension refers to understanding the author's meaning or message. Teachers must address both vocabulary and contexts or background knowledge when they teach.

I strongly suggest that elementary and secondary teachers search for picture trade books that frequently provide a clearer explanation of principles through more simplistic vocabulary and clearly drawn diagrams than textbooks provide. Many nonfiction books are written at approximately the fifth- through eighth-grade level and may be used with high school as well as middle school students. Seymour Simon has written a number of nonfiction books that address scientific principles, such as *Poisonous Snakes* (1981), *Earthquakes* (1991), and *The Heart: Our Circulatory System* (1996). Laurence Pringle is another author who has written nonfiction books for young adolescents that may be used at the high school level, such as *The Animal Rights Controversy* (1989) and *Smoking: A Risky Business* (1996). A local bookstore can be a valuable source of materials for you after you peruse your textbooks and note complex principles and phenomena that your students will study throughout the year.

You should choose several reading levels of books for students. Even though students may be studying similar themes and principles, different books are likely to be required for different students. Anita, a Philadelphia middle school teacher, recognizes an important corollary for teaching urban students: "We've realized for a while now that giving every child the same book is just not in the best interest of the child."

Low-ability readers including some SLL students may learn some principles better with audiotape books than with print. Queiruga (1992) discovered significant gains in reading comprehension abilities of high school students with low reading levels after they spent a few months listening to several books on tape at reading levels from second through tenth grade. You and other students can read materials on audiotape, or you can buy fictional books on tape. Books on audiotapes are generally read at a slower pace and with greater expression than other reading.

I know reading materials and additional resources are often unavailable to urban teachers due to budget constraints. However, effective educators dig around every place they can for additional materials, such as family members' attics and garages. Old children's books, magazines, or pictures from old editions of *National Geographic* can be great sources for your classroom. Friends who are ready to part with their own children's childhood books or adolescent novels can help add to your school library. Soliciting orders from students for the children's book club provides opportunities to obtain free books each month. Check local children's bookstores and public libraries to determine if they give books away. Solicit funds from private organizations for the purchase of trade books. Be resourceful instead of throwing up your hands in defeat about not having developmentally appropriate materials. Many urban schools receive federal grant monies for curricular materials. By asking questions about these possibilities, you can attain additional resources for students who are not able to comprehend standardized curriculum materials.

What Should Students Know and Be Able to Do?

When adults think about what students should be able to do as a result of years of schooling, of course they think of the basics: perfect varied literacy skills; perform mathematical computations; possess basic geography and history knowledge; and, have a comprehensive knowledge of science content. Computer skills are also required of all graduates regardless of the jobs they will seek. Literacy and mathematics abilities are crucial for maneuvering through life as students obtain their first job, find their own place to live, and start a family. Some of the information we require students to know from the social sciences and science areas represent knowledge that is static and useful only in the context of trivia. However, critical themes can be associated with social science and science disciplines that affect human interactions, the nature of relationships, the power of politics, and ethical behavior.

It is the ability to integrate the so-called basics of education—reading, writing, and arithmetic—with the issues inherent in the science and social science disciplines that defines meaningful and genuine curricula for students. Think of the significance of these issues as they relate to our students' lives:

cloning   parenting   social-class struggles   disease

health care   social security   equity in educational spending

gender equity   immigration laws   police profiling

environmental safety   declining oil reserves   terrorism

peace in the Middle East   political relationships with China

the spread of AIDS   civil rights   misuse of technology

Of course, the list is endless! The challenges these issues currently present to humans are the reasons that we want our children to become critical readers, to understand mathematics, to unravel the mysteries of science, and to embrace social theory to protect others. When you imagine curriculum, think about empowering your students to help solve these problems instead of how your students will fare on *Jeopardy*, or *Who Wants to be a Millionaire*, or whether they will understand everything in *What Your Sixth Grader Needs to Know* (Hirsch 1993) by the end of sixth grade! Answering questions that have known answers is the easy part of living. Solving problems that seriously affect humans is the challenging part of life, but a primary purpose of education. The question is, "How does what I choose to teach in the classroom positively affect students' awareness of, interest in, and affinity for wanting to address these issues?" Let this question be your guide in seeking appropriate curricular materials and experiences.

Teachers are often uncomfortable taking the lead in altering curricula due to the pressures from central office and local administrators to prepare students for standardized tests. However, providing students with developmentally appropriate and culturally responsive curricula is a greater obligation and does result in improved test scores, despite teacher fears to the contrary. Many urban teachers are expected by local administrators to focus on teaching the basics; but the effect of such an emphasis is lower expectations for students and a stifling curriculum that prevents urban students from engaging in meaningful learning.

If you believe that in 180 days you can teach students all they need to know, think back on your education. Just how much of what you learned in those thirteen years of schooling have you continued to draw upon in your successes in life? I realize that's difficult to answer in some respects, but if you really examine that question, I think you will recognize the absurdity of the belief that the purpose of schooling is to pack students full of isolated facts. The isolated facts that we learned have no purpose for us unless they are connected to our lives in a meaningful manner and unless they help us to hone broader lifelong learning strategies. When you imagine, for instance, what strategies are needed for you to maneuver through your adult life on a daily basis, what comes to mind? Let me help you. I see these activities occurring regularly in my life:

- I need information on how to replace the heating system in my house.
- I want to know where I can find the safest new tires at low cost.

- I want my state representatives to know I am opposed to vouchers.
- I want to find a reputable preschool for my daughter that shares the same philosophies about raising children as I do.
- The principal wants me to teach fourth grade next year in another building instead of sixth grade in the middle school.

Do you see what all these questions have in common? I need information, and I want it now! Getting the answers and solving these problems require logical and organized critical thinking skills supported by basic research skills. I must determine where to find telephone numbers, which questions to ask, where to find the answers, and how to communicate my needs effectively and in an assertive manner. Is there an emphasis in your curriculum guides on improving research strategies? Do the activities used in language arts classes genuinely help students to communicate respectfully and assertively?

So I began to solve my problems by collecting all the information I needed, and now I have the following needs:

- What does a good preschool look like? What should three-year-olds be doing in school? Why should I choose this school over the other one? I like the teachers, but not the facility. The location is too far from home, and my wife and I won't be able to adjust our schedules to pick my daughter up in time at the end of the day. But I know how important good teachers are to a child's enjoyment.
- A new heating system costs at least $3,800, but that only has a warranty for ten years. I know I want to live here for twenty-five years, but should I spend the money on the system that costs $5,000 with a twenty-year warranty, especially since I need that extra $1,200 for preschool costs?
- Most of the residents in my representative district vote in a partisan way; but, many of those ideas misrepresent my views of life—especially when education issues arise. How can I convince my representatives that this voucher idea

is wrong for children when I know many people want educational vouchers?

- I've never taught fourth graders before. I know sixth graders well, but I've had it with my sixth-grade colleagues, so I need a change in scenery from this building. That other school is twelve miles in the other direction from my daughter's preschool. What's the best decision to make?

Do you see what real life is like? Decisions, decisions, and more decisions to make—every hour it seems. How can we help students to make decisions that are in their best interests and also reflect their needs? What are some good decision-making models and how do we encourage students to make ethical decisions about controversial issues that affect their lives?

How often do you need creative solutions in your life? I found myself in these situations over the past year:

- What's the best way to get to school when the usual route is blocked by an accident?
- How can I create a lesson for this class that will encourage students to think about the three most important topics of this unit?
- How can I get my daughter to want to brush her teeth?

I know these seem like minor issues; yet, I find myself bombarded with challenges to my creative energies on a daily basis. What parts of the curricula you teach encourage students to think creatively in solving problems? What do you use in the classroom to encourage students to develop hypotheses for problems, then find ways to prove or disprove those theories?

Prioritizing Curricula

When you imagine an appropriate curriculum for your students, focus on these questions:

- What skills and strategies should students build on throughout this grade level in their schooling?

- What are some typical cognitive and social abilities of students at this grade level that I can expand on?
- How can I personalize the topics that we cover to encourage students to think critically?
- What experiences can I introduce with which contextual situations to encourage creative thinking in my students?
- What themes can we study that will hone students' analytical skills?
- How can I help students improve their communication processes so that they know what to say, how to say it, and when to say it?

Answering these questions provides you with the BIG picture strategies that we want all students to gain, as well as a list of basic strategies or tools for learning literacy and mathematics. Saving the complex skills for students to learn after they leave high school is foolish at best and can be dangerous, particularly for many urban children and adolescents. Effective instruction involves the introduction and direct teaching of these thinking processes through meaningful curricular experiences that encourage students to use these strategies.

Adrienne, from Los Angeles, shares her philosophy of curricula: "I no longer think school is about imparting information. I prefer to help students develop critical thinking, to impart ways of seeing and knowing things, essential skills of analysis—especially with literature, and how to handle a charge account. I believe this because as a teacher, I don't know what you're going to need to know in twenty years. I need to teach you how to get your own education. Those who are going to succeed will learn how to learn."

Colette, who teaches English in a Philadelphia high school, describes an activity she uses with her students: "I have debates on Fridays. We pick a topic, and I have students choose sides of the room to sit on based on their beliefs. Some sit in the middle if they don't know how they feel. I'm trying to teach them to think about things. If they can think logically and talk logically, I'm hoping they can write logically." Adrienne's and Colette's thoughts reflect the research on teaching for thinking, where the emphasis is on the development of thinking processes rather than a focus on memorization of discreet facts and skills (Costa 1991; Perkins 1992).

If you feel compelled to use some aspects of mandated district guidelines for curriculum, then choose those concepts and principles that promote thinking processes and that you can connect to your students' lives. Colette handles the curriculum guides this way: "I divide my lesson plans. What I'll do is pick a standard from the state guidelines, look at the district benchmarks, and then try to create a lesson plan that way. There is some articulation going on now that we have the benchmarks so I know what students have read before they get to high school." *Benchmarks* are the school district's content standards; in other words, what all students are expected to learn. Curriculum emphasis should be based on students' needs. That often means departing from the list of things mentioned in the school's curriculum guides.

Beyond teaching thinking processes, teachers must make decisions about which content they will use to guide students into thinking, analyzing, synthesizing, and applying information. The decisions about what your students will read in fourth grade, or what mathematics principles will be attempted in seventh grade, or which science topics should be discussed in tenth grade biology are ultimately determined by you, the teacher. The reason that the decisions belong to you is because no one knows your students like you do.

Wise educators realize that alterations to the curricula are necessary based on students' interests, needs, and developmental stages. Jackie suggests this idea as she describes some of the frustration with accepting curriculum guides from New York City administrators: "To have this faceless group saying to you, 'This is what you have to teach and these are your goals,' is very difficult for everybody—and that's what stinks about it. If they gave teachers some time during the summer, and we decided what's reasonable to expect in all of these areas, then I think it would be much better."

Even those summer forays into curricular revision must be accepted with caution—summer becomes fall, and an entirely new set of students walks through the door for another school year. For instance, Lisa, a primary grade teacher from Los Angeles, describes her frustration with curriculum guides in meeting the needs of many second language learners: "They really focus on the basics—instead of opportunities for using manipulatives in science, math, and social studies. These students are missing out when most of the information is from books only. These students need many more opportunities for hands-on learning." Shanika characterizes the strengths of her Philadelphia middle school students: "The majority of them love drawing and other artwork. They love working with their hands. I've seen an increased motivation to learn science since I have been doing more hands-on experiments. They are less afraid of making predictions now, and they are better at answering questions through experimentation." It took Lisa and Shanika a couple of years of teaching to realize curriculum guides and textbooks severely limit students' learning.

Involving Students in Determining Curricula

Every semester as I plan for my courses at the university, I ponder how to elicit from my students their questions about the course and content. I question my role; that is, should I play the role of a giver of knowledge, or should I encourage students' questions and use those as the basis for deciding what we will learn? If I choose the traditional role as a giver of knowledge, there is an assumption that *I* ultimately know what the students' questions are about these topics—even though I have no idea. The alternative is to elicit their questions at the beginning of the semester and use those to guide our readings and discussions.

This constant struggle of mine leads us to the missing step in designing a meaningful curriculum—student involvement in deciding what will be studied. Wlodkowski and Ginsberg (1995) posed a critical question: "For us as teachers, the question is not *should* we but *how can* we provide learners with choice and minimize pressure on them to perform in specified ways while encouraging their initiation of new learning with a respect for their perspectives, values, strengths, and needs?" (113). If you understand young adolescent and adolescent growth patterns, you realize the power of their cognitive growth and thus their ability to ask meaningful questions about their world. In my own observations as a teacher, nine-year-olds have the cognitive maturity to ask questions, formulate hypotheses, and perform reasoned research analyses to meet many of their own learning needs. Yet, with all of these cognitive abilities, the traditional education system denies students opportunities to engage in inquiry of their interests. Instead, we typically design courses of study that completely ignore students' cognitive strengths and innate curiosity about their cognitive, social, physical, and emotional concerns.

The typical teacher's response to the idea of permitting student responsibility for choosing content is, "They'll choose topics that are too simple, easy to solve, and not related to what they need to know as adults"; or, "If I tried that, my students would choose to study nothing, and all go home for the day." It's amazing, however, that I have never heard anyone make these comments who has actually allowed students to make decisions about curricula. In classrooms where students are permitted to make decisions about what to study, their choices are highly significant, futuristic, creative, and integrative (Knowles and Brown 2000; Wraga 1996; Bergstrom 1995; Burnaford, Beane, and Brodhagen 1994; Beane 1993).

Pete, the Philadelphia high school ESL teacher, speaks of the agreement that must be negotiated between students and teacher: "I beat myself up for a long time thinking I wasn't providing a meaningful curriculum. Now I'm much more relaxed, so that I am able to pursue things that are interesting to them. You can't force the curriculum. It's something that has to be agreed on by the group—a willingness to work together must be shown by all involved."

The process of eliciting students' questions to develop themes for study may appear to be overwhelming, yet it is relatively simple. Several strategies exist for developing themes, and the ideas generated by students may be integrated with many principles that are recommended as part of your district's guidelines. I suggest reading the works of James Beane (1993); Brazee and Capelluti (1995); and Knowles and Brown (2000) who describe the philosophy and practical aspects of eliciting students' interests to guide curriculum.

Student-generated themes do not fit into separate subject areas of study. Teachers who have implemented student-driven curricula usually elicit common topics from students such as peace, violence, the study of money, social-class issues, environmental concerns, and other clearly integrative topics. Clark's (1996) middle school students identified the following themes after he initiated this process with them: "[C]rime and violence, war, prejudice, disease, rights and freedom, environment, immigration, starvation, employment, poverty and welfare, taxes, drugs, and education" (cited in Knowles and Brown 2000, 101). These are significant issues that beg to be studied and can be connected to all of the separate subjects that exist in traditional school curricula.

Kline (1995) explained the advantage and power of interdisciplinary study to stimulate thinking processes: "Interdisciplinary projects promote thinking strategies that cross content areas and transfer solidly into real-life application—analytical observation, for instance, or critical thinking, comparison and contrast, evaluation, perspective, and judgment" (27). Thematic and interdisciplinary learning approaches produce learning advantages for SLL students also, as Saravia-Shore and Garcia (1995) explained: "For students learning English as a second language, thematic approaches enhance learning and comprehension, because the new learning is incremental and added to a theme that the students already understand" (68).

Teachers and students work together to determine how they will study the themes, how the themes may be connected to district curricular guidelines, and what kinds of products will be produced to verify students' learning. Timelines are also developed to insure that students understand their daily responsibilities and establish specific products or presentations as part of their summative assessment and evaluation. Daily student goal setting is a meaningful activity that encourages student self-evaluation and planning. Teachers have many responsibilities in this process including

- insuring that students are involved in daily activities that lead to desired learning outcomes
- helping students evaluate their daily progress
- encouraging the use of primary research processes
- identifying, locating, and collecting information and resources

- presenting mini-lessons on various topics for which students show a need for improvement
- working with other teachers at the secondary school level to encourage integrative studies (Knowles and Brown 2000).

Problem-Based Learning

An alternative strategy for involving students in curricular decisions is the use of problem-based learning strategies (Reed-Victor and Stronge 1995). Students identify genuine problems that exist within their lives, their communities, or internationally and develop questions to guide their study of the problems. Problem-based learning is culturally responsive because the topics originate from the diversity of backgrounds and experiences of students. Reed-Victor and Stronge explained the value of problem-based study: "Problem solving requires students to define issues, retrieve pertinent information, formulate potential solutions, analyze options, select and implement a solution, and evaluate outcomes" (25). The thinking required in this curricular focus makes problem-based learning a valuable process for students.

Remember that curriculum is what you, the teacher, decides will occur in your room each day. Every event that occurs in your room is perceived by students as a part of what they should learn while in your presence. You have only nine to ten months with these children or adolescents. There's nothing hidden about what you want them to know because all of your actions reveal that message. Make your message a significant one—design a curriculum that's developmentally appropriate to help all of your students grow in the way each needs to grow. Design a curriculum that treats students as though they have minds—get them involved in the process. Deliver a curriculum that appeals to the social, emotional, and cultural needs of your students so they can use the information they receive to benefit their circumstances; to better their lives now, not in some distant future. Be responsible for your students' growth—take control of how curricula are designed—it's your personal and professional responsibility!

References

AMERICAN HERITAGE DICTIONARY. 2000. 4th ed. Boston, MA: Houghton Mifflin.

APPLE, M. W. 1985. "The Culture and Commerce of the Textbook." *Journal of Curriculum Studies* 17, no. 2: 147–162.

BEANE, J. A. 1993. *A Middle School Curriculum: From Rhetoric to Reality*. Columbus, OH: National Middle School Association.

BERGSTROM, K. L. 1995. A Student Retrospective on Integrated Learning: Seven Years After "Go with the Flow." Paper presented at the National Middle School Association annual conference, November, New Orleans, Louisiana.

BISHOP, R. 1992. "Extending Multicultural Understanding." In *Invitation to Read: More Children's Literature in the Reading Program*, edited by B. Cullinan. Newark, DE: International Reading Association. 80–91.

BRAZEE, E., AND J. CAPELLUTI. 1995. *Dissolving Boundaries: Toward an Integrative Curriculum*. Columbus, OH: National Middle School Association.

BURNAFORD, G., J. BEANE, AND B. BRODHAGEN. 1994. "Teacher Action Research: Inside an Integrative Curriculum." *Middle School Journal* 26, no. 2: 5–13.

CAINE, R. N., AND G. CAINE, 1994. *Making Connections: Teaching and the Human Brain*. Menlo Park, CA: Addison Wesley.

CARY, S. 2000. *Working with Second Language Learners: Answers to Teachers' Top Ten Questions*. Portsmouth, NH: Heinemann.

CLARK, S. 1996. Unpublished presentation materials. Westfield, MA: Westfield State College.

COSTA, A. L., ED. 1991. *Developing Minds: A Resource Book for Teaching Thinking*. Rev. ed. Vol. 1. Alexandria, VA: Association for Supervision and Curriculum Development.

DARIGAN, D. L., M. O. TUNNELL, AND J. S. JACOBS. 2002. *Children's Literature: Engaging Teachers and Children in Good Books*. Columbus, OH: Merrill/ Prentice Hall.

Diamond, B. J., and M. A. Moore. 1995. *Multicultural Literacy: Mirroring the Reality of the Classroom.* New York: Longman.

Dick, G. S., D. W. Estell, and T. L. McCarty. 1994. "Saad Naakih Bee'enootiltji na'aikaa: Restructuring the Teaching of Language and Literacy in a Navajo Community School." *Journal of American Indian Education* 33, no. 3: 31–46.

Elkind, D. 1987. *Miseducation: Preschoolers at Risk.* New York: Knopf.

Ennis, R. 1985. "Goals for a Critical Thinking Curriculum." In *Developing Minds: A Resource Book for Teaching Thinking*, edited by A. L. Costa. Alexandria, VA: Association for Supervision and Curriculum Development. 68–71.

Gay, G. 2000. *Culturally Responsive Teaching: Theory, Research, and Practice.* New York: Teachers College Press.

Hirsch, E. D., Jr., ed. 1993. *What Your Sixth Grader Needs to Know.* New York: Delta.

Jensen, E. 1998. *Teaching with the Brain in Mind.* Alexandria, VA: Association for Supervision and Curriculum Development.

Kline, L. W. 1995. "A Baker's Dozen: Effective Instructional Strategies." In *Educating Everybody's Children: Diverse Teaching Strategies for Diverse Learners*, edited by R. W. Cole. Alexandria, VA: Association for Supervision and Curriculum Development. 21–45.

Knowles, T., and D. F. Brown. 2000. *What Every Middle School Teacher Should Know.* Portsmouth, NH and Westerville, OH: Heinemann and National Middle School Association.

Mason, J. M., and K. H. Au. 1991. *Reading Instruction for Today.* Glenview, IL: Scott Foresman.

National Association for the Education of Young Children. 1988. "Position Statement on Developmentally Appropriate Practices in the Primary Grades, Serving 5- Through 8-Year-Olds." *Young Children* 43: 64–83.

Ohanian, S. 1999. *One Size Fits Few: The Folly of Educational Standards.* Portsmouth, NH: Heinemann.

Perkins, D. 1992. *Smart Schools: From Training Memories to Educating Minds.* New York: Free Press.

PRINGLE, L. 1989. *The Animal Rights Controversy.* San Diego: Harcourt.

————. 1996. *Smoking: A Risky Business.* New York: Morrow.

QUEIRUGA, L. 1992. *A Reading Styles Experiment with Learning Disabled, High School Students.* Syosset, NY: National Reading Styles Institute.

REED-VICTOR, E., AND J. H. STRONGE. 1995. "Diverse Teaching Strategies for Homeless Children." In *More Strategies for Educating Everybody's Children,* edited by R. W. Cole. Alexandria, VA: Association for Supervision and Curriculum Development. 10–32.

RODRIGUEZ, C. E. 1992. Student Voices: High School Students' Perspectives on the Latino Dropout Problem. Report of the Fordham University, College at Lincoln Center Student Research Project. New York: Latino Commission on Educational Reform.

RUDDELL, R. B. 1999. *Teaching Children to Read and Write: Becoming an Influential Teacher.* 2nd ed. Needham Heights, MA: Allyn & Bacon.

SARAVIA-SHORE, M., AND E. GARCIA. 1995. "Diverse Teaching Strategies for Diverse Learners." In *Educating Everybody's Children: Diverse Teaching Strategies for Diverse Learners,* edited by R. W. Cole. Alexandria, VA: Association of Supervision and Curriculum Development. 47–74.

SIMON, S. 1981. *Poisonous Snakes.* New York: Four Winds.

————. 1991. *Earthquakes.* New York: Morrow.

————. 1996. *The Heart: Our Circulatory System.* New York: Morrow.

TEEMANT, A., E. B. BERNHARDT, M. RODRIGUEZ-MUNOZ, AND M. AIELLO. 2000. "A Dialogue Among Teachers That Benefits Second Language Learners." *Middle School Journal* 32, no. 2: 30–38.

THARP, R. G. 1992. "Cultural Compatibility and Diversity: Implications for the Urban Classroom." *Teaching Thinking and Problem Solving* 14, no. 6: 1–4.

WADE, R. C. 1993. "Content Analysis of Social Studies Textbooks: A Review of Ten Years of Research." *Theory and Research in Social Education* 21, no. 3: 232–256.

WLODKOWSKI, R. J., AND M. B. GINSBERG. 1995. *Diversity and Motivation: Culturally Responsive Teaching.* San Francisco: Jossey-Bass.

WOLFE, P., AND R. BRANDT. 1998. "What Do We Know from Brain Research?" *Educational Leadership* 56, no. 3: 8–13.

WRAGA, W. G. 1996. "A Century of Interdisciplinary Curricula in American Schools." In *Annual Review of Research for School Leaders*, edited by P. S. Hlebowitsh and W. G. Wraga. New York: Scholastic. 117–145.

SIX

Responsive Instruction

If teaching were simply a question of giving children assignments then trying to force compliance, anybody off the street could be a teacher. The knowledge we need teachers to bring in the classroom is how to elicit interest and engage learners in wanting to do the work of learning.

HABERMAN (1995, 28)

Sometimes school is like a shoe that's shaped for someone else's foot.

TOMLINSON (2001, 10)

Understanding Teachers' Responsibilities

As I listened to conversations in the teachers' lunchroom at an urban middle school recently, I heard a teacher say, "These kids just don't have the backgrounds to learn." Another teacher responded, "I know it, and they don't put any effort into school, and their parents sure don't care!" I turned around to see who was speaking because I wondered just how many years these two had been teaching. I noticed that they were first- and second-year teachers. I was surprised that they had already developed the attitude of, "It isn't my fault these kids aren't learning!" If you want your classroom to be a place of meaningful learning for every student, blaming children won't improve your chances of accomplishing that outcome.

If you want to help every child to grow, then you must be the one who adjusts your instructional processes to meet your students' needs. That's an entirely different perspective from the views expressed in comments such as, "My students have a lot of problems," or "They don't have the basic skills to be in this grade level." This "blaming the victim" (the students in this case) attitude does nothing to help students learn or succeed at school (Weiner 2000, 371). You're an unsuccessful teacher if many students are consistently unwilling to learn in your classroom. Successful teachers discover and implement strategies that help students grow. Haberman (1995) refers to ineffective teachers of children of poverty as "quitters and failures" (2). Those may be strong words, but Haberman values what many educators believe is their job: that as a teacher, you're responsible for students' engagement in the learning process. You're in control. You have the power do something to help your students grow!

A number of questions must be answered to create a positive learning environment for every child:

1. How will you create a trusting and caring environment in which students comfortably take the risks associated with learning new content?
2. How will you identify and capitalize on the learning profiles of each student—including cultural learning preferences?
3. How will you personalize learning so that each student enjoys learning and succeeds at it?
4. How will you engage and challenge students while also providing developmentally appropriate learning activities?
5. How will you encourage students to work productively—independently and collaboratively?

These questions must be asked and answered for every student in your room if you hope to have an impact on each one's learning. You will not be able to answer these questions without engaging in frequent conversations with students and observations of students.

Genuinely knowing students refers to the fact that you know about their lives in and out of school. Delpit (1995) explained, "If we do not have some knowledge of children's lives outside the realm of paper-and-pencil work, and even outside of their classrooms, then we cannot know their strengths. Not knowing students' strengths leads to our 'teaching down' to children from communities that are culturally different from that of the teachers in the school" (173). What many urban teachers may fail to recognize is that students have cognitive strengths in many areas that may not necessarily be associated with a linear view of intelligence; that is, a focus on literacy and mathematical skills. American schooling practices have prioritized improving students' linguistic and logical mathematical abilities. Some urban students may not yet have achieved grade level writing, reading, or speaking skills, or may not be able to demonstrate strong computational skills. These same students, however, may have exceptional or above-average skills in areas such as music, writing poetry, negotiating conflicts, exhibiting a strong sense of humor, artistic talents, strength in their interpersonal skills, or exceptional intrapersonal abilities.

Immigrant students are particularly cognitively resourceful as they navigate a new language and an entirely new cultural experience. Do you recognize the cognitive strengths of immigrants? Valuing students' other capabilities is explicit evidence of your belief in them as capable learners who already possess strategies for successful learning. Students who are armed with the knowledge of a teacher's confidence in their learning potential are much more likely to engage in tasks that will build their knowledge and skills in areas where they need extensive growth—which may be their writing, reading, and mathematics skills.

As an educator, you must recognize and build on these other talents and strengths through creative lesson design. Shanika, from Philadelphia, recognizes that some of her fifth-grade students are good artists, so she designs activities to build on those skills: "They love crafts, so I build hands-on activities into science lessons." When teachers focus on a standardized curriculum and traditional ways of teaching, they will not recognize the many other multiple intelligences that students demonstrate regularly outside of class. Every student has strengths—you have to uncover those if you expect students to improve their skills in other academic areas. Teachers who realize students' varied talents use this information in planning and delivering instruction. Let's examine the research on effective instructional practices.

Encouraging Risk Taking

Think about what it means to take a risk in life. As adults, the kinds of risks we took as children hardly seem like risks at all. Do you remember climbing to the top of the rope in gym class; sliding to the bottom of a snowy hill on a sled until you almost crossed a busy street; jumping off the high dive; asking someone to dance at the junior high Halloween dance; sneaking out of the convenience store without paying for an ice cream sandwich; or asking your parents for money to pay for the window you accidentally broke. You obviously survived those experiences, but each time you took the risk, you felt fear—enough fear to hesitate and possibly refuse to do what you had originally planned.

Because you're reading this, you have obviously succeeded academically and are comfortable taking more cognitive risks as you complete college or begin your first teaching position. But think about the fear of student teaching—the first time you were or are in front of students and things weren't or aren't going well. It can be a horrifying experience! If you passed your student teaching, you overcame your fears about teaching (at least I hope so). Despite the fact that you continue to experience fear in different contexts, you may never understand the fear that many students experience when they try to learn in school.

Some students' fears are caused by the fact that they can't read as well as many of their classmates. Their fears are compounded every time they read orally and someone snickers in the background. Fear exists because students have been called *stupid* by teachers and classmates because they were not able to memorize all of those multiplication tables in fourth grade. Many immigrant students experience fear because they don't speak English well, and at fifteen years of age, they don't want to be made fun of every time they use the wrong word or pronounce words incorrectly. Many students are afraid because they can't write a one-page essay without help from a teacher. Some feel fear because every time they are called to the board to do a mathematics problem they freeze and can't think clearly. These are genuine concerns that students have to live with every day of the school year for as many as thirteen years! Your job is to create a place where these fears are cast aside and students feel comfortable saying, "I don't get this, but I'm willing to try," or "Let me try this on my own."

A Safe Learning Environment

Students are not likely to take academic risks if your classroom is a threatening social and academic environment. Students shouldn't experience ridicule from fellow students or teachers when they try to pronounce words, falter while working on mathematics problems, or struggle in their attempts to write an essay. Teachers are responsible for creating a family; a small community of caring students where all are protecting one another. These expectations must be explicitly stated. An expectation such as, "No one makes fun of anyone in this classroom—especially when we're learning!" should be announced. It's a rule that must be rigorously enforced if you expect students to respect one another's learning challenges.

Second language learners, for instance, need to feel comfortable experimenting with English. Challenged readers need to know that they won't be ridiculed for reading a book below grade level, and those students who need assistance with writing must be assured that their efforts and products will be valued despite the level of their work.

Eliminate Competition

Eliminating competition among students will also help encourage risk taking. Children and adolescents who have historically performed poorly academically are even more convinced of their perceived failure as students if they are constantly compared to those students who will always perform better. Make it clear that in your classroom each student is judged by her or his efforts and products of learning. Each student should be held to reasonable expectations for what he or she should accomplish. Teachers who assign grades based on an evenly distributed bell curve ignore an obvious fact of human behavior: each student has different strengths and areas of need that must be fostered and developed. Students' dreams of academic growth shouldn't be destroyed by having their test and homework assignment scores placed on a bell curve. In classrooms where competition is emphasized and used in an attempt to motivate students, few students succeed and most fail because only one person or a small group of students can actually win the top prizes. Meaningful learning has nothing to do with students competing with one another. Setting individual and realistic academic outcomes and expectations insures that every student has an opportunity to succeed, and not at the expense of another. Academic success is measured against each student's progress toward separately established learning outcomes.

Provide Frequent Assistance
When students don't understand concepts and principles, they want help—not a frustrated attitude from teachers. Lee (1999) reported that urban students at one high school would often cut classes because they couldn't comprehend content. Lee stated, "They saw their teachers as impatient with their lack of understanding because instructors often failed to take the time to provide needed individual attention" (225). Teaching requires taking responsibility for helping students to develop and improve their skills and knowledge in areas that they may be completely ignorant of prior to entering a classroom. If they are already experts at the strategies and knowledge you teach, then they won't need to spend ten months in first grade or fifth grade or as a junior in high school. Take students from their current knowledge base and ability levels and extend their growth as far as possible.

In their interviews with over 300 urban middle schoolers, Wilson and Corbett (2001) elicited the following advice for how teachers should help students:

- simply responding to a student's question in front of the class
- visiting students individually at their desks as they worked on assignments
- suggesting that students with questions, "Ask three before me" as a way of getting them to view one another as resources
- allowing students to work on a task in groups
- being available at nonclass times—before school, after school, and at lunchtime (33).

"One student concluded simply that the teacher had to, 'teach the way we understand'" (33). You won't hear a more simplistic or clearer explanation of your role as a teacher than that statement, no matter how many books you read.

Don't decide that the effort you put into your teaching will match the effort extended by your students. Don't determine your level of commitment based on the past academic abilities of your students. You are responsible for educating all those who enter your classroom each year, regardless of whether they are bound for an Ivy League college or a job in the local mall. Students also expect equal attention and assistance from their teachers. Students do not expect to be given less attention based on previous poor academic performance.

Provide Encouragement

Most students desire and need frequent encouragement. It is critical for middle and high school teachers to be as encouraging as the best elementary teachers frequently are. Jackie speaks of the needs of her middle school students in Philadelphia: "I find that many students can't direct themselves to finish a task or reach goals. It's very hard for these students to work individually. They need to hear constantly, 'You're doing a good job,' or 'Take another look at this.'" Lee (1999) interviewed low-achieving high school students from the San Francisco area and found that students needed teachers to believe in their abilities to learn despite past failures; to push them to come to class and complete their work; and to become more involved in their personal lives. Some high school students might be ready to give up on schooling, but they don't want their teachers to give up on them, too! Students from this same study indicated that teachers often contributed to their apathy in school due to, ". . . [L]ack of personal teacher-student relationships as reflected in teacher apathy, lack of caring, and low expectations" (225).

Lee (1999) provided a list of student-generated recommendations for how teachers should encourage students in the context of learning:

- get to know students on an individual level both inside the classroom and out
- be more encouraging of all students despite what they did in the past
- improve communication with students, asking them if they need more help, why they're having trouble, and how you can help
- provide more individualized attention
- communicate that you believe in students, and that they have the ability to learn
- interact with all students in the same way regardless of race (239).

These may seem like commonsense actions for educators, yet many teachers are not able to perceive how they violate these student-friendly behaviors on a regular basis.

Demonstrate Personal Interest in Each Student
Each student needs regular, individualized attention. Effective educators develop specific strategies for getting to know students. These strategies may not be conventional, but they are deliberate attempts to establish a relationship with each student. Learning more about your students' lives can occur as you schedule individual conferences with students, eat lunch with them, sit beside them in small group activities, speak to them outside during recess, and maintain a shared journal in which you correspond in writing with each student.

I know urban classrooms are frequently overcrowded; however, effective teachers find strategies for meeting regularly with individual students for the purpose of

- establishing and discussing their academic outcomes for the year
- assessing their reading and writing abilities through oral reading activities and feedback on their writing pieces
- eliciting questions they have about the classes and subjects that you teach
- determining students' areas of academic need
- demonstrating your interest in their personal experiences— particularly finding time to discuss their families' cultural heritage
- providing feedback on their progress toward previously established learning or behavior outcomes
- helping students to recognize their learning profiles and develop strategies for academic success.

Locke Davidson (1999) interviewed urban high school students and reported that, "[A] substantial portion of students emphasize also that they want teachers to personally and consistently communicate interest in their personal well beings and futures" (345). The students Locke Davidson interviewed described specific actions that teachers could employ including, "[R]egularly taking time during class to visit a struggling student individually at his or her seat, noticing a look of confusion on a student's face during a discussion and making sure to clarify material, or taking care not to schedule tests on a day that students have many others" (346). Polly, from a Chicago high school, explains how teachers at her school encourage frustrated students: "We don't put students in a position where they can fail often. We encourage our students to set goals, and then we take the time to meet with students to help them keep their eyes on those goals."

The Significance of Community Spirit to Learning

I addressed the need to create a community spirit in your classroom to promote cooperative behavior in Chapter 4. Building a community

143

spirit in your classroom also can reduce students' fear and encourage risk taking in the learning process. In a safe community, others are trusted and students feel more comfortable taking the risks required for learning. For some urban students, however, trusting relationships are rare, promises are broken, responsibilities ignored, and sharing resources or ideas may not be common. Many students who are in the same classroom may originally be from different countries and not know how to communicate, or are afraid of communicating with others who are culturally different. As a result of this fear and ignorance, students from similar backgrounds sit together in classrooms or during lunch. Saravia-Shore and Garcia (1995) suggested, "To break down this defensive withdrawal into ethnic groups, students need to have time to get to know each other and to find that they share common ground, common problems and common feelings" (58).

Many students want to collaborate with others, primarily because that's how learning is viewed in their cultures (Reyes, Scribner, and Paredes Scribner 1999; Ladson-Billings 1994). The motivation exists to establish a community, but the strategies for attaining it are elusive to students. Adolescent gang activity is evidence that students desire to be a part of a group that is accepting; a group that bestows power, offers recognition, and provides a sense of status (Lee 1999).

Teachers can create a community by modeling treasured characteristics that all humans seek; particularly safety, trust, and camaraderie. Marino Weisman (2001) reported the opinions of four Latina teachers who suggested that, "Teachers should develop strategies that are designed to improve the social, psychological, and moral growth of students. Giving informal lessons about personal pride, common courtesy, and showing respect to peers and elders are examples of how to incorporate nonacademic issues in pedagogical practices" (200).

Many students who have struggled academically blame someone else for all of their failures rather than shoulder their share of the responsibility for unsuccessful learning. Veteran urban teachers advise novices to explain and demonstrate to students how to succeed academically. An urban teacher of primarily African American students in Howard's (2001) study suggested, "We should have high expectations, and we should tell them that we have high expectations, and I do all of those things. But it isn't just enough to tell a child that you can do it. You also have to show the child how he can do it" (194). Recognizing students' initial and small successes begins to help them build the confidence it takes to attempt more challenging tasks.

Remember that you want students to take risks. When they feel safe, valued, encouraged, and recognized they are more likely to engage in the kind of risk taking required for genuine learning to occur. Locke Davidson (1999) summarized, "In short, students who feel stigmatized say they are more receptive to and appreciative of teachers who treat them with respect and who convey confidence in their abilities, no matter how poorly they are performing" (352).

Gathering Baseline Data

In Chapter 4, I provided several strategies for establishing caring and trusting relationships with students as part of creating safe places for learning. Most of those ideas are based on a single critical aspect of effective teaching: developing caring relationships with each student. That kind of relationship forms the foundation to support meaningful learning. Beyond building that relationship is the dance that ensues between students and teachers as they negotiate learning experiences. The "dance" involves teachers' efforts to entice students to actively produce and learn and students' requests that the requirements for learning be reasonable with attainable outcomes that match their level of energy, their attitudes, their interests, and their abilities.

Reducing academic fear begins with discovering what each student is capable of doing. Detailed strategies for gathering information about students' academic backgrounds and current levels of ability are discussed in Chapter 8. Influential teachers are constantly researching the lives of their students to discover their academic, social, and emotional statuses. A few general data-collection strategies to provide information about students include

- administering pretests to assess prior knowledge
- maintaining individual folders on each student and stocking

them with notes as you notice their growth in specific skill areas

- initiating journaling with students on their perceptions of their academic progress and understanding of principles and concepts learned
- recording notes from conversations with caregivers and past teachers
- visiting students' homes to meet caregivers and parents
- helping students establish learning outcomes and general goals for the academic year.

Once you establish some baseline data on students' characteristics, then you can begin to design learning experiences that match the cognitive, social, physical, emotional, and cultural needs, and effort levels of your students. This is a substantial list of "needs," but if you don't know something about these personal characteristics, you won't touch students' minds or hearts—necessary requirements for insuring meaningful learning. Tomlinson (2001) explained, "We go about learning in a wide variety of ways, influenced by how our individual brains are wired, our culture, and our gender" (9). Influential teachers discover what those ways are for their students—especially in a classroom with diverse students.

Learning Profiles

Helping students succeed academically requires knowledge of learning profiles. A person's learning profile is a description of the classroom conditions, cognitive styles, and intelligence preferences needed to establish a comfortable and productive learning environment. Students have preferences for how they learn based on personal characteristics affected by physiology, socialization interests, and external factors. A few examples of preferences may be a student's desire to either

- work independently or collaboratively
- be physically active during learning or passively listening
- prefer people-oriented to task-oriented activities
- need concrete as opposed to abstract explanations

- learn new principles from part-to-whole or from whole-to-part (Tomlinson 2001, 61).

These are not fixed cognitive and social preferences that remain the same for every learning experience. A student's learning preferences may change based on background knowledge, time of day, motivation for learning, socialization needs, or developmental abilities. This is a short list of the many factors that may be a part of a student's learning profile. For a more extensive explanation, read Tomlinson's book, *How to Differntiate Instruction in Mixed Ability Classrooms* (2001). To identify all of the specific needs of all of your students is, of course, impossible! You need to know, however, that many possible learning profiles exist so that when you choose curriculum, plan a lesson, decide how to instruct students, and develop assessment plans, you realize the many factors that influence students' attitudes, abilities to focus, and motivation for learning. Urban teachers must be particularly aware that learning profiles are highly influenced by students' cultural backgrounds.

Your role is to share information on learning profiles with students and help them identify the preferences they have for learning. You can assess students' profiles through several methods: administering formal instruments and surveys; teaching students about profiles so that they begin to recognize their personal styles; and observing their behaviors during the day to see which instructional strategies appear to have a positive influence on your students. Don't merely observe—take extensive notes and refer to them at the end of the day so that in your next lesson-planning session you can make adjustments based on your observations. Because culture affects our learning profiles, let's examine the idea of culturally responsive instruction.

Instructional Needs of Diverse Learners

Inductive Teaching and Learning

Gay (2000) supported the need for more active instructional processes for culturally diverse learners. She described that many prefer learning by studying phenomena and principles from an inductive approach; that is, from whole-to-parts instead of learning about the parts then moving to the big picture. Those of you familiar with reading processes, realize that the idea of teaching reading using the "bottom-up approach" (beginning with a solitary focus on sound-symbol relationships, followed by instruction on whole words, and then sentences) has limited benefits for many African, Hispanic, or Native American learners. If you were teaching science using the inductive learning process, that is teaching about the broader picture of principles while examining the micro components, you might begin by having students explain how they think an airplane is able to lift off of the ground instead of having them memorize the parts of the wing the first two days of the unit. Caine and Caine (1994) emphasize that a component of brain-based learning (learning theory supported by cognitive science) is that, "The brain processes parts and wholes simultaneously" (91). Gay's (2000) recognition of a need for the inductive approach for African, Hispanic, and Native American learners supports this theory.

The knowledge of students' needs for a whole-to-parts approach should provide a valid warning to all educators: spending fifteen minutes teaching vocabulary words to students before they read the science, social studies, or health book, or the next literary selection is, at best, a poor strategy for insuring that students will comprehend the text. Believing that a minimal explanation of vocabulary is sufficient to students' understanding is a common misconception among teachers. Urban teachers also need to know that primary-aged children from high socioeconomic families generally have twice the number of vocabulary words as children from lower-income families (Scott and Nagy 1997; Graves, Brunetti, and Slater 1982). Many urban students, therefore, need more background information than a mere twenty minutes of vocabulary instruction before reading new text. Deductive teaching leaves many holes in students' text comprehension, especially for second language learners who often need much more background information or the wholes of principles and concepts to clearly understand them.

Contextual Learning

Related to students' needs for more concrete information to enhance their understanding of abstract principles is a need to explain complex principles and phenomena in a context that is meaningful to the learner. Delpit (1995) described the ineffectiveness of decontextualized teaching in which educators attempt to disseminate information without effectively relating it to the background experiences or current environmental circumstances of students in their classes. Curriculum taught using references, vocabulary, or examples that are unimaginable to students decreases the chances for meaningful learning. Based on this understanding, how could schools use the same materials across the United States or even within each state to teach a common curriculum to students with such diverse background experiences? Each child and adolescent has different learning needs and requires different experiences to learn new principles!

What do you think it means to someone who's never left the city to "tap a tree"? What does an adolescent living in rural, southern Illinois know about catching "the L" in Chicago? How do you explain side-angle-side to a student who has never constructed anything? How do I bring unfamiliar vocabulary to life for city students who are reading a story about a hunting trip in the wilds of Canada? When teachers focus on covering as much of the curriculum as possible, they are almost forced to ignore students' needs for more time and direct instruction to establish the familiar context needed to insure understanding of new concepts and principles. Gay (2000) reminds us that learning is highly context bound in African and Hispanic cultures. In Chapter 5, I explained that many textbooks are written at readability levels beyond the instructional levels of many urban students. In short, urban teachers need to spend additional time providing comprehensive contextual information in many content areas to insure greater understanding. Teachers should engage students in activities such as

- telling stories
- sharing experiences related to story topics

- engaging students in kinesthetic reenactments of historical events
- using pictures, films, diagrams, and videos to provide clarity for students
- designing graphic organizers that clarify confusing topics
- encouraging students to design physical models of topics being studied
- inviting guest speakers to provide accurate descriptions and explanations of topics studied
- taking field trips whenever possible to any site (even on school grounds) that provides clarity to students on unfamiliar topics.

Colette, the Philadelphia high school English teacher, speaks of providing her African American students with learning activities that recognize multiple intelligences: "Kids learn in different ways. I try to do things with the kinesthetic because I know I have certain kids that can't sit still. I have kids who are musical, so I try to draw upon their prior knowledge. I do the KWL [Tell me what you KNOW now, WHAT more would you like to know about this topic, and what did you LEARN from this unit?] and then, based on their responses to that, I try to make connections to their lives. Whatever it takes, I try to make those connections." The list of possible activities teachers can use to increase students' background knowledge is endless. Influential educators are constantly developing new strategies for teaching complex principles. Susan uses the city to bring learning to life for her fifth-grade students in San Francisco: "I take students outside into the community. We do lots of environmental education projects, and we visit the museums, and a local ship at the waterfront."

Just remember one phrase, "Make it real," when it comes to explaining new principles to students. Avoid using confusing jargon and rely more on genuine events than on only linguistic teaching. Kathleen, from a Chicago elementary school with many SLL students, speaks of her instructional focus: "I'm a visual learner, so I use a lot of visual cues also, and I demonstrate mapping techniques. I use pictures and diagrams to build background knowledge for my students. I do think alouds to demonstrate and model my thinking for them. I get every student involved by calling on all of them." These are real learning experiences that touch students' lives.

Collaborative Learning

One serious deficit of traditional American educational processes is an insistence on individualized and competitive learning. Despite years of overwhelming statistical support for and value of collaborative learning experiences (Walberg 1999; Lipsey and Wilson 1993; Slavin 1991), many teachers still refer to any type of group study as "cheating." There are few activities related to American business success that are accomplished individually. In many job listings, companies are seeking a "team player." I'll be the first to admit, when I need help or I'm confused, I seek assistance and feedback from others. I believe that most American adults consider it a sign of maturity and intelligence to seek help when needed (with the exception, of course, of males who are lost while driving). So, why do teachers persist in forcing students to work in isolation? As Kline (1995) stated, "Only in U. S. classrooms are individuals expected to find every answer, solve every problem, complete every task, and pass every test by relying solely on their own efforts and abilities" (23).

Gay (2000) stated that collaborative learning is preferred among many Asian and African Americans and Latinos. The use of collaborative discussions, group problem solving, and team research activities can create opportunities for more comprehensive learning among students. The exchange of student-to-student questions, solutions, hypotheses, and background experiences can help students to develop confidence as learners as they engage in learning activities without constant direct teacher intervention. Fullilove and Treisman (1990) noted that mathematical achievement was much higher among African and Hispanic American students when they modeled the group learning processes used by Chinese Americans in which students shared problem-solving solutions while studying in groups. Diane, who

151

teaches fifth graders (many who are SLL) in San Francisco, explains that in her teaching, "I use a great deal of socialization activities for my second language learners."

One of urban teachers' greatest complaints is the constant attention they need to provide to many students who refuse or don't have the confidence to complete schoolwork independently. Teachers won't be so taxed by the constant need to provide assistance, feedback, and encouragement to each student if they develop a culture of collaborative learning in their classroom. Students can assist each other as grade level partners who share common developmental abilities. Older students in each building can be involved in helping younger students complete challenging assignments. Anita, from a Philadelphia middle school, talks about how she accommodates her primarily African American students in a room with so many diverse ability levels: "I find that in a classroom where you have a real mixed group, most kids don't mind working with someone. I just think they do better, and I think they learn more from each other rather than when they are forced to do it by themselves." Teachers who design and initiate collaborative activities should require a student evaluation at the end of the project on the effectiveness of team members in working together. Common collaborative learning activities that may be implemented in classrooms include

- writing workshop including collaborative brainstorming, peer revision, and peer editing
- literature circles for the discussion of commonly read books
- team book talks where partners make oral presentations of trade books they have read
- group investigations of hypotheses developed in science or history
- reader's theatre in which small groups of students present scenes from stories read
- groups of students working together at stations to complete mathematics problems or science experiments
- paired reading partners who read text orally to one another.

These are a few activities that can be initiated for group learning. Use your own creativity in designing collaborative learning projects. Match students with classmates who can assist them in areas of need. You'll also need to notice which students can work well together and which ones aren't able to cooperate. Experimenting with different grouping configurations will be necessary until you find students who genuinely help each other. I provide a caution: avoid forming groups so that all students with similar ability are on the same team. You will soon realize what research clearly demonstrates: homogeneous grouping practices do not improve the achievement levels of low ability students (Lou et al. 1996).

Students need direct instruction on the strategies, challenges, and solutions for working collaboratively whether working as formal, cooperative group teams or merely in other creative collaborations. Training students for group activities is a necessary component for assuring successful group engagement. Encouraging students to assess the value of group work and contributions of team members will help students improve their social skills and group's effectiveness. For SLL students, group activities provide the necessary discourse to improve language skills and increase vocabulary development.

Differentiated Instructional Strategies

What can you possibly do to insure that every student's cognitive needs are being met during the day? Each urban class has a wide range of academic abilities. Many urban students who are referred for testing to determine whether they need additional assistance from a resource teacher are never diagnosed or tested due to many roadblocks and constraints. The inability to receive needed services prevents many students from succeeding and drives many teachers from urban schools because they cannot meet the needs of these students.

Carol Ann Tomlinson (1999, 2001) explained the theory and practice of differentiated learning. *Differentiated instruction* looks much like the kind of teaching that occurs in one-room schools that still exist in several western states. The reason that this is an appropriate comparison is because those schools have perhaps one to three students at each grade level from kindergarten through eighth grade. In a class of twenty students, only one or two are at the same cognitive developmental stages. It's highly likely that in your urban classroom you'll have students that, although near the same chronological age, are far apart academically for many reasons:

- They possess considerable differences in reading and mathematical abilities.
- Students are from several different immigrant backgrounds.
- Immigrant students have lived in America for a varying number of years—for some it's their first year, others have been here much longer.
- Their parents and caretakers have limited English proficiency.
- Some students excel academically and are in gifted education programs.
- Some have strong mathematical abilities but weak literacy skills.
- Some have few mathematical strengths but excel in reading and writing.
- Some students never complete assignments.
- Some students need constant attention and support to complete assignments.
- Some children and adolescents are independent learners.
- Some children and adolescents need constant reassurance to complete assignments.
- Some students have a series of special needs because of their learning disabilities.

The list of variable cognitive and social characteristics can be added to forever. If you are already an urban teacher, you have experienced the variations—you know how challenging it is to help them all when their needs are so diverse. Students need to be cognitively challenged while working on projects, reading, and writing. They need reading materials that are close enough to their independent level to improve their growth without being so challenging as to discourage their efforts. Students need instructional processes that match their learning profiles and offer individual assistance when needed. They need assessment practices that encourage creativity and integration of curricula. The strategies for meeting the needs for each child or adolescent are varied. Differentiated instruction can be designed to address all of their needs.

Tomlinson (1999) characterized differentiated learning as

- individual and group assessment of students
- flexibility in assignments given based on the ability levels and academic needs of students
- differing curricula chosen to meet the interests and developmental characteristics of students
- varying sets of expectations for what each student will learn
- flexibly designed time frames for learning
- a variety of grouping arrangements for studying topics (adapted from Tomlinson 1999, 2).

Teachers should alter instruction based on students' needs on three levels: they can alter the content, the process of how they teach, or the way that students are assessed. I would like to focus on different strategies for how students learn. Tomlinson (1999) suggested several strategies for differentiating instruction.

1. *Learning stations:* This is not an original instructional strategy, but it is effective in meeting the needs of diverse learners all crowded into one room. You may have designed learning centers for primary-age children as a part of your course work at the university. Learning stations should not solely be reserved for kindergarten or first-grade students. Any concepts or principles that you believe students should learn can be taught using separate learning stations within the classroom. Each station can be designed to engage students in scientific explorations, hypothesizing, comparing, reading short stories, writing

poetry, peer editing for writing, and other thinking processes and skills. I recently witnessed two valuable learning station activities. In one, fourth graders were studying geology. At various stations across the room, students were involved in testing the hardness of rocks, placing a chemical on minerals and recording the reaction, and looking through stones to establish a level of clarity. Each station involved students working in pairs and students rotated through the stations during an hour-long period.

In another station activity, students in third grade were involved in doing taste tests at two stations; comparing the amount of calories among several food items; identifying the roots of a variety of foods at another station. Each station may be designed to assess different levels of ability based on students' backgrounds. Perhaps only half the students will go through four of the six stations. Your job is to design the stations to challenge students, but not frustrate them. Students with higher-ability levels may be paired with those who struggle. One station may be designed as a mini-lesson point where you meet with a small group of students who need additional support with the principles being taught. Variations on the design and implementation of stations are advised so that they meet your needs for what you believe students should learn and students' needs for how they need to learn.

2. *Centers:* Learning stations are similar to centers. Centers have been used for at least thirty years in American classrooms. "Centers differ from stations in that centers are distinct" (Tomlinson 1999, 75); that is, they are not connected to one another through a common theme of study or integrated unit of study. Each center provides activities for students to improve their skills in a specific content area. Each center is designed to be self-contained for students to insure that they can complete the activities independently. Activities are usually designed to "[F]ocus on mastery or extension of specific understandings or skills"

(Tomlinson 1999, 76). Students working at centers are able to improve their skills and add to their knowledge base as they practice some of the principles they previously learned. Centers are commonly used in multiage classrooms to allow the teacher to focus on direct instruction with groups of students at different ability levels while others are completing center activities.

3. *Agendas*: When students engage in an agenda, they complete "[A] personalized list of [learning] tasks" within a specific time frame (Tomlinson 1999, 66). The assigned work for an agenda usually lasts from two to three weeks. Teachers establish a contract for each student working on agendas that outlines the tasks required, time frame for completion, and special instructions for each student. Each student works on his or her agenda independently from other students but receives teacher assistance during the time allotted for agenda studies each day. Agenda contracts involve studies in several content areas simultaneously: mathematics, social studies, science, and writing that are usually connected assignments. A student, for instance, may have a contract requiring the identification of three resources from the library on the influence of air pollution on trees. A connecting writing assignment is to a draft a letter to a local city council member to explain the impact of air pollution and inquire about local ordinances on air pollution. An associated mathematics assignment might require the student to figure how many miles per gallon of gasoline five vehicles in the school's parking lot consume. You can see the interdisciplinary nature of an agenda. Tomlinson (1999) suggested that students become responsible for monitoring their progress and establishing daily outcome plans to insure focused study.

Students will need daily assistance with their agendas. Agendas are not designed as individualized study for an entire day of learning. Specific time periods are established during the day based on grade levels and how the agendas fit into other studies within your classroom. The advantages of agenda study are the individualized study required among students, the chance to conference with students individually, and the opportunities for integrating curricula.

4. *Orbital studies:* Like agendas, orbital studies involve independent study of topics that are related to the curriculum (Stevenson 1997). Stevenson believes middle school students generally possess the appropriate cognitive skills for orbital studies. With orbital studies students choose the topics to study; whereas, the choice is teacher directed with agendas. Investigations for orbital studies are recommended to last from three to six weeks. Topics may originate from student suggestions as long as they relate to curricula being studied. Each student works individually to investigate topics.

   An African American student may choose to study historical and current health characteristics of her family as related to a science unit on the cardiovascular system. Students and teachers work together in orbital studies to develop a timeline for completion of the project, strategies for researching information, ideas for how they will present their findings to the class, and may develop a set of rubrics for evaluating their final projects. The teacher and student are in daily contact to evaluate progress and establish daily outcomes.

5. *Complex instruction:* Complex instructional activities involve students learning in small groups (Tomlinson 1999). The activities associated with complex instruction are more open ended than the previous strategies mentioned because they are not necessarily related to curricular guides. Tomlinson described complex instructional activities: "Complex instruction seeks tasks that call on a much wider range of intellectual skills, such as generating ideas, asking probing questions, representing ideas,

hypothesizing, or planning" (69). They are investigations initiated by students that represent their interests and permit flexibility in how students research topics and acquire new knowledge. Students are grouped heterogeneously to design and implement their area of study.

A small group of urban students engaged in complex instruction may choose to investigate the differences among their families who immigrated from different Southeast Asian countries. Their research would involve generating questions about how their families arrived in the United States, where they lived in Southeast Asia, and how their place of residence affected their cultural development during the last hundred years. Students are responsible for presenting findings to the class through a variety of methods following the completion of their projects. Projects can be evaluated using student-generated rubrics. Each aspect of complex instruction builds on students' thinking processes and reflection on their learning.

6. *Tiered activities:* Tiered learning experiences expand on content learned in previous lessons. Teachers design tiered activities when they recognize that several students have not grasped the principles taught during teacher-directed instruction and want to insure that students better understand the essential principles studied. Teachers design separate learning activities for the different developmental levels of students. Tomlinson (1999) explained that the idea is that, "(1) each student comes away with pivotal skills and understandings and (2) each student is appropriately challenged" (83). Each student or group of students is required to complete a different learning activity related to the principles being studied based on their ability levels.

Tiered learning activities may be used with students to further expand their understanding of the value of knowing how to use latitude and longitude. Several students who are second language learners may be required to explain their understanding of the two principles by designing a chart with diagrams. Students who know English well may be required to research which professions use latitude and longitude and explain in a presentation to the class how they are used in those professions. Other groups of students may be required to identify several cities along the same latitude and explain how their weather could be different despite their similarities in distance from the equator. Each of these activities extends students' learning because they use creative and critical thinking processes to further develop their knowledge.

These are a few instructional strategies that provide greater opportunities for individualizing instruction in classrooms of multiability students. Many advantages exist for using differentiated instructional techniques. First, differentiated instruction provides opportunities for independent study activities at students' developmental levels. Differentiated instruction provides teachers with the time and structure for individualized assistance and conferencing with a classroom of diverse students with vast differences in academic abilities. Certain differentiated activities permit teachers to acknowledge and respond to the differences in English-language skills of immigrant students. Using differentiated instructional practices, permits teachers to adjust instruction to match and improve students' background knowledge in certain areas. Students' reading levels can be matched to their instructional levels through using differentiated activities.

Because many differentiated activities are based on students' learning interests, the probability exists that differentiated instruction will increase students' motivation for learning. Curricula can be designed to challenge students through appropriate differentiated activities. Integrating curricula, which is an aspect of differentiated learning, can improve the meaningfulness of many learning experiences. Perhaps the greatest advantage of using differentiated learning, for urban teachers is the way in which the activities provide the time and structure to meet the needs of students at several levels of academic ability, language acquisition, and cultural knowledge. This characteristic of varied ability levels sharply defines the populations of students in urban classrooms. Urban teachers are faced with the challenge of presenting learning experiences to their students that match their varied levels of learning to insure academic success.

Listening to Students to Plan Instruction

Planning meaningful learning activities for diverse populations of learners requires an understanding of the lives, cultures, and learning preferences of every student you teach. I hope you have discovered this critical fact from reading this chapter. No one learns exactly like you learn, so you can immediately dispel that personal egocentric influence on how you teach or plan to teach. Many separate cultural factors, age characteristics, maturity issues, and personal preferences determine how students learn best. Every opportunity that arises during the course of the school year should be used to gather more information from each student about his or her learning profile. Lee (1993) discovered in his interviews with high school students from an urban school that these adolescents wanted the following components to exist in their classes:

- more group work
- more enthusiasm in teaching class material
- more interesting, upbeat lectures and discussions
- more communication, discussion, freedom of expression
- more culturally relevant materials
- more activities, projects, field trips
- greater student voice in deciding classroom topics
- classroom materials that directly relate to real life
- grading based not just on tests and quizzes but also on projects, papers, and individual improvement
- ongoing feedback on performance in class (238–239).

This student-generated list mirrors the research presented throughout this chapter on effective pedagogy for diverse learners. Locke Davidson (1999) discovered similar calls for better teaching among urban high school students including their interest in receiving "teachers' explanations [that] are clear and accessible. Students prefer teachers who

161

help them understand material and who take time to explain concepts and ideas carefully and thoroughly" (355).

References

CAINE, R. N., AND G. CAINE. 1994. *Making Connections: Teaching and the Human Brain*. Menlo Park, CA: Addison Wesley.

DELPIT, L. 1995. *Other People's Children: Cultural Conflict in the Classroom*. New York: New Press.

FULLILOVE, R. E., AND P. U. TREISMAN. 1990. "Mathematics Achievement Among African American Undergraduates at the University of California, Berkeley: An Evaluation of the Mathematics Workshop Program." *Journal of Negro Education* 59, no. 3: 463–478.

GAY, G. 2000. *Culturally Responsive Teaching: Theory, Research, and Practice*. New York: Teachers College Press.

GRAVES, M. F., G. J. BRUNETTI, AND W. H. SLATER. 1982. "The Reading Vocabularies of Primary-Grade Children of Varying Geographic and Social Backgrounds." In *New Inquiries in Reading Research and Instruction*, edited by J. A. Harris and L. A. Harris. Rochester, NY: National Reading Conference. 99–104.

HABERMAN, M. 1995. *Star Teachers of Children of Poverty*. West Lafayette, IN: Kappa Delta Pi.

HOWARD, T. C. 2001. "Powerful Pedagogy for African American Students: A Case Study of Four Teachers." *Urban Education* 36, no. 2: 179–201.

KLINE, L. W. 1995. "A Baker's Dozen: Effective Instructional Strategies." In *Educating Everybody's Children: Diverse Teaching Strategies for Diverse Learners*, ed. R. W. Cole. Alexandria, VA: Association for Supervision and Curriculum Development. 21–45.

LADSON-BILLINGS, G. 1994. *The Dreamkeepers: Successful Teachers of African American Children*. San Francisco: Jossey-Bass.

LEE, C. 1993. "Signifying as a Scaffold to Literary Interpretation: The Pedagogical Implications of a Form of African American Discourse." National Council of Teachers of English Research Report No. 26. Urbana, IL: National Council of Teachers of English.

162

Lee, P. W. 1999. "In Their Own Voices: An Ethnographic Study of Low-Achieving Students Within the Context of School Reform." *Urban Education* 34, no. 2: 214–244.

Lipsey, M. W., and D. B. Wilson. 1993. "The Efficacy of Psychological, Educational, and Behavioral Treatment." *American Psychologist* 48, no. 12: 1181–1209.

Locke Davidson, A. 1999. "Negotiating Social Differences: Youths Assessments of Educators' Strategies." *Urban Education* 34, no. 3: 338–369.

Lou, Y., P. C. Abrami, J. C. Spence, C. Paulsen, B. Chambers, and S. d'Apollonio. 1996. "Within Class Grouping: A Meta-Analysis." *Review of Educational Research* 66, no. 4: 423–458.

Marino Weisman, E. 2001. "Bicultural Identity and Language Attitudes: Perspectives of Four Latina Teachers." *Urban Education* 36, no. 2: 203–225.

Reyes, P., J. D. Scribner, and A. Paredes Scribner, eds. 1999. *Lessons from High-Performing Hispanic Schools*. New York: Teachers College Press.

Saravia-Shore, M., and E. Garcia. 1995. "Diverse Teaching Strategies for Diverse Learners." In *Educating Everybody's Children: Diverse Teaching Strategies for Diverse Learners*, edited by R. W. Coles. Alexandria, VA: Association for Supervision and Curriculum Development. 47–74.

Scott, J. A., and W. E. Nagy. 1997. "Understanding the Definitions of Unfamiliar Verbs." *Reading Research Quarterly* 32, no. 2: 184–200.

Slavin, R. E. 1991. "Synthesis of Research on Cooperative Learning." *Educational Leadership* 48, no. 5: 71–77, 79–82.

Stevenson, C. 1997. "An Invitation to Join Team 21!" In *In Search of Common Ground: What Constitutes Appropriate Curriculum and Instruction for Gifted Middle Schoolers?*, edited by C. Tomlinson. Washington, DC: Curriculum Studies Division of the National Association for Gifted Children. 31–62.

Tomlinson, C. A. 1999. *The Differentiated Classroom: Responding to the Needs of All Learners*. Alexandria, VA: Association for Supervision and Curriculum Development.

———. 2001. *How to Differentiate Instruction in Mixed Ability Classrooms*. 2nd ed. Alexandria, VA: Association for Supervision and Curriculum Development.

WALBERG, H. J. 1999. "Productive Teaching." In *New Directions for Teaching Practice and Research*, edited by H. C. Waxman and H. J. Walberg. Berkeley, CA: McCutchen Publishing. 75–104.

WEINER, L. 2000. "Research in the 90s: Implications for Urban Teacher Preparation." *Review of Educational Research* 70, no. 3: 369–406.

WILSON, B. L., AND H. D. CORBETT. 2001. *Listening to Urban Kids: School Reform and the Teachers They Want.* Albany, NY: State University of New York Press.

SEVEN

Language Considerations in Instructional Processes

[T]he achievement of students is increased when teachers modify their instruction to make it more congruent with the cultures and communication styles of culturally diverse students.

HOWARD (2001, 183)

Culturally Responsive Instructional Communication

Communicating effectively through nonverbal, oral, or writing processes is a powerful way to achieve outcomes. Nonverbal actions are more meaningful and powerful than oral communications. Every action by teachers from how discussions are held to how much individual assistance is provided is an opportunity to either encourage or frustrate students. As you go through a day of teaching, reflect on how all of your social behaviors, especially nonverbal cues, might affect students' perceptions of their ability to grow and succeed academically. Think about how you respond to students' mispronounced words, different dialects, syntax mistakes among second language learners, and classroom discussion patterns. How do you provide feedback to students to validate their cultural norms? How accepting are you of those speaking patterns that differ from what you expect? The importance of communicating with students from diverse backgrounds is made clear by Saravia-Shore's and Garcia's (1995) finding: "The aspects of culture that influence classroom life most powerfully are those that affect the social organization of learning and the social expectations concerning communication" (57).

You will likely discover more about your verbal and nonverbal communication styles by videotaping a few lessons. Notice your actions *and* student reactions to your behaviors when you review the tape. You may discover that some students are not reacting well to your non-verbal or verbal behaviors. Review the tape with a colleague of a different culture to help you evaluate your discourse styles.

Two middle school teachers, one European American, Karen, and the other African American, Jennifer, conducted a study in which they took turns observing one another teach (Obidah and Manheim Teel 2001). They each naturally had preconceived notions about how students should communicate in school. Karen perceived her African American students' communication characteristics as a demonstration of

1. an aggressive communication style
2. unfamiliar expressions
3. the need to save face in front of peers
4. a demand for respect from peers and the teacher
5. vocal and honest expressions of dissatisfaction with the class
6. a tendency to test her as a person of authority.

The communication styles of Karen's African American students didn't match how she, as a white middle-class person, believed students should respond to each other or an adult figure. Because of her ignorance of African American cultural communication patterns, Karen often engaged in power struggles with students. At other times, her negative reactions to their verbal behaviors discouraged students from participating at all. Jennifer identified these culturally biased teaching behaviors and was able to help Karen understand more about African American discourse patterns. Fortunately, Karen was professional enough to listen with patience and accept the advice from Jennifer about how she could alter her communication style and accept students' discourse patterns to become a better teacher.

Teachers often discourage student learning because many don't realize that discourse styles and preferences and the social rules associated with communicating are all influenced by a person's culture. Geneva Gay (2000) described the relationship between culture, communication, and teaching: "Culture provides the tools to pursue the search for meaning and to convey our understanding to others. Consequently, communication cannot exist without culture, culture cannot be known without communication, and teaching and learning cannot occur without communication or culture" (77). Teachers judge their students' growth, understanding, and potential based on how they communicate with each other. The high percentage of culturally diverse students in urban schools naturally creates a challenge to effective communication exchanges between students and their primarily white Anglo female teachers. If you expect to communicate effectively with your students, you will need to comprehend their preferred discourse styles, and if your students are from several different ethnicities and cultures, you'll have much to learn from each student.

Saravia-Shore and Garcia (1995) provided research support for the fact "[T]hat students learn more when their classrooms are compatible with their own cultural and linguistic experience" (57). They added,

> When the norms of interaction and communication in a classroom are very different from those to which the student has been accustomed, students experience confusion and anxiety, cannot attend to learning, and may not know how to appropriately seek the teacher's attention, get the floor, or participate in discussions. By acknowledging students' cultural norms and expectations concerning communication and social interaction, teachers can appropriately guide student participation in instructional activities. (57)

Now, urban teachers must know what specific norms their students expect and how they can accommodate those communication needs.

Accepting Nonstandard English Discourse Patterns

Approximately sixty to seventy percent of African Americans often speak in a different dialect than standard English, referred to as Black English Venacular (BEV) (Wiley 1996). Other nonstandard forms of

English exist in the United States including Hawaiian Creole English and Appalachian English, but less students are speaking those dialects than BEV (Ruddell 1999).

I have worked with in-service teachers who want to know if students should be corrected and asked to use standard English every time they use BEV. The answer is "No!" Correcting students has the effect of frustrating them. Howard (2001) explained, "Teachers should recognize that any attempts to invalidate or denigrate the use of nonstandard English might have detrimental effects on the academic prospects for African American students" (200). Ruddell (1999) provided an important philosophy and instructional statement about BEV: "Standard English should not be viewed as a replacement for children's nonstandard dialects but as an alternative dialect that can be used in school and work when appropriate and necessary" (292). Permitting students to use BEV to engage in discussions, exchange ideas with classmates, respond to teachers' questions, and speak to you privately or publicly are appropriate because, in listening nonjudgmentally, you recognize and honor a child's cultural personality.

If you're like most teachers, holding your tongue may be challenging at first. You will need to get used to it. When you demonstrate respect for African American children and adolescents in this manner, you have a much greater opportunity for establishing positive relationships. As Delpit (1995) stated, "To suggest that this [BEV] form is 'wrong' or even worse, ignorant, is to suggest that something is wrong with the student and his or her family" (53). Constant correction of language differences leads to the development of severe negative feelings toward teachers. Furthermore, no evidence exists that permitting the use of BEV negatively affects academic achievement (Dwyer 1991).

Providing advice on the appropriate time and place to use standard English should become part of specific lessons that demonstrate to students the oral and writing rules of standard English in context with meaningful learning experiences. Delpit (1995) described how one white teacher had her students teach her rules that govern creating rap songs. Following their teaching, she compared their rules to some of the rules expected in speaking and writing standard English. In this exchange, the teacher recognized students' language while sharing the knowledge that they needed to successfully maneuver through different cultural and economic communities.

Appropriate Instructional Activities

Although you don't have to speak BEV to your students, in a few studies, academic achievement improved in classrooms where teachers frequently spoke BEV and permitted its use as acceptable discourse (Howard 1998; Williams 1997; Lee 1993). Gay (2000) described some of the communication styles of African American students' culture that contributed to their academic success:

- dramatic presentation styles
- conversational and active participatory discourse
- gestures and body movements
- rapidly paced rhythmic speech
- metaphorical imagery (87).

Adrienne, from a Los Angeles high school, uses conversational instructional processes with her African American students: "I use activities such as book talks, literature circles, plays, and courtroom trials." Jackie, who taught in New York City and now in Philadelphia, discusses the kinds of strategies that are successful with her primarily African American students: "I place a great deal of emphasis on theatre and art activities. For example, having students act out *Charlotte's Web* (White 1952) and then write a play much like it. I'll have students design a stage set and do all the painting of props. I have huge success also with videotaping their reenactments of books."

Lee (1993) discovered that high school students made gains in their literary analysis skills when they were permitted to use *signifying* or *sounding* in classroom discussions. *Signifying* involves using insults, insinuation, and exaggeration during class discussions to insult each other (Gay 2000). This strategy may not match your views of proper protocol for classroom discussions, yet its use improved student engagement and understanding of text. Students who use *sounding* during class discussions may brag in a demonstrative manner, using exaggerated phrases and a loud voice as if arguing with others rather than merely sharing information.

The participatory interaction style referred to as *call-response* is related to signifying. During call-response, students may provide encouragement, give compliments, or loudly disagree *while* teachers are speaking (Gay 2000). For some European Americans, these behaviors may seem rude; yet they are a part of expected discourse patterns in some African American communities. Effective teachers accept frequent indirect comments during class discussions and recitations as long as students aren't emotionally hurt. Accepting these types of discourse may be more challenging for female teachers whose perspectives on appropriate communication styles may be less assertive than that of males. Tannen (1990) and Sadker and Sadker (1994) explained how it is common for many women to use much less aggressive conversational practices than males. Many women may also prefer to avoid conflictual communication situations. Accepting a more varied discussion pattern than the traditional turn taking, raising hands, and an "Only one person talks at a time" policy, means renegotiating both cultural perspectives and gender roles for many women teachers. Each of these seemingly different discourse characteristics meet the learning needs of many African, Hispanic, and Asian American, and Native Hawaiian students in the sense that they provide more active student involvement in the learning process.

Communicating with Second Language Learners

It seems that many Americans share the egocentric view that if someone enters our borders they should be able to speak English well, especially if they plan to stay for any length of time. That response shows the limited experiences of many Americans who have been isolated from other countries by geographic boundaries, thus requiring no need to learn of or share in the culture and language of other peoples. Some Americans who have visited other countries are more understanding of the challenges and processes of effectively communicating in another language. Perhaps when they return to the United States they are more sympathetic of SLL students.

Please recognize that achieving enough English-speaking proficiency to succeed academically can take from four to seven years, depending on the backgrounds of second language learners who enter school (Collier 1989). California's recent educational policy to limit bilingual instruction to one year suggests that some legislators and residents think one year of English instruction is sufficient for students to succeed in school without further assistance (Ohanian 1999).

Helping SLL students succeed academically begins with establishing a comfortable and stress-free learning environment, particularly for adolescents who face the fear of making mistakes and being embarrassed by peers. The classroom rule of insuring that no students will be ridiculed must be explicitly stated and enforced to encourage SLL students to practice their English. If English isn't spoken at home, school must be the environment where students are able to practice and experiment with the language with classmates and teachers.

Becoming Acquainted with Second Language Learners

An integral aspect of a teacher's role for creating an optimal learning environment for SLL students is demonstrating a respect for and value of their familial cultural heritage. Teachers must validate the cultural backgrounds of students rather than deny that differences exist, especially because the larger society often denigrates the cultures and languages of diverse populations. As mentioned earlier, understand that students are clearly cognizant of your feelings and attitudes about them by the way you act individually with each one and in large group situations.

Effective educators of SLL learners do as much personal research as possible to understand the social, linguistic, and other cultural characteristics of their students. Your role in helping immigrant students is to acquaint yourself with how different their languages are, that is, to attempt to understand the rules for the structure of their language. You need to determine, for instance, syntax patterns (the order of words for speaking and writing), challenges they experience in pronouncing certain English sounds, and discourse styles; that is, is the language more orally based than written? Consider for instance, the differences in vowel pronunciations between Spanish and English; subject-verb agreement challenges for some Asian SLL students; syntax differences between the Hmong language and English; and, the fact that many sounds in English do not even exist in other languages (Cary 2000). An awareness of these language differences will help you assist students in English-language development. Added aspects of cultural awareness include understanding a child's perspectives and expectations about learning and being in America. Attitudes affect students' interests, effort, and motivation to learn English.

Your research also should provide information on a student's native country: geography, historical information, and current political status. Knowing more about your students' backgrounds will assist you in creating a friendly place to learn—an environment where students are comfortable taking risks. Knowing all of this information is necessary if you expect students to begin to engage in classroom conversation freely and comfortably. You'll know if you have connected with your SLL students by their eventual oral involvement in class discussions. Despite their need to listen for extended periods to learn language, they also need to engage in genuine conversations to extend their growth. Your encouragement is a needed component, and the more you know about their native lands and culture the better chance you have of drawing them into conversations. Ramirez (1985) discovered in his research that the more positive the attitude toward the culture of the people that spoke the new language, the higher language proficiency was among those learning it.

Accepting Code Switching

Deciding how to engage SLL students should be based on the research on how a second language is learned. First, realize that students do not completely ignore or cease to speak their native language once they begin second-language acquisition. Many of their utterances involve *code switching*, that is, using words from both languages simultaneously while speaking. This is typical and does not prevent SLL students from understanding or learning standard English conventions (Padilla and Liebman 1975). For older students, code switching may involve their own construction of mixed language with its own specific language rules, as in the use of Spanglish or Calo—combinations of Spanish and English (Garcia 1999).

The implication for teachers is to accept and understand those utterances without providing unnecessary negative responses to code switching. As with students who use BEV during class discussions, teachers should not correct the mistakes made by SLL students as they speak and code switch, but instead, provide modeling later through their own use of standard English. As Garcia (1999) indicated, "It [code switching] is not to be taken as evidence of a language disability or confusion" (184). The development of second language parallels original development of language by native speakers (Dulay and Burt 1974). If you know children between the ages of two and four, listen to how they develop language, and you will ultimately understand how language develops for anyone learning a new language. It is truly amazing how patient adults are with toddlers learning the language compared to the attitudes they have about second language learners. You can understand how constant correction of SLL students can discourage speaking and development in the language.

Understand that language and cognition are closely linked; therefore, it is imperative that SLL students maneuver through their learning of English with many opportunities to speak in both languages without undue pressure to pronounce every word correctly or use the appropriate word. Preventing code switching negates the child's opportunities to use the brain efficiently in learning a new language (Garcia 1999). Cary (2000) explained the advantage of a teacher ignoring the mistakes of her SLL students: "Giving students permission to get language wrong went a long way in helping them to get it right" (59).

Bringing Text to Life

A common challenge for second language learners is making sense of miles of confusing text material. Because one goal of American educators is to encourage students to read, interpret, and react to decontextualized text, many urban teachers falsely believe that pushing abstractly written texts at SLL students and having them memorize aspects of language growth is appropriate. Many students do not succeed at learning English or interpreting text through decontextualized teaching or books. SLL students need reality—real materials, videos, pictures, reenactments, plays, presentations, and demonstrations to connect principles while learning language. They need to use all the senses while they are learning to fully comprehend the principles being taught. Researchers refer to this type of experiential teaching as *contextualized* language instruction; in other words, content is connected to realia—real events, objects, and authentic discussions (Duquette 1991).

Discussion Discourse Patterns

The type of discussions that occur in traditional American classrooms are not typically discussions at all—they are actually recitations. *Recitations* are like the game Jeopardy: the teacher asks a question; a student responds (usually the first one with a hand up); the teacher responds with a "That's right!" or "No, not exactly," or "That's not it, anyone else have an answer?" Then, another question is asked and the pattern is maintained. This pattern—teacher question, student response, teacher response, then another teacher question—might continue for an entire period. In an hour's time, perhaps students spoke for ten percent of class time. There is no discussion when teachers speak this much! Students are denied opportunities to speak to each other or to respond for long enough periods of time to actually learn language. The pace of the class is too fast for many students, particularly SLL students. As a result, students are not likely to engage in the recitation if they have limited English proficiency.

A recitation discourse pattern does not correspond to the cultural, oral interaction patterns of many SLL students. Recitations are primarily teacher directed with little, if any, student engagement. Naturally, families (including African, Hispanic, and Native Americans) use more conversational discourse at home than the question-answer format commonly used in many American classrooms. The discourse practice of raising hands to gain permission and taking turns to speak is not culturally congruent with these families either. The result among students placed in recitation-learning formats is typically silence due to reluctance to participate. These passive language-learning activities are unproductive for SLL students.

SLL students need opportunities to speak to each other and to the teacher as equal-status participants in a genuine discussion format in which the teacher acts merely as any other student in the class who wants to occasionally add something to class discussions. Class discussion topics should be genuine issues that address the interests and tap the background knowledge of students in the class. In support of greater student-to-student discourse during class discussions, Boggs (1972) reported a "[R]eluctance of Native Hawaiian children to respond to direct questioning" strategies used by teachers (cited in Garcia 1999, 189). The Hawaiian students became more verbally engaged when teachers permitted discussions among students with multiple speakers to support one another.

Altering the format alone will not correct the problems of many traditional American instructional practices for SLL students. Many teachers, for instance, ask short, known-answer questions of students that require minimal thought and even less verbal interaction between and among students and teachers. These types of questions further discourage the development of language acquisition for SLL students because they aren't allowed much time to respond either. Children and adolescents need time—time to think in their language and respond in English, or time to respond with more elaboration, which can increase English acquisition. Language acquisition is a complex process. Designing instruction so that students have extensive time to engage in both large and small group discussions increases the probability of greater gains in language knowledge (Garcia 1999).

Culturally responsive instructional discourse patterns for some learners should also permit and encourage spontaneous verbal interruptions and additions in a discussion rather than one person speaking at a time after being recognized by the teacher. Native Hawaiian students respond in discussions with a strategy referred to as "*talk-story* or *co-narration* which involves several students working collaboratively,

175

or talking together, to create an idea, tell a story, or complete a learning task" (Gay 2000, 92). Talk-story is similar to the interactive conversational styles of African Americans referred to as call-response, explained earlier (Gay 2000). Teachers must demonstrate acceptance of these multiple conversations to recognize students' cultural discourse patterns while encouraging the development of their language acquisition.

Research indicates that Chinese American students prefer independent help while learning with a focus on teacher-directed instruction (Garcia 1999). You'll certainly be challenged when you have an equal number of Chinese American and Chicano students in your classroom because each group has a different preferred discourse pattern.

Realize that every suggested strategy in this chapter is based on the experiences of many successful teachers and a supportive research base. However, research studies provide generalizations in many instances that naturally do not apply to every student from that cultural background. Many urban classrooms do, however, contain wide variations of students from a diverse set of cultural heritages. Responding appropriately to the learning needs of your students requires as much individualization as generalization. Providing for the needs of all students requires adapting instructional strategies for each child or adolescent in some way.

Specific Instructional Strategies for Second Language Learners

The single most effective and appropriate assistance for SLL students is for learning to occur in their native language *and* English (Cary 2000). *Bilingual education* provides students with opportunities to learn in both languages daily. If you want to have a significant educational impact on your classroom of primarily Spanish-speaking students, for instance, then learn Spanish and speak both languages when the situation calls for it during the day. Learning at least some of students' native languages will have a positive impact on many features of culturally responsive teaching!

Because you may not be well versed in Spanish, Hmong, Chinese, or Russian yet, knowledge of how to incorporate components of

Specially Designed Academic Instruction in English (SDAIE) will go a long way in helping your SLL students. SDAIE is often referred to as *sheltered instruction*. Sheltered instruction involves many active instructional processes to help make the abstract content in textbooks and other instructional materials clear for SLL students. Cary (2000) described some of these meaningful learning activities:

- organization of students learning into "small collaborative work groups"
- peer assistance for most learning activities
- extensive use of objects, drawings, maps, graphs
- videos to build background knowledge
- teacher modeling of how to do activities
- storyboarding
- kinesthetic activities
- role playing and dramatic presentations
- art activities to extend concept development
- pairing of SLL students with native English speakers during learning activities (55–56, 84).

An example of using sheltered instruction is described by Pete, a Philadelphia high school teacher. He relies on socialization processes to teach his students: "I get them up and moving around and interacting with each other. I allow students the freedom to talk to each other and exchange ideas during class. When you're learning language, you have to allow students to speak it! I also use videotaping as they orally present their written autobiographies. We did a unit on fables, and the students wrote them and illustrated them. Then we invited kindergarten students in as judges, and my students had to perform their fables in front of the kindergarten students as they graded the fable presentations. We videotaped all of those also." Pete obviously found a way to create genuine language activities for his SLL students that matched their instructional level while challenging them at the same time.

Ruddell (1999) provided the following philosophy for using sheltered instruction: "The key purpose of SDAIE is to make information accessible to students through careful planning and scaffolding, while at the same time avoiding oversimplication of the curriculum" (299). To that end, Ruddell provided the following four goals for SLL students engaged in sheltered instruction:

- learn to communicate in English
- learn content-area material
- advance in higher-level thinking skills
- master literacy skills (299).

Be realistic about your influence in a single year on the growth of SLL students' English proficiency. Use instructional processes that match their developmental levels and language ability skills.

Garcia (1999) provided an additional list of instructional ideas that can assist you in teaching SLL students:

- increase wait time following your questions and after their responses to promote elaboration and more processing time
- simplify your language—don't speak louder, rephrase comments or questions instead
- don't force students to speak
- pair SLL students with proficient English speakers
- adapt instructional materials to make them more comprehensible
- build on students' prior knowledge
- support the student's home language and culture (adapted from 315).

Responding to Questions and Writing

Classroom learning activities in many American classrooms are often dominated by a focus on oral discussions, or reading and writing processes. You know how the game is traditionally played: the teacher initially provides an orderly explanation of what you need to know to complete an assignment or provides detailed information on a specific content area. These are typically teacher-centered activities in which students are asked to passively consume information. Gay (2000) described this traditional practice as *topic-centered* instruction. In Gay's description of topic-centered teaching, when educators speak they, "[F]ocus on one issue at a time, arrange facts and ideas in logical, linear order; and make explicit relationships between facts and ideas" (96). This is indeed a linear approach to teaching that mirrors deductive learning. You have seen and experienced this structured approach to learning. Au (1993) contended that African, Native, and Hispanic Americans as well as Native Hawaiians prefer *topic-associative* speaking and writing over topic-centered. Gay described the topic-associative style of speaking and writing as "[E]pisodic, anecdotal, thematic, and integrative" (96). Also called *topic-chaining*, this style of speaking is much less structured than topic-centered instruction, with speakers weaving stories into comments and text while disregarding a linear delivery. This type of speaking or writing may sound to others like the speaker is completely disorganized.

If teachers take the initiative to deliver instruction in a topic-associative manner, such as using story telling to explain principles, then lessons may have more meaning for African, Hispanic, and Native American learners. Accepting the fact that students respond orally to teacher questions using topic-chaining discourse will also assist in reacting appropriately and with support of students' speech patterns.

Another noticeable communication characteristic of some African and Hispanic American students is their more highly charged emotional state while engaged in discussions. Teachers must learn to accept that some African and Hispanic Americans may act emotionally in their support for issues and that these emotions may be unleashed during class discussions, even on teachers, as a way for students to communicate their support. Discussions for many African American students may be more like debates (Kochman 1981).

Topic-associative writing may also be a challenge for teachers to accept. Because many African American students write using topic-associative style, it may appear to you that they are writing in a manner to merely fill the page with words unrelated to one another and that their response is quite indirect. Upon closer scrutiny, you will

179

realize that their paragraphs are connected to one another in a more fluid manner than topic-centered writing. Topic-chaining writing appears as narrative with storytelling evident in the text (Kochman 1985). Again, your evaluation of and feedback to students' writing must demonstrate specifically how you support their progress. The focus should initially be on story line, characterization, or descriptive processes. Mini-lessons may be used later to demonstrate the differences between discourse writing patterns among cultures and how writing may be altered or structured for different purposes.

Appropriate Questioning Strategies

Other traditionally Eurocentric instructional patterns are in direct conflict with the cultural communication and learning needs of many urban students. The types of questioning strategies employed by teachers may easily discourage students through their simplistic expectations for responding. For instance, Delpit (1995) spoke of the ineffective practice of asking students questions that have known answers. You know the kind: "Please raise your hand and tell me what the main character's occupation is in this story?" or "Which number in the problem is the dividend?" Please realize, if the answer can be found in the book, no critical or creative thinking is required, no problem solving is needed, no introspection is encouraged, and you need to find more appropriate strategies for designing questions. These traditional questioning strategies do nothing to engage students in genuine learning! It appears European American students are the only ones who have the patience to listen and respond to these types of questions.

Heath (1983) described how the practice of asking more complex questions matched the discussion styles of African American students' home situations. African American students were more likely to become engaged in discussions when they were required to make connections between text and their lives or use problem-solving strategies to answer questions. Lee (1993) explained that African American students demonstrated more complex understanding of literature when discussions "[W]ere more student-initiated" rather than teacher directed, "As well as consistently focused on difficult, inferential questions" (cited in Gay 2000, 89). The back-to-the-basics curricular focus, intense phonetic approaches to teaching reading, or use of known-question-answer recitation formats appear to be ineffective in engaging African American learners despite a call for these kinds of pedagogy every time someone takes an interest in urban students' test scores (Kohn 2000).

Responding to the needs of students whose family and cultural backgrounds differ from yours is a continuous learning process. You have to learn to accept and understand how students communicate differently to help them develop. Sure, you're done with your undergraduate days at college, but your education on how to reach the lives of many urban students is just beginning. May you be open minded enough to grow as a professional educator as you accept and build on these strategies for helping urban students.

References

Au, K. H. 1993. *Literacy Instruction in Multicultural Settings*. New York: Harcourt Brace.

Boggs, S. T. 1972. "The Meaning of Questions and Narratives to Hawaiian Children." In *Functions of Language in the Classroom*, edited by C. Cazden, V. John, and D. Hymes. New York: Teachers College Press. 299–330.

Cary, S. 2000. *Working with Second Language Learners: Answers to Teachers' Top Ten Questions*. Portsmouth, NH: Heinemann.

Collier, V. P. 1989. "How Long: A Synthesis of Research on Academic Achievement in a Second Language." *TESOL Quarterly* 23, no. 3: 509–531.

Delpit, L. 1995. *Other People's Children: Cultural Conflict in the Classroom*. New York: New Press.

Dulay, H., and M. Burt. 1974. *Natural Sequence in Child Second-Language Acquisition*. Toronto: Ontario Institute for Studies in Education.

Duquette, G. 1991. "Cultural Processing and Minority Language Children with Needs and Special Needs." In *Language, Culture, and Cognition*, edited by G. Duquette and L. Malve. Philadelphia: Multilingual Matters. 200–213.

Dwyer, C. 1991. "Language, Culture, and Writing." Working Paper No. 13. Berkeley, University of California: Center for the Study of Writing.

Garcia, E. 1999. *Student Cultural Diversity: Understanding and Meeting the Challenge.* 2nd. ed. Boston: Houghton Mifflin.

Gay, G. 2000. *Culturally Responsive Teaching: Theory, Research, and Practice.* New York: Teachers College Press.

Heath, S. B. 1983. *Ways with Words.* Cambridge: Cambridge University Press.

Howard, T. C. 1998. Pedagogical Practices and Ideological Constructions of Effective Teachers of African American Students. Ph.D. diss., University of Washington, Seattle.

————. 2001. "Powerful Pedagogy for African American Students: A Case Study of Four Teachers." *Urban Education* 36, no. 2: 179–201.

Kochman, T. 1981. *Black and White Styles in Conflict.* Chicago: University of Chicago Press.

————. 1985. "Black American Speech Events and a Language Program for the Classroom." In *Functions of Language in the Classroom,* edited by C. B. Cazden, V. P. John, and D. Hymes. Prospect Heights, IL: Waveland. 211–261.

Kohn, A. 2000. *The Case Against Standardized Testing: Raising the Scores, Ruining the Schools.* Portsmouth, NH: Heinemann.

Lee, C. 1993. "Signifying as a Scaffold to Literary Interpretation: The Pedagogical Implications of a Form of African American Discourse." National Council of Teachers of English Research Report No. 26. Urbana, IL: National Council of Teachers of English.

Obidah, J. E., and K. Manheim Teel. 2001. *Because of the Kids: Facing Racial and Cultural Differences in Schools.* New York: Teachers College Press.

Ohanian, S. 1999. *One Size Fits Few: The Folly of Educational Standards.* Portsmouth, NH: Heinemann.

Padilla, A. M., and E. Liebman. 1975. "Language Acquisition in the Bilingual Child." *The Bilingual Review/LaRevista Bilingue* 2: 34–55.

182

RAMIREZ, A. 1985. *Bilingualism Through Schooling*. Albany, NY: State University of New York Press.

RUDDELL, R. B. 1999. *Teaching Children to Read and Write: Becoming an Influential Teacher*. 2nd ed. Needham Heights, MA: Allyn & Bacon.

SADKER, M., AND D. SADKER. 1994. *Failing at Fairness: How Our Schools Cheat Girls*. New York: Touchstone.

SARAVIA-SHORE, M., AND E. GARCIA. 1995. "Diverse Teaching Strategies for Diverse Learners." In *Educating Everybody's Children: Diverse Teaching Strategies for Diverse Learners*, edited by R. W. Coles. Alexandria, VA: Association for Supervision and Curriculum Development. 47–74.

TANNEN, D. 1990. *You Just Don't Understand: Women and Men in Conversation*. New York: Morrow.

WHITE, E. B. 1952. *Charlotte's Web*. New York: Harper.

WILEY, M. S. 1996. "Environmental Education in the School Culture: A Systemic Approach." *Clearing House* 94: 25–27.

WILLIAMS, R. L. 1997. "The Ebonics Controversy." *Journal of Black Psychology* 23, no. 3: 208–214.

EIGHT

The Real Meaning of Assessment

*This is what I have been given. These are the students
who have walked into my room; so, I need to give them
something valuable, useful, and meaningful.*

ADRIENNE, LOS ANGELES HIGH SCHOOL ENGLISH TEACHER

Critical Components of Assessment

The amount of information students learn as they progress through
each academic year is not determined by the scope and sequence of
the district's curriculum guides. Students' growth rate is not controlled
by the state guidelines for what every fifth grader should know by June.
Student learning is minimally affected by those questions asked on
state and national standardized tests, and it is not determined by your
pre-established plan for how much of the textbook you intend to complete during the year.

Discovering the extent of students' learning is much more complex than administering state tests or implementing guidelines established by legislators, administrators, textbook writers, school board
members, or teachers. Knowing what students have learned as a result
of instruction is a component of assessment. Discovering their beginning knowledge is a more critical piece of assessment.

Identifying exactly what students learn during the year is an in-
exact science. There is little value in determining what students know
if their learning is measured by externally imposed state and national

standardized tests. State and national standardized tests fail to address the contextual circumstances of your students' academic histories, are often totally unrelated to a school's curricula, and are normed with a population of students completely different from your students (Kohn 2000). Standardized tests fail to determine the genuine growth that your students actually make within a year. Those tests don't assess students' growth, they label and classify students—which does nothing to improve your teaching effectiveness or improve students' learning.

The primary purpose of conducting meaningful assessment activities is to provide you with useful information about students' growth during the year: to improve your teaching and help students grow. Teachers always know more about the level of their students' learning through their own observations than they do through tests, especially tests designed by someone else.

A teacher's role in appropriately assessing students is to discover a child's or adolescent's knowledge base in reading, mathematics, language acquisition, and the content areas you teach. Furthermore, assessment enables teachers to respond to each child's needs through the use of appropriate curricula, effective instructional activities, and meaningful assessment strategies. Assessment is not as simple as examining a student's standardized test scores and past grades. Those activities won't do anything to help students this year while they are in your classroom. Academic backgrounds and current levels of ability can be extremely diverse among students in the same classroom. Providing appropriate assistance to students requires responding to their diverse ability levels. Susan, from San Francisco, explains how she addresses the differences in her fifth-grade students' abilities: "My curriculum is open ended. There's a buy in place for every kid. They go as far as they can. Those that can't fit in—we find their beginning place, and it's always level appropriate."

Assessment is a personalized process for each student that involves answering these questions prior to teaching:

1. What does this student know?
2. What is the student able to do at this point in time?

3. Based on these data, what information does this student need to know to succeed at the numerous tasks and understand information appropriate for his or her level of development?
4. What strategies can I use to help this student succeed?

Notice, I didn't say on question number three, "appropriate to their grade level." Grade level guidelines are predetermined and based on an assumption that all students learn at the same rate, are at comparable developmental stages merely due to age similarities, and possess equal amounts of and similar background knowledge. Every teacher realizes the absurdity of the probability that all students in a classroom are at similar places in their background knowledge and skill areas! Think about the variable ability levels in Kathleen's third-grade classroom in Chicago, as she describes her student population for this year:

> I have four African American students, one white, eighteen who are mostly Puerto Rican and some of those are Mexican Americans. Three of these students go to speech classes during the week. I referred four more students for speech classes during the year. Two of my students are probably gifted. Approximately one-half of them are able to work at grade level. Three students probably would be identified as ADHD, and three have serious asthma that affects their learning. Three or four definitely have emotional and social problems that affect their learning. One kid comes from a family that sleeps in their car at night. I've never had every child work on grade level.

Teaching a standardized curriculum to these third-grade students is a serious disservice to each of them!

The following are four additional questions you need to ask to complete the assessment process after students are engaged in learning:

1. What is this student learning?
2. What is she or he able to do as a result of learning this content or engaging in planned learning experiences?
3. What are some meaningful ways for this student to dem-

onstrate what she or he knows or can do as a result of studying this unit?

4. What should I do differently to improve this student's learning?

Every teacher must understand that the role of an educator is to help each student progress academically at a rate that matches his or her cognitive abilities at the time. Learning is set at a separate pace with a different set of challenges, while attempting to reach diverse outcomes for each child. Keep the assessment process simple: discover what information and strategies students need in order to grow, provide instructional activities to help them grow, then gather evidence that verifies that they are growing.

One assessment can't tell you enough about a student to help you teach him or her effectively all year long. What is it you want to know about each of your students to teach them effectively? Let me propose some of the possible questions you'll need to answer to assess students in meaningful ways:

1. What are a student's reading strengths and weaknesses?
2. What specific reading strategies has the student mastered?
3. On which reading strategies does the student need assistance?
4. What kind of background knowledge does a student have in the areas we will study this academic year?
5. What attitudes does the student hold about school in general?
6. What are some specific interests of this student?
7. What has this student read for leisure or written outside of school?
8. What mathematics abilities does this student possess?
9. What is this student's life like after school?
10. Who are this student's friends, and how do they influence her or his learning?
11. What can the parents or caregivers tell me about this student?

12. Do any health issues affect the child's ability to learn?
13. Does the student have special learning needs such as a learning disability, attention deficit disorder, or emotional difficulties?
14. What are some components of this student's learning profile?
15. What classroom environment will support this student's learning profile?
16. What materials will I need that match this student's developmental abilities and will push her or him to the next level?
17. Which motivational strategies and instructional strategies help this student to succeed?
18. What are some of this student's personality characteristics that may affect his or her learning?
19. Which instructional strategies were effective in past years?
20. What is the student's English-language proficiency level?
21. How is this student progressing weekly?

Notice that not all of these questions are focused on academic factors. Learning is affected by all of the issues mentioned in these questions and more. Collecting an adequate amount of information about your students' learning needs doesn't merely occur in the first few weeks of school. Discovering students' strengths and needs is year-long, ongoing process. As the school year progresses and you notice more about each student, you'll develop more questions than you'll actually get answers to! Shanika, a Philadelphia middle school teacher, describes how she observed one of her student's growth throughout the year:

> One of my students is from Sierra Leone. He recently came to the states. He hadn't been in a consistent school in Sierra Leone because of the war. They [the family] were constantly moving. He could hardly write, couldn't speak or read anything when he arrived. He was pretty insecure about being in class because it was all unfamiliar to him. He has grown so much! He is more outgoing now. His

enthusiasm about doing things is very high. He believes he is part of the classroom.

Can you understand how many factors can affect the learning of a student as you reflect on this student's background? How can a standardized test provide comprehensive information about this student to a teacher? Think about how you will make decisions about how and what to teach students who bring these kinds of experiences into your classroom.

Gathering Student Data

The historical origin of the word *assess* is Latin, *assidere*, meaning "to sit by" (*American Heritage Dictionary* 2000, 108). Seems a perfect description of the requirement to determine what students really know—sit by them! You begin assessment by getting to know students' personalities and their backgrounds. Strategies for gaining information on students' backgrounds are mentioned in Chapter 2. The more you understand about a student's home environment, academic effort, and interpersonal skills, the better prepared you will be to motivate him or her. It takes more than an awareness of students' personalities, however, to help them grow academically. Discovering a student's knowledge base and developmental levels is a necessary prerequisite to providing appropriate instruction and curricular materials.

Students' past grades are poor indicators of what they know or are able to do academically; examining them is a futile exercise in determining how or what to teach students. Tombari and Borich (1999) explained that grades, "[A]ssume equal amounts of learning have occurred for individuals who achieve the same grade, fail to acknowledge continuous progress or development in learning, and may mask an individual student's learning strengths and needs" (39). As Knowles and Brown (2000) described, "Assessment is a comprehensive act that includes consideration of a student's goals for learning, processes of learning, progression toward established goals, and revision of goals when needed" (127).

Assessing Reading Ability

It is imperative that you initiate specific steps to determine students' reading abilities—especially for those who you recognize are struggling. Secondary teachers have as much responsibility for discerning students' reading abilities as elementary teachers because learning new information at the middle and high school levels occurs primarily through reading text. Students will not make academic progress unless they have access to instructional materials that match their reading abilities. Students' personal files may have standardized test scores that provide a minimal amount of information on reading abilities. Standardized tests, however, do not provide enough specific information to assist teachers in designing appropriate learning experiences or in choosing developmentally appropriate instructional materials. These tests will be particularly inappropriate for providing useful information about second language learners. Several options exist to avoid administering or using standardized reading tests to determine students' reading ability.

Your first clues about a student's reading abilities are derived from personal observations each day. You may notice a student's reading skills when he or she is asked to read orally. You'll notice that some students' inability to complete assignments is a clue to their reading deficits. A student who approaches you with many questions about how to complete assignments may have reading problems. If you have second language learners who have difficulty speaking English, they are likely struggling with reading text. You may determine more from observing which books a student selects for independent reading. If a student shows little or no interest in reading books for pleasure, a clear message is sent about the student's perspective on reading. How students respond in class discussions, the rate at which they complete assignments, and their ability to focus during assigned reading activities during the day all provide more pieces to the reading-ability puzzle. You can see how your own observations are initial clues and provide powerful information about students' reading abilities.

Teachers can add to their informal observations by administering a reading interest inventory to obtain a broader picture of a child's or adolescent's reading interests and attitudes about reading. Ruddell (1999) developed a reading interest inventory and a "developmental inventory," for teachers to assess students' personal reading habits and interests and their speaking and writing developmental stages (339–340). May (1998) provided an "Observation Checklist for Reading and Language Disabilities" that should be used to assess students who are experiencing difficulty with classroom reading and writing tasks (527). An explanation of the types of questions provided on these inventories is in Figure 8.1. These inventories and observation instruments provide a broader perspective on students' reading attitudes and backgrounds than you will discover with standardized tests. You don't need any special training to administer these inventories.

You can obtain a more detailed analysis of students' reading strengths and weaknesses by finding time in the beginning of the year to have an individual conference with each student to listen to her or him read. The purpose of an individual "reading" conference is to determine which strategies students use in reading. Listening to students read while specifically noting their strengths and weaknesses is an aspect of an *informal reading inventory* (IRI). Ruddell (1999) provides three purposes for administering an IRI:

1. It helps you understand how a student constructs meaning and applies word-analysis strategies. This is especially useful for a student you believe is encountering special reading problems.
2. It provides a rough indication of reading placement level for a student.
3. It offers insight into a student's comprehension and use of word-analysis strategies as he or she reads aloud and interacts during small group instruction (342).

Informal reading inventories are published by several companies. Burns and Roe (1995) publish IRIs for all grade levels, and Silvaroli (1994) has published the *Classroom Reading Inventory*.

Reading abilities are affected by many factors, but four abilities are directly connected to successful reading: a student's background

Reading Assessment Instruments

1. Reading Interest Inventory

A survey used to determine students' interests and motivation to read. Several interest inventories exist in addition to one provided by Ruddell (1999, 337). An individual conference is established with a student to determine her or his reading interests and personal feelings about reading. Questions include:

- Do you like to read, and if so, what are your favorite books?
- Do you have any books of your own?
- What are your special interests outside of school (337)?

2. Developmental Inventory

A method for recording observations of students' typical classroom literacy skills. Ruddell's instrument can be used to evaluate reading, listening, writing, and speaking abilities (338). A teacher notes student's use of the following:

- How does a student "[G]uide self through reading a text"?
- Does a student, "[D]raw inferences from spoken and written text"?
- Does a student, "[R]aise questions about unknown information"?
- Does a student "[D]emonstrate fluency and confidence when engaged in text" (339)?

3. Observation Checklist for Reading and Language Disabilities

A checklist for observing and noting students' general behavior, reading, and writing behaviors. The categories that May (1998) provided include:

- Tends to get frustrated easily
- Has far too much energy

- Has trouble making lasting friendships
- Informal reading inventory is at least one year below grade level in grades two and three, and two years below in later grades
- Asks teacher to decode words rather than using word-analysis skills
- Transposes words, letters, and syllables in writing
- Writing is very laborious (568).

4. Informal Reading Inventory

An individually administered reading assessment to identify specific reading difficulties demonstrated by students at any level. It requires twenty to forty minutes of time alone with a student. The teacher listens to the student read while marking a copy of the same text with specific codes to note the student's mistakes. Standardized forms are provided to mark text as students read. Comprehension questions are provided to note student understanding of text. Burns and Roe (1995) provide assessment forms for every grade level. The inventory helps in identifying a student's grade level reading abilities and frustration, instructional, and independent reading levels.

5. Miscue Analysis

An individually administered reading assessment that identifies a student's reading mistakes or miscues. The teacher listens to a student read and notes the specific miscues made. It requires twenty to forty minutes of time alone with a student. The teacher can identify whether miscues negatively affect a student's comprehension, enhance comprehension, or have no impact. Miscues can be analyzed to determine which instructional strategies would most effectively target student's reading deficits (Wilde 2000).

Figure 8.1 Description of Reading Assessment Instruments

knowledge, basic vocabulary, knowledge of syntax (word order and sentence structure), and grapho-phonemic (sound and letter) awareness. These are four cueing systems readers use to identify text features to understand a writer's message. Effective readers use all four systems to decipher text. Deficits in any one of these areas affect a student's ability to comprehend text.

The most accurate means of determining which cueing systems challenge students is to use a miscue analysis of a student's reading. *Miscues* refer to any departure a reader makes from the written text; such as omitting, substituting, inserting, or reversing text. Wilde (2000) indicates that by noting miscues that students make while reading we, "[U]nderstand what strategies struggling readers are using and how effective those strategies are, in a way that doesn't focus on weaknesses, doesn't oversimplify, and doesn't label readers" (4). Wilde's book, *Miscue Analysis Made Easy: Building on Student Strengths* (2000), provides a clear and detailed explanation on how to assess students' reading to determine which cueing systems students need additional assistance with to improve their reading strategies. Conducting a miscue analysis involves listening to a student read orally from approximate grade level material you have selected. Wilde explains how to note miscues students make and how to analyze those miscues to determine how they affect reading. Darigan, Tunnell, and Jacobs (2002) provide a companion website with their book, *Children's Literature: Engaging Teachers and Children in Good Books*, at which you can observe a child reading text and practice conducting a miscue analysis.

Following a miscue analysis, you may discover that a student needs specific instruction in

- developing background knowledge
- comprehending appropriate sentence structure and word order (syntax)
- pronouncing words correctly
- understanding letter-sound relationships
- building vocabulary.

You may also note the extent to which students are comprehending text by asking them to retell the story they have read and then following with specific questions about the text. The depth and breadth of their retelling and responses to your questions indicate their degree of understanding the text.

Other assessment strategies beyond an IRI should be used to determine a student's reading level. An IRI relies on oral reading to determine reading ability, which may not be an accurate measure of how a student reads silently or comprehends text during silent reading (Rhodes and Dudley-Marling 1996). Teachers can ask questions or have students complete reading-response logs following silent reading of text.

Meeting with students after school, during lunch or recess, or before school are more efficient ways for conducting individualized reading assessments than attempting to conduct reading analyses during class time. If you are fortunate to have a reading specialist who has the time to assist you, then encourage that person to administer a reading analysis for those students who appear to be struggling.

The value in identifying the reading needs of students is discovering a student's reading proficiency level. You want to find appropriate reading materials for students so that they are able to understand text. The three labels used to describe a student's reading level are *instructional*, *independent*, and *frustration*. Students ideally should be reading content and other forms of learning materials at their instructional level. Reading materials that are too challenging for students are at their frustration level and do little to promote learning. Students are able to easily comprehend text written at their independent level.

Identifying the reading abilities of students is an ongoing assessment process that should be used to establish additional instructional activities and collect appropriate curricular materials for students. I believe it is important for all educators to have some basic knowledge of reading development. I strongly suggest that you find a reading specialist who can provide you with more information on how to assess your students' basic reading abilities; or better yet, who is willing to assess some of your students for you.

Assessing Writing Skills

Identifying a student's writing interests and abilities is also a necessity for helping students to progress in all subject areas. Rhodes and Dudley-Marling (1996) suggested two general questions for assessing student's writing:

1. How well does the writing fulfill its purpose—to report, persuade, elicit feeling, and so forth?
2. What do students know about writing, including writing conventions that help them fulfill their intentions? (59)

Many opportunities for writing occur during the week. Teachers can gather information on students' writing strategies in any subject area. You will want to observe writing activities to determine if a student is able to

- self-initiate writing
- choose writing topics
- focus on writing during the time permitted without excessive prompting
- reread, revise, and edit what is written
- focus the content of writing when writing for a specific purpose
- organize a piece of writing for fluency
- use appropriate language structures such as syntactic rules, word endings, and various sentence patterns
- use a variety of vocabulary
- take risks in writing
- use conventions (punctuation, capitalization, spelling) in writing appropriate for stage of development (adapted from Rhodes and Dudley-Marling 1996, 59–60).

Discovering students' writing abilities is another continuous process that occurs over the course of a year. As in assessing reading abilities, you'll need to "sit beside" a student to collect information on writing strategies. Asking students questions about how they choose a topic for writing, the challenges they perceive in writing, and how they evaluate their writing provides more information to help them improve. Content area high school and middle school teachers, as well as language arts teachers at any level, need to make observations about their students' writing strategies. Observing students' proficiency in writing laboratory reports, research papers, or literature reviews can provide clues to students' writing strengths and needs.

As in discovering a student's reading needs, once you realize a student's writing abilities, you can begin to design developmentally appropriate activities and assignments that help this particular student progress. Comparisons with other students will most likely fail to improve the effort or products produced by students who need additional assistance.

Identifying English-Language Proficiency

Assessing a student's English-language proficiency should be a high priority for assisting immigrant students. The most appropriate way to begin assessing an SLL's knowledge of English is to listen to the student during conversations at recess, lunch, or in the hallways. Personal conversations and other informal observations should lead to a perspective on a student's understanding of spoken English, ability to speak English, knowledge of reading and understanding written English text, and ability to write using English.

Taking descriptive notes during observations provides the opportunity for more accurate instructional decision making when you review notes later. Taking notes from a variety of settings will provide a broader picture of a student's abilities than using only two or three observations from the same activity each day. SLL students may interact more in different classes or with other teachers. I suggest gaining permission to observe your SLL student during physical education, art, or music class to gain a perspective on how she or he interacts in those classrooms. Eliciting information on how an SLL student acts in colleagues' classrooms can also provide another viewpoint that can add to the development of strategies for helping these students.

When SLL students speak English, it's important to realize that, although they may not use standard English well due to their unfamiliarity with conventions, they may clearly understand directions, comprehend principles, or be able to complete assignments. That's why it is so important to record their abilities in all four areas previously mentioned. Additionally, you should listen to students read certain materials to determine their proficiency as readers of grade level content. Administering an informal reading inventory will provide some specific information about a student's reading knowledge.

These informal and semiformal observations alone will not be enough, though, to determine additional needs for many SLL students. Cary (2000) suggested administering either the Language Assessment Scales (1991), which are normed oral and written English tests for SLL students, or the IDEA Oral Language Proficiency Test (IPT) (1994). Basic information about a student's English proficiency is provided by these tests.

As with all assessment information, learning about immigrant students' needs is a continual process throughout the academic year. Your observations, notes, and personal conversations with SLL children and adolescents provide a constant source of information about their needs while creating a more relaxed learning environment for the students.

Assessing Mathematics Knowledge

Mathematics teachers at any grade level need to know where to begin teaching students. Discovering what students know about mathematics is also a multifaceted process based primarily on gathering data on students' computational skills and background knowledge of mathematical operations, formulas, and theorems. Many schools have textbook unit pretests that accompany adopted textbooks. If you intend to follow the textbook as an instructional guide, I strongly suggest using their assessment instruments to determine students' competence on specific concepts and principles. Another option is to create and administer your own assessment instrument that reflects your curricular focus for each unit you teach. You can design a simple assessment on students' knowledge of basic computational skills; that is, do fourth-grade students have automaticity in using multiplication tables; can tenth graders independently use basic algebraic formulas; are sixth graders able to choose the appropriate operation to use in mathematical problem solving; and, how skilled are seventh graders at reducing fractions? These are a few basic questions that you'll need to have answered prior to beginning a unit of study. The information you gather from students can be used as a guide to how instruction will be delivered and where to begin a specific mathematics unit.

I caution you not to use any assessment results for sorting students into homogeneously grouped classrooms. The feedback received from various standardized tests should help teachers develop and implement developmentally appropriate curriculum and instructional practices for all students—not to sort them! You may discover from your mathematics assessments that you need to find additional instructional sources and activities than those suggested by central office curriculum guides or textbooks. You may realize from students' pretest scores that some students are well above grade level norms and others lack background knowledge in basic computational skills. Use the information to choose appropriate curriculum and instructional practices!

Assessing Students' Content Area Knowledge

Social studies, science, foreign languages, and health are other traditional academic content areas. As a content area teacher, you may not have received training to initiate assessment activities in reading, mathematics, or in working with SLL students. However, you are interested in knowing what your students' background knowledge is in the content areas that you plan to address during the year. Much like the standardized mathematics pretests used, you may find pretests that accompany a textbook in your area of teaching.

Pretests provide invaluable data to teachers about a student's knowledge base in a specific area. Another useful tool is implementing the *KWL* strategy at the beginning of a unit (Kauchak and Eggen 1998). The KWL instructional strategy is used to determine what students know about specific concepts and principles within a unit. Teachers begin a KWL process by asking students to respond to the question, "What do you *know* about a specific principle and these numerous concepts or vocabulary words we will be studying?" Students may work individually or collaboratively to brainstorm a list of items that represents their background knowledge. Students' responses may reveal significant gaps or, perhaps adequate ability and understanding in their knowledge base.

The second aspect of a KWL may also reveal quality information about students' backgrounds. The *W* in KWL represents the question, "*What* more would you like to know about this particular topic; that is, what questions do you have concerning this topic?" Witnessing the development of student-generated questions provides a picture of students' preliminary motivation and interest in studying specific topics. Student-generated questions should be used for designing instructional events that support students' levels of background knowledge while adding to them.

The last component of KWL is framed by the question, "What have you *learned* as a result of studying these topics?" Asking this question gets to the heart of assessment—gaining an understanding of what students have learned or can do after they have studied a unit. An elaborate response can be gained from students if they are required to develop specific products that demonstrate their learning such as dramatic presentations, designed pamphlets, or Powerpoint presentations.

Establishing Reasonable Student Outcomes

Wise teachers begin the school year by using the various assessment strategies just mentioned to identify where they should initiate instruction within each subject area. Having knowledge of students' basic reading levels, mathematics skills, English proficiency, and writing abilities provides a starting point for developing a set of individualized learning outcomes for some students and a broader set of outcomes for the rest of the class.

Outcomes are the gains expected of students within a specific time frame. One-on-one conferencing with a student provides the opportunity to establish a set of outcomes for the study of a particular unit or for establishing individual objectives for each week. The level of a student's motivation is likely to increase if you can personalize outcomes and they are realistic and achievable.

Keep in mind that students may not reach some established outcomes. Reevaluation of what students can accomplish may be necessary if you realize that students lack the ability to complete outcomes. You need to be flexible in developing outcomes for students while maintaining high, but realistic expectations.

Rubrics

It is your responsibility to make learning expectations known to students. Students should have a clear sense of how they can improve their performance and what is expected. Developing a set of rubrics for certain tasks creates a clear picture to students of expected performance levels. *Rubrics* are descriptive statements that provide detail concerning specific performance levels. I have provided an example of a simple rubric for the completion of assignments for a fifth- or sixth-grade classroom in Figure 8.2. Notice that each level describes what students must accomplish. Many teachers are familiar with rubrics that are used to evaluate students' writing. Rubrics can be designed for any type of assignment including projects, presentations, performances, or portfolios. I included in Figure 8.3 a sample rubric that high school teachers might use to evaluate effective student participation during class discussions. A class discussion is a culturally responsive instructional strategy and a powerful way to create relevant and meaningful learning for many urban students. Providing students with a rubric for expected behaviors may increase student involvement.

Rubrics are valuable for promoting student learning because they clarify expected behaviors and products. Critical, reflective processes occur when students are asked to design rubrics. Imagine how engaged students become in understanding the levels of acceptable performance when they must describe what is expected. Naturally, you have a better perspective of acceptable levels of performance than students do. Once you have a list of students' ideas for a rubric, you should add your words to their initial drafts to complete the rubric. Student-designed

High-Quality Assignment

All parts of the assignment are completed. You have responded to all questions and problems with complete answers. Your answers show that you understand the assigned work. Appropriate books or other resources are used to answer questions. At least ninety percent of the problems/answers are correct. Assignment was checked over after it was completed to be sure that it was done correctly. Answers are neatly written.

Better-Than-Average Assignment

Most parts of the assignment are completed. You have responded to most questions/problems with complete answers. Your answers show that you understand almost all of the assigned work. Most of the answers are from the appropriate book or sources. At least eighty-five percent of the problems/answers are correct. You checked over most of the answers after it was completed to see that they were correct. Most answers are written neatly.

Poor-Quality Assignment

About one-half of the assignment is complete. You have responded to approximately half of the questions/problems with complete answers. Your answers show that there is quite a bit of the assignment you don't understand. You didn't use the appropriate books or other sources to find answers. Fifty to sixty percent of the answers/problems are correct. You only checked over a few of the answers/problems to see that they were correct. Only a few answers are written neatly.

Unacceptable Work

Most of the assignment is *not* completed. You have the right answer for only a few questions/problems. Your answers show that you do not understand much or any of the assignment. You failed to use any books or resources to find the answers. Almost all of your answers are incorrect. Most of your paper is illegible (I can't read it and neither can anyone else).

Figure 8.2   Sample Rubric for Completing Assignments

rubrics are effective tools for garnering more information about students' background knowledge.

A philosophy associated with using rubrics is that they are not to be used as a method of grading students. Rubrics have value due to their ability to encourage student growth rather than when used to evaluate students. They create opportunities for students to better understand areas where they need to improve, rather than providing feedback that indicates that they either passed or failed an assignment. Keep in mind that any chosen assessment process should increase students' knowledge.

Discovering What Students Learn

Discovering what students learn from the activities in your classroom is a question for which everyone wants an answer; from legislators to parents and all the "middle men" in between. The learning occurring in urban schools has become everybody's business lately; for instance, on June 14, 2001, the United States Senate passed a bill tying federal monetary support of urban schools to students' test score results in reading and mathematics (Koszczuk 2001). Only you and your students have an honest appraisal of the abilities and knowledge each student brings as she or he enters your room in September and departs with in June. Finding appropriate strategies for students to demonstrate their learning is primarily yours and your students' jobs. No one else is as close to the learning, the students, or the knowledge of what each student can do and accomplish.

Remember that before you can tell what students have learned, you need to know the levels of ability and knowledge they entered your classroom with on the first day of school. That is the reason that this chapter begins with data-gathering strategies. Once you realize students' needs, you design learning activities to improve their knowledge and skills in those areas. The final piece of assessment is determining what students have learned or can do as a result of their time in your room. The strategies you choose should encourage and motivate students as they gain knowledge and skills throughout the year. Many

Exceptional Discussion Abilities

You demonstrate interest, motivation, initiative, and awareness of responsibilities as a learner, as exhibited through the following actions every class session: you ask questions that relate to specific content from readings; you respond to questions from the teacher every class session regarding reading assignments and analysis of readings; you voluntarily provide information that is pertinent to discussions; you provide examples of concepts and principles related to discussions; you lead small group discussions in responding to questions asked of group; you explicitly synthesize discussion topics; and you exhibit initiative and high motivation.

Better-Than-Average Discussion Abilities

You occasionally demonstrate interest, motivation, initiative, and awareness of responsibilities as a learner, as exhibited by the following actions: in some class sessions, you occasionally ask questions regarding assigned readings and topics of discussion; you occasionally respond orally to assigned readings; you are called on by the teacher to respond to topics of discussion rather than volunteering information; you occasionally provide examples of discussion topics; you participate in small group discussions, but never lead discussions; and you occasionally discuss topics not pertinent to task in small groups.

A Few Discussion Skills

You demonstrate minimal interest, motivation, initiative, or awareness of responsibilities as a learner, as exhibited by the following actions: you seldom become involved in discussions related to topics of interest; your verbal responses indicate you often do not read assignments; you seldom volunteer information pertinent to discussions; you seldom asks questions regarding course principles and concepts; you seldom add pertinent information to small group discussions; and you often discuss topics not pertinent to intended topics in small groups.

Figure 8.3   Sample Rubric for Class Participation

Minimal Discussion Skills

You fail to exhibit interest, motivation, initiative, or awareness of responsibilities as a learner, as exhibited by the following actions: you don't become involved in class discussions; you only occasionally read assigned readings; you never volunteer information pertinent to discussions; you never add information to class discussions; you constantly lead small group discussions off task.

Discussion Skills Nonexistent

You appear to be "brain-dead" as you are in class physically only. The teacher has no clue that you are missing from class when you are absent, and the teacher never learns your name because you never speak in class.

Figure 8.3   *continued*

traditional forms of assessing students provide evaluation but not feedback to students. You have experienced some of the useless means of providing feedback about learning: grades, multiple-choice standardized tests, unannounced quizzes, and timed tests. Most of these assessments lack validity; that is, they don't measure what they claim to measure in many circumstances. Most standardized tests measure discreet skills typically unrelated to the general way in which reading, writing, and mathematics are used in our lives as adults or adolescents. Timed tests prevent students from processing and reflecting on information for effective hypothesizing, decision making, problem solving, critical thinking, and creative thinking. Tests that are given to surprise students prevent them from understanding beforehand what is expected or how to get prepared for the assessment. Traditional standardized tests are generally culturally biased, developmentally inappropriate, and invalid measures of what urban students gain as a result of schooling. If you expect to learn what your students have gained from the activities that occur in your classroom, you'll need to implement some alternative assessment strategies that relate to their learning.

Genuine Assessment Activities

Realistic assessment activities provide students with a variety of options to demonstrate their learning that are quite nontraditional. Generally termed *alternative assessment*, these strategies are closely related to what students are studying and provide opportunities for students to gain even more knowledge as they engage in assessment activities. Alternative assessment activities may begin with student involvement in establishing the outcomes they hope to attain as a result of studying individual topics or units. Once individual or whole classroom goals are established, students collaborate with you, the teacher, in deciding how they will demonstrate their learning.

Students need guidance during this process for two reasons. First, you want to insure that the assessment activities students choose are appropriate to their ability levels—that is, challenging, yet not impossible for them to achieve. Secondly, be certain that the activities that students complete are connected to the desired unit outcomes and encourage students to use thinking processes and skills. Students must use thinking processes (critical, and creative thinking, problem solving, and research) to acquire, produce, and apply knowledge they learn. Effective assessment activities can be designed by you to encourage students to expand these skills.

Some possible alternative assessment activities include

- performing drama
- writing a health or travel pamphlet
- painting a mural
- illustrating
- building models
- writing poetry, prose, essays, letters, etc.
- developing Powerpoint presentations
- reenacting historical events
- designing experiments
- conducting interviews
- analyzing water, air, or soil samples
- performing a dance

- designing a computer program
- developing a portfolio
- writing a newsletter
- designing a game
- writing and performing songs
- creating a map
- drawing political cartoons
- conducting debates.

This is merely the beginning of a list of possible activities that students can engage in to demonstrate what they have learned following the study of any topics in any subject area. We all want students to be able to succeed at basic skills, but it is through the alternative assessment activities listed here that students are given the time and avenues to use those skills in authentic ways.

Providing Feedback—Promoting Growth

Students learn when they receive feedback in a manner that encourages self-evaluation and further growth. You may believe that you are the only one who will be concerned about whether students grow from being in your classroom, but Wilson and Corbett (2001) reported that urban middle school students wanted teachers who would, "[T]ake a keen interest in unmotivated students, give students the opportunity to make up work, invite students to come in for after-school tutoring, [and] go over work until everyone understood it" (66). You can see from these students' responses that merely providing a grade on a paper or failing a student for not doing the work does nothing to encourage student learning. Feedback means so much more than evaluation. Providing meaningful feedback involves

- one-on-one conferencing with students to help them understand how and why their answers are incorrect
- providing details to students about how to correct mistakes they make to help them improve future performances

- guiding students through challenging assignments by providing the skills and knowledge they need to complete them successfully
- conducting an item analysis on homework assignments to determine which processes students clearly understand and with which ones they need additional assistance
- conferencing with students during the process of completing portfolios, projects, presentations, and demonstrations
- presenting mini-lessons to students when needed to correct misunderstandings
- assisting students in restructuring their questions and research processes to reach desired outcomes
- nudging students to increase effort or output
- meeting with small groups of students
- grouping students for learning who share similar problems
- recommending students for additional assistance through initiating observations from an instructional support team (IST) member
- initiating after- and before-school tutoring sessions
- calling parents and caregivers to provide information on children's and adolescents' educational progress and areas of needed improvement
- rewriting specific goals and objectives with students that better meet their learning needs based on current progress
- choosing alternative assignments and curricula to meet students' learning needs
- reestablishing deadlines for completed projects and assignments to insure higher-quality products.

These are explicit actions that encourage student growth based on children's and adolescents' levels of knowledge, abilities, efforts, and attitudes toward learning. Providing meaningful feedback is a continuous process throughout the year. Teachers have the responsibility to be honest and subjective with students when feedback is given. Students must be made aware of their strengths and their areas of need and provided with the information and tools to improve on those weaknesses.

I contend that little about assessment should be objective. No one knows students as well as their teachers. The information needed to help students improve must come from you! Information that is subjective, genuine, useful, and accurate can help students. Many forms of assessment, particularly standardized tests, unfortunately are not specific enough, are unrelated to meaningful learning activities, ignore the nature of learning, and are unrelated to the context of genuine learning to be useful to students or teachers.

Student Involvement in Assessment

Motivating students is an elusive art. Any teacher would readily admit that much of gaining students' cooperation, insuring their greatest effort, or exciting them about learning is often based on luck rather than science. As teachers, we wonder exactly how our efforts influence student decisions about becoming involved in learning. I have attempted throughout this book to describe how teaching processes, socialization skills, curriculum choices, and management issues may affect student learning. There is an adequate body of science to support specific strategies in these areas that affect student attitudes and perhaps effort. The amount of student decision making in assessment processes may also influence their motivation to learn. Many opportunities exist for involving students in assessment. The most meaningful assessment activities are those that encourage students to reflect on their efforts and the products of their work and, as a result, make decisions about how they need to improve.

The assessment activities that students engage in should be genuinely related to circumstances that affect their lives. *Authentic assessment* is the term used to describe assessment experiences that connect curriculum to events that reflect the concerns and people in students' lives. Authentic assessment affects students emotionally due to its connection to their lives (Schurr 1999). Examples of authentic assessment in urban settings include designing a mural in a local neighborhood representing students' cultural history; writing letters to state and local representatives about local environmental conditions; reporting data on the water quality within area homes; or researching and presenting a budget for improving the traffic flow in a busy neighborhood. Students must be involved in authentic assessment if we expect learning to be significant. Authentic assessment activities embody the philosophy of student-generated learning that encourages the use of thinking processes such as problem solving, creative thinking, and research. "Students are motivated when they are engaged in these activities because they are the creators of their own learning— not recipients of a contrived curriculum evaluated by externally devised tests" (Knowles and Brown 2000, 134).

Providing Students with Choices and Responsibility

Providing students with choices in how they will be assessed encourages greater student effort and involvement. Some student decision making may occur at the primary-grade levels. Primary age children can be given choices about what items will be placed in a portfolio, deciding between two or three ways to present a book they have read to the class, or deciding between a presentation or a short report for their independent study of a social studies or science topic. They can explain why certain pieces of their work represent their best or why some items need improvement. The earlier teachers begin asking children to make these decisions, the earlier they begin to internalize their responsibility for learning and improving efforts.

Intermediate students are ready for more advanced decision making about how they will be assessed. Fourth through twelfth graders can be involved in numerous assessment decisions. They can make choices about

- adding and deleting items from a portfolio
- which writing genre they will use during writing workshop
- which books to read and report on as part of literature circles
- how to present their findings for independent study or research projects

- establishing outcomes for units they study
- how to explain to teachers, parents, and caregivers how they have progressed in certain areas throughout the year.

The possibility for increasing motivation rises when these decisions are made by students. Identify other means of involving students in assessment as you design alternative assessment activities. Opportunities for self-reflection and thus greater learning are increased each time students are involved in assessment decisions.

Another meaningful role for middle and high school students is the role they can play in student-led parent-teacher conferences. At these conferences, students are responsible for guiding parents and caregivers through their portfolios and other evidence of their work. Parents have the opportunity to directly ask their own child about her or his progress instead of hearing about it from the teacher. The value of placing this responsibility on students is that they become responsible for monitoring their own learning early in the academic year so that they are able to explain the content and extent of their learning to their caregivers. Students can also explain the reasons for their lack of progress or effort if those are issues that affect their learning. Teachers must provide students with the knowledge and communication skills necessary to successfully express their progress to parents. Class time should be set aside to assist students in developing the necessary skills to successfully and accurately communicate their growth (Kinney, Munroe, and Sessions 2000). Student-led conferences provide the greatest responsibility for students in monitoring their goal setting for learning, their growth in academic areas, and for understanding their progress well enough to explain it to caregivers. It is a genuine, comprehensive assessment process that provides students with the keys to direct their own learning.

Student-led conferences ultimately lead to self-evaluation. When asked to self-evaluate, several processes occur as students

- identify desired outcomes prior to and while learning
- reflect on the effort and attitude required to successfully complete assignments

- establish personal expectations and standards of effective work
- compare their performance with expected levels of success
- assume greater responsibilities for monitoring their work
- discover their strengths and weaknesses as learners.

Opportunities for genuine learning are improved when students are engaged in these self-evaluative and reflective processes. Self-evaluation improves with the use of portfolios, as mentioned in the next section.

Portfolios

Portfolios are collections of students' work that demonstrate their "[E]fforts, progress, or achievement in one or more subjects" over the course of an academic year (Schurr 1999, 4). Almost any age student can and should be involved in deciding what goes into a portfolio. Portfolios can provide a variety of information about the growth of a child within an academic year. Teachers at all grade levels and in all subject areas should establish a system of using portfolios with guidelines and lists of items that are to be placed in them. Teachers should exercise flexibility in determining which items go into the portfolio.

Reviewing portfolios should be a routine process for students and teachers throughout the academic year to assess both effort and growth. Students who become frustrated learning new principles during the year may need to review the items placed into the portfolio earlier in the year to encourage more effort and assure them that they are progressing in their learning. Portfolios should be on display for parents and caregivers and students during conferences with adults and students.

Concluding Thoughts

Effective assessment occurs when teachers are willing to engage in creative thinking about how students can demonstrate their learning in developmentally appropriate ways. Be flexible in how students may present their growth to you within all areas that they study. Appropriate assessment activities do not compare students to one another. Each student has a separate growth pattern and avenue based on ability and background knowledge. Keep in mind that valuable assessment processes provide you and students with accurate information about their strengths and their areas of need and actually promote more growth as students engage in them.

References

AMERICAN HERITAGE DICTIONARY. 2000. *American Heritage Dictionary*. 4th ed. Boston: Houghton Mifflin.

BURNS, P. C., AND B. D. ROE, 1995. *Burns/Roe Informal Reading Inventory: Preprimer to Twelfth Grade*. 2nd ed. Boston: Houghton Mifflin.

CARY, S. 2000. *Working with Second Language Learners: Answers to Teachers' Top Ten Questions*. Portsmouth, NH: Heinemann.

DARIGAN, D. L., M. O. TUNNELL, AND J. S. JACOBS. 2002. *Children's Literature: Engaging Teachers and Children in Good Books*. Upper Saddle River, NJ: Pearson Education.

IDEA ORAL LANGUAGE PROFIENCY TEST. 1994. Brea, CA: Ballard & Tighe.

KAUCHAK, D. P., AND P. D. EGGEN. 1998. *Learning and Teaching: Research-Based Methods*. 3rd ed. Needham Heights, MA: Allyn & Bacon.

KINNEY, P., M. B. MUNROE, AND P. SESSIONS. 2000. *A School-Wide Approach to Student-Led Conferences: A Practitioner's Guide*. Westerville, OH: National Middle School Association.

KNOWLES, T., AND D. F. BROWN. 2000. *What Every Middle School Teacher Should Know*. Portsmouth, NH and Westerville, OH: Heinemann and National Middle School Association.

KOHN, A. 2000. *The Case Against Standardized Testing: Raising the Scores, Ruining the Schools*. Portsmouth, NH: Heinemann.

KOSZCZUK, J. 2001. "Bush School Proposal Advances." *Philadelphia Inquirer*, 15 June, suburbs edition.

LANGUAGE ASSESSMENT SCALES. 1991. Monterey, CA: CTB Macmillan McGraw-Hill.

May, F. B. 1998. *Reading as Communication: To Help Children Write and Read.* 5th ed. Upper Saddle River, NJ: Merrill/Prentice Hall.

Rhodes, L. K., and C. Dudley-Marling. 1996. *Readers and Writers with a Difference: A Wholistic Approach to Teaching Struggling Readers and Writers.* 2nd ed. Portsmouth, NH: Heinemann.

Ruddell, R. B.1999. *Teaching Children to Read and Write: Becoming an Influential Teacher.* 2nd ed. Needham Heights, MA: Allyn & Bacon.

Schurr, S. 1999. *Authentic Assessment: Using Product, Performance, and Portfolio Measures from A to Z.* Columbus, OH: National Middle School Association.

Silvaroli, N. J. 1994. *Classroom Reading Inventory.* 7th ed. Dubuque, IA: Brown and Benchmark.

Tombari, M., and G. Borich. 1999. *Authentic Assessment in the Classroom: Application and Practice.* Upper Saddle River, NJ: Merrill.

Wilde, S. 2000. *Miscue Analysis Made Easy: Building on Student Strengths.* Portsmouth, NH: Heinemann.

Wilson, B. L., and H. D. Corbett. 2001. *Listening to Urban Kids: School Reform and the Teachers They Want.* Albany, NY: State University of New York Press.

NINE

Reasonable Expectations or Impossible Standards?

Are you going to expect a kid in a wheelchair to run the 100-yard-dash as fast as a kid who's running on two feet?

PETE, PHILADELPHIA HIGH SCHOOL TEACHER

Using only one set of standards for the entire city cheats students from differing neighborhoods because you're lowering standards for one set of students and setting the bar too high for others.

JACKIE, NEW YORK CITY ELEMENTARY TEACHER

Decisions about whether or not students are learning should not take place in the legislature, the governor's office, or the department of education. They should take place in the classroom, because that is where learning occurs.

DOUGLAS CHRISTENSEN CITED IN ROSCHEWSKI, GALLAGHER, AND ISERNHAGEN (2001, 611)

What Are Standards?

Standards is such a powerful word because for many it signifies excellence, a quality product, and a promise of "the best." There are two types of educational standards: content standards and performance

215

standards. *Content standards* are explicitly stated learning outcomes designed for a specific grade level, unit of study, or content area. Content standards, or what students should know, are developed by state boards of education, local school districts, professional organizations, and in rare cases, local teachers. Most classrooms in America contain a copy of the document that describes a school district's or state's standards for learning.

Content standards have different names depending on where one teaches. The school district of Philadelphia, for instance, calls its standards *curriculum frameworks*; other districts have their *benchmarks*; and, the state education department in Virginia has its Standards of Learning (SOLs) for students across the state. Generally, teachers are responsible for teaching both local school district standards and state standards as well. You might be surprised to discover that the standards from the two organizations don't always match, placing teachers in a precarious position of attempting to help students meet both sets of standards.

Performance standards describe expected levels of success, usually on standardized tests. Performance standards may also specify how students will demonstrate their learning and the "[K]nowledge they need to demonstrate" (Lewis 1999, 19). In general, the word *standards* is issued in reference to performance standards. Politicians and legislators foolishly believe they can improve students' test scores merely through enacting legislation linking test scores to teachers' compensation or funding for the schools. In these circumstances, higher scores lead to more funding and lower scores less state monetary support.

The premise of linking test results to funding is that with enough pressure from legislators, educators will work more diligently (assuming that they haven't been doing their jobs already) so that their students will attain higher test scores; and, that those higher scores represent more learning. A number of fallacies exist in this belief:

- Teachers are primarily responsible for student academic success.
- All students are capable of performing at or above grade level.

216

- Students enter school with similar backgrounds of academic success.
- Standardized tests are valid indicators of student growth.
- Standardized tests reflect local and state content standards.
- Standardized tests measure meaningful learning.
- Effective teaching can erase the significant barriers to learning that many students experience.
- Urban students are less entitled to receive funding due to their academic backgrounds.

Every one of these statements is false. When you hear the words *high standards*, listen carefully to the remarks that follow, because they are likely to be based on these entirely inaccurate statements about teaching, learning, and testing. Anyone who accepts the belief that students' performances on state assessments is an accurate indicator of effective teaching and learning has never really taught children and adolescents—especially in urban environments!

Teachers' Limitations

It is absurd to believe that your efforts as teacher will help *all* of your students score above the fiftieth percentile on certain standardized tests. You should understand the limitations of standardized tests to accurately assess the growth that your students will experience in a year and comprehend the realistic limitations of effective teaching on your students. Falk (2000) reported that New York City's Board of Education recently passed a policy that no student would be promoted from the third, sixth, or eighth grade unless she or he passed the district's reading and mathematics tests (22). Falk added, "Nearly one-third of the more than one million student population (more than three hundred thousand students) are expected to be retained in their grade this year" (22).

How will this testing policy improve teaching and learning, or help failing students? Students need help *before* the tests are given. Why give students a test to identify weaknesses of which their teachers are already aware, and then tell students and teachers that they have failed?

217

Students and teachers obviously know about their needs. Members of the New York City Board of Education are responsible for seeing that students' learning needs are met now—not a year from now. Administering a high-stakes test and holding students back a grade to learn the same things will do nothing to advance students' knowledge or improve teaching. Using test scores as punitive measures is not an equitable means of helping urban students. As a matter of fact, when students are retained, it increases their risk of dropping out by as much as forty to fifty percent (Carnegie Council on Adolescent Development 1989).

Academic performance standards should never be associated with students' standardized test scores in any school, and especially not in urban schools. Urban students are not at all "standard." Standard American children would all have similar academic backgrounds, motivation for learning, support for learning at home, speak English from birth, possess reasonably high reading and mathematics skills and would all come to school every day ready to learn. The probability of this occurring is impossible in any suburban school district in America, much less in urban schools. Susan Ohanian (1999) clearly explains in her book, *One Size Fits Few: The Folly of Educational Standards*, that educational performance and content standards should never be applied to students as a way of determining which schools receive more funding; which teachers receive raises or are fired; or, which students receive the resources they need to succeed.

Teachers' Perceptions of Standards

Standards Linked to Tests

Jeff, who teaches high school English in Wichita, shares a valid concern among many teachers about the value of standardized tests: "We shouldn't worry about high-stakes tests because we need to help the kids. They don't care about the tests. They don't see how it affects them. I lost four weeks of teaching time giving tests this year." Effective teachers don't need a standardized test to explain learning gaps or students' strengths. They become familiar with their students' learn-

218

ing needs and design instructional activities and curricula to meet those needs. Standardized state and national test demands create time and instructional barriers to the learning progress teachers could be making with their students if these tests weren't used.

Shanika, a fifth-grade teacher in Philadelphia, agonizes over her students' preparedness for their curriculum and tests: "Sometimes I think the expectations for students are realistic. I think, maybe I haven't expected enough of them. I may be lowering my expectations. When I gave out the state tests and realized what students are supposed to know by fifth grade, I felt so sad. Many students said, 'What's this?' and 'We don't know what this is!' I felt like I had really failed them because there were so many concepts and questions that were beyond them that we hadn't even touched." Taking *some* responsibility for how much students learn throughout the year in your room is reasonable; but being responsible for how students score on standardized tests is unrealistic considering students' baseline knowledge.

Kathleen teaches third graders in Chicago and indicates that the school has developed quarterly assessment tests for all of the five subject areas. Every third-grade teacher gives the same test in her school. Teachers at this school have developed their own performance standards, hopefully designed to indicate students' growth throughout the year within their curriculum. Local assessment instruments provide a more valid link with the school's curricula than externally administered state or nationally designed tests.

Lisa teaches third grade in Los Angeles and speaks of how her district has restructured standards to address the needs of her students: "We reworded the state standards to create our own here. We now have criterion-referenced tests that are linked to report card grades." Lisa wasn't especially happy about the test scores representing report card grades. However, I do see the advantage of the school district adapting state standards to local students' needs. Standards can be more appropriately matched to specific students' needs when locally rather than state determined.

Shanika is not satisfied with the unrealistic standards external tests impose on her fifth graders: "I think the fourth-grade standards would be more realistic for these fifth graders. There are certain general standards that these students can do, like writing creatively, but certain concepts we can't do! Mathematics and grammar are the greatest challenges I see for my students." Student performances on standardized tests frustrate teachers and parents, and provide no information about how students are growing or enough specifics about how they can be helped to improve reading and mathematics achievement. Shouldn't standardized tests at least help students and teachers, considering all the money and time spent purchasing, administering, and scoring them?

The result of using high standards for high-stakes decisions such as graduation requirements frequently causes:

- an increase in the dropout rate (Kohn 2000; Darling-Hammond 1991)
- a decrease in teachers' use of effective teaching strategies (Kohn 2001; Madaus et al. 1992)
- a decline in students' ability to transfer discreet skills to more complex learning situations (McNeil 2000).

These are a few negative impacts of using high-stakes tests to determine the educational future of students. Wasley (2001) stated, "The standards are a very good thing from kids' perspectives when they feel that their school, their teachers, their principals, and community members are going to make sure that they can meet the standards. It's when the standards feel punishing to kids that they really have problems with them" (7). Many districts and states unfortunately have adopted "punishing" rather than "helpful" standards within the past few years.

Dealing with Content Standards

Kathleen speaks of the Chicago school district content standards she adheres to for her third-grade students: "We all have a copy of both state and city standards. I think the math and reading standards are fine; but the science and social studies standards are much too difficult to cover in a year. The system is very bureaucratic: the curriculum supervisor comes around to check off which standards we've covered."

Shanika faces similar challenges with the expected content students will learn in fifth grade: "Because these kids are the product of kindergarten through fourth grade as well as this year, the concepts that they've been missing snowball. I don't think these [external standardized] tests are appropriate. At the same time, I do think I've brought down my expectations. I think about math . . . so few of my students understand division, so after a while I say to myself, 'Let me just move on because I'm wasting time.' When I make a decision to move on, it's based on my frustration and their frustration." Shanika adds, "I don't really follow the school district standards because I don't think they're realistic. The things that the standards suggest really don't apply to my kids."

Teachers are often forced to make decisions concerning how they will use standards primarily due to time constraints. Stoskopf (2000) reported, "[T]hat it would take 6,000 extra hours of classroom time to cover all the information required on most state standards" (38) (cited in Falk 2000). This information provides a valid reason for you as the teacher to use discretion and professional judgment in choosing which standards students will meet and which ones will need to be postponed until students acquire the skills and developmental abilities to successfully learn them.

Susan, from San Francisco, shares her perceptions of California's content standards: "The state standards are bad—they are developmentally inappropriate. I refuse to use those state standards to determine my students' levels of ability. They are absurd, and I refuse to adhere to them piece-by-piece. I have my own standards for students. I like to see where they are, and then challenge them." That last statement describes the appropriate level of teacher responsibility for assessment and standards in all schools!

Jackie, from Philadelphia, has similar concerns about standards: "The difficult thing about standards is that it's an outside entity giving you goals—and it never works! If you want to lose weight, you have to decide you want to do it. If you want to quit smoking, you have to decide that that's your goal. Standards have to be more individualized. What's going to work in one area of Philadelphia is very different from what's going to work in areas of North Philly. Or, standards for the upper-East Side of New York are going to be very different from what is expected from students in East Harlem."

Teachers realize how inappropriate standards can be when they are established behind closed doors, thereby preventing the developers from comprehending the lives of the learners they intend to affect. Students' backgrounds *should* be a factor in designing curricula, choosing instructional strategies, and establishing standards for learning. What if every automobile repair shop provided the same repairs for every car even though each one has a different problem? What if the state automobile repair examiner declared that every mechanic spend only forty-five minutes changing all mufflers regardless of the problem or type of car being worked on? That idea sounds absolutely absurd to me; yet, that's what state content standards do to teachers—require educators to teach the same material to every child, at the same pace regardless of students' backgrounds and genuine academic needs and interests.

The Difference between Expectations and Standards

The Absurdity of Standards

Imagine you're a seventh-grade student standing in the gymnasium watching the physical education teacher adjust the height of a hurdle used for track meets. Your job is to jump over the hurdle to show that you can meet the "standard." The teacher places the hurdle height at a foot and a half. Your twenty-nine classmates and you line up forty feet away and run to jump over it. Everyone makes it over. The teacher announces, "OK, that was great work. Now, I'm going to raise the hurdle to two feet." You all run and jump again, but two students aren't able to jump over it. Those two students failed to meet the two-foot standard. The teacher explains to the students how disappointed she is at their inability to clear the hurdle. They are considered failures despite their limited physical abilities, attitudes about jumping hurdles, and poor background knowledge about hurdle jumping. The two students are asked to sit down and think about how they can improve their jumping ability before the next class session.

222

The teacher, meanwhile, decides to raise the hurdle to two and a half feet and asks the remaining students to jump over that height. Several more are asked to sit out because they can't meet the standard. They are given low grades for the day and discouraged from practicing hurdle jumping in the future. The hurdle is raised three more times within the hour and each time fewer and fewer students are able to jump over it. Finally, class ends and grades are distributed to students based on how high they were able to jump. Only three of thirty students were able to clear the height the teacher designated as a "reasonable standard." The worst part was watching how the teacher treated those students who were not able to jump over each height. Students were not provided with any feedback for how to improve their jumping ability, were not encouraged by the teacher to try different strategies, and were only provided with one opportunity to jump over the hurdle at each height.

This physical education class experience describes how raising standards works against many students in American schools—especially urban schools. Performance standards are most frequently designed and mandated by nonschool personnel; ignore students' varying developmental needs; are unrelated to school curricula, textbooks, or instruction; ignore students' baseline academic data; are measured using an invalid assessment instrument; and are completely unrealistic measures of students' growth potential. How can these externally imposed standards improve educators' teaching strategies or improve student learning based on these enormous inconsistencies?

Establishing Realistic Performance Expectations

Teachers who recognize students' differences in growth rates, ability levels, background knowledge, English proficiency, reading levels, and learning profiles clearly comprehend that individual students need distinct, personalized standards for learning. I prefer to use the term, *expectations* to describe the level of improvement expected of students in learning processes, cognitive strategies, and basic knowledge. Expectations are realistic levels of learning based on each student's

223

baseline data gathered from previous teachers' reports about each child and your own observations and experiences. Expectations are established throughout the first few weeks of the school year and revisited and revised as teachers conference with each student.

Reasonable expectations are

- challenging to students, but not frustrating
- developmentally appropriate based on students' abilities
- temporarily established to allow for flexibility when needed
- aligned partially with district curricula
- supported through effective instructional strategies to help struggling students improve with reasonable effort.

Standards are not characterized by the same statements. Establish reasonable performance expectations for each student in your class based on his or her abilities if you actually believe in the idea of success for all students. Students will refuse to engage in learning if the tasks they are required to do are greatly beyond their cognitive capabilities. Some states' content and performance standards are frequently beyond the abilities of many urban students.

You can make a difference in children's or adolescents' learning despite the barrier unrealistic standards create to your perceived success as a teacher. "Success for all" implies that teachers identify the starting point of each student's abilities and establish realistic expectations built on this baseline knowledge.

Implementing expectations that strike a balance between students' academic needs and a set of benchmarks that students may reasonably achieve within a school year is an urban teacher's responsibility. Asking questions about what your students know and can do is the most effective strategy for establishing the appropriate expectations for student learning. You role is to discover what each student needs to accomplish to reach success in your classroom. Data gathering starts when you ask, "What do my students know at this point?" You want to collect information on issues such as students' basic skills, English proficiency, learning profiles, attitudes toward learning, and other information, as mentioned in Chapter 8. You will be able to establish a set of reasonable outcomes for each student by using the responses to those questions. Realistic performance expectations should vary for each student based on all of the factors in a student's life that affect learning, including issues such as family dynamics and socio-economic levels.

Anita, who has twenty-five years of teaching experience with Philadelphia middle school students, shares her views of how standardized curricula affect urban students. "You must know that when you complete a year of teaching seventh graders, many of them are still going to be at the second and third grade level in reading ability. Unfortunately, we don't do enough here to help these kids because of money. These students need more individualized help. They get lost in the large group. The way curriculum is set up, kids get hurt academically, and it gets worse! When they get to high school, what we find is that they just drop out because they just can't keep up—they can't do it! Many students are coming in academically well below where they should be. You can't penalize them for what they can't do!"

Jeff, from a Wichita high school, experienced challenges establishing realistic expectations: "I vary my expectations from honors classes to frosh classes. I expect them to get work done. I was failing so many kids that I had to reevaluate. I changed the way I ran the class. Homework isn't as important as it was before to me. These students are at home babysitting their brothers, working too much at home because Mom and Dad are working two or three jobs. I do more in-class projects now to find out what they know." Jeff has found a strategy for helping students to succeed instead of applying unrealistic expectations with the result of many failures. Striking a balance between appropriate expectations and standards that are much too high is the ideal for students; however, it will take some time each academic year before you are able to determine which of your expectations are appropriate for each student or an entire class of students.

Colette, from a Philadelphia high school, shares her philosophy on student expectations: "I expect students to do their work, and I try to make the projects interesting enough to motivate them. But students make all kinds of excuses. They're so full of excuses; they really are!

So I tell them, 'It's not personal, it's just business. You have to do your work. As much as I like you, I'm still going to fail you if you don't do your work!' Sometimes I'll ask them if this is too much work, and the honest students will say, 'This is reasonable; we just don't feel like doing it.'"

These homework expectations hopefully focus more on student effort than on performance. One of the greatest challenges facing urban teachers is getting students to complete assignments. Performance standards are insignificant for students who refuse to complete assigned school tasks. It may be necessary for teachers to develop rubrics for completing assignments so students have a clear indicator of how their effort and finished products affect their potential for learning.

Kathleen, who teaches in a Chicago elementary school, explains how eight of her third-grade students attended summer school following their unsuccessful completion of third grade. Four of those eight students did not pass summer school and repeated third grade. Kathleen applied a set of standards based on the quarterly tests given to students at the end of each grading period. She believes the standards are appropriate based on her knowledge of third-grade curricula and her students' abilities.

You can see from these stories that each teacher is charged with determining which standards have significance for his or her students, and how they are applied. You will also decide which students will receive acceptable passing grades based on your knowledge of what students should know, be able to do, their strengths, and their areas of need. These are both personal and professional decisions based on each individual case every year you teach. No one has a special formula for choosing appropriate standards and applying them. Although many legislators, parents and caregivers, and administrators may mandate specific standards, many of those standards are too inflexible, unrealistic, and inappropriate to measure students' growth in a meaningful manner. You are the judge, the jury, the prosecutor, and the defender of every student you encounter as a teacher. No one has as much knowledge as you do about your students; therefore, you must be the one to protect students by providing them with the greatest opportunities for growth when you teach them.

Balancing Content Standards with Reasonable Expectations

Falk (2000) described the role of teachers as one of "[F]inding ways to *uncover*" the critical concepts and principles mentioned in content standards that your students will need for further learning and to advance their own understanding of how their world works (104). I suggest you collaborate with your grade level colleagues as you evaluate mandated state and local content standards to determine which ones are essential for your students to learn. You will have to prioritize principles because completing all of the mandated standards will be difficult for some students. I suggest developing this list early in the year, keeping in mind that it will need to be altered based on your specific students' personal learning profiles and needs. Teacher decision making in establishing reasonable levels of learning should always take precedence over any pre-established state or local content standards.

Establishing Reasonable Levels of Performance

Another component of establishing appropriate expectations for students' growth is to determine reasonable and acceptable levels of student performance that indicate understanding of prioritized learning principles. This may be the most challenging piece of assessment due to the distinct variations in students' background knowledge as they enter urban classrooms. Finding one standard of acceptable performance and applying it to all students is not a sound educational practice. A critical aspect of effective assessment is providing students with multiple measures and means to determine their level of understanding.

Kohn (2000) suggested that, "Each school should be encouraged to develop its own criteria for self-evaluation, inviting students, teachers, parents, and others in the community to decide what will help them determine how effectively they've been meeting their goals" (48). One particular school district in Wisconsin, for example, requires students to learn content benchmarks. Students' progress is determined as they reach a certain level of mastery on these general concepts and principles (benchmarks) in each subject area (Hughes 2001). Following completion of each unit of study (benchmarks), success is determined by students' scores on locally developed rubrics in four categories:

advanced, proficient (where students are expected to perform), basic, and minimal (6). Students who perform well on various assessments receive an advanced rating. Students receiving a proficient score have also mastered a unit's concepts and principles at a satisfactory level. A basic or minimal rating indicates less than adequate demonstration of knowledge; thereby requiring review of those concepts and principles. The expectation is that students who reach the proficient level require no more instruction or practice in that content, skill, or process area. Appropriate assessment does not compare students' performance to other students as most tests do; but instead, is criterion or standards-referenced—indicating the extent that students comprehend the principles they are expected to learn. As a teacher, you need to know how you can help students, not where they rank with their classmates either in your school or across the state or country.

Benchmarks and rubrics are shared with students in this Wisconsin school district so that they clearly understand what's expected. Hughes (2001) reported that these benchmarks also help teachers monitor students' progress and use those results in planning further instruction.

Carr and Harris (2001) suggested aligning acceptable standards for performance and content standards with report cards. Redesigning report cards to reflect acceptable performance and content standards can be a lengthy process. The advantage, however, of doing so is the possibility of clearly communicating to students, teachers, parents and caregivers, and administrators the most important strategies and knowledge students should learn and what levels demonstrate acceptable learning.

I realize, with much disappointment, that externally developed and mandated student performance standards are a fact of life in most urban schools. However, I encourage you to use other measures of students' performance to determine to what extent each is growing. The few urban schools (Central Park East Schools, Urban Academy, and others in New York City) in which teachers develop standards based on their knowledge of students and instructional expertise have much greater success in helping students to grow (Falk 2000). Teachers are the last line of defense for students. You must be an advocate for every student you encounter to insure that each receives what he or she needs.

How Do Teachers Measure Success?

The 2000 Phi Delta Kappa/Gallup educational issues poll indicated that sixty-eight percent of all respondents preferred that *teachers* measure student achievement rather than standardized test scores (Rose and Gallup 2000). Respondents to this survey added that the primary purpose of tests should be to determine the kind of instruction that students need rather than measuring the amount of information learned. Determining whether you are successful with students or not depends on so many factors. Reaching success with all students will be elusive if you use one level on the measuring stick as your indicator of success—much as standardized assessments are applied. Success needs to be measured one child at a time and with different instruments for many students.

Diane, who teaches fifth graders in San Francisco, states a broad definition of how she often measures success: "Sometimes I measure success by the fact that everyone [students] comes back the next day." For many of the urban teachers I interviewed, succeeding with students means designing learning experiences that are developmentally appropriate and can be successfully completed. Success means gaining the cooperation of students who are gang members, helping a struggling middle school student read a novel for the first time, and helping a high school student complete a science project during your planning period. The gains may not be immense or noticeable on a large scale.

Influential urban teachers address the needs of every student they can and evaluate their influence based on broader victories than those that are merely academic. Pete, who teaches SLL students in Philadelphia, explains, "I provide as much support as possible with the tools they need. My job is to provide them [students] with as many keys as I can. I can't open all the doors for them, and I can't give them all the information they need. I *can* provide them with the small pieces that help them to open up the larger pieces."

Carr and Harris (2001) suggested that teachers measure success on several levels:

- *Individual success:* How well has this student learned?
- *Instructional success:* How successful was my instruction?
- *Curriculum success:* How successfully is the curriculum addressing our students' learning needs?
- *Program success:* How well is our instructional program working? (65)

I strongly suggest that teachers look at success beyond academic indicators. Carr and Harris (2001) advised school personnel to consider improvements in attendance, fewer dropouts, greater numbers of students promoted or retained as other indicators of success (65). Classroom teachers should also consider these as signs of success:

- more students engaged in class discussions
- higher percentages of students completing assignments
- students taking more risks with their learning
- greater effort among certain students
- students cooperating with each other and demonstrating respect
- fewer discipline referrals
- more parents and caregivers involved in their children's schooling.

These are positive signs that you are making a difference in the lives of your students. These signs are much more reflective of you and your students' successes than test scores!

References

Carnegie Council on Adolescent Development. 1989. *Turning Points: Preparing Youth for the Twenty-First Century.* New York: Carnegie Corporation of New York.

CARR, J. F., AND D. E. HARRIS. 2001. *Succeeding with Standards: Linking Curriculum, Assessment, and Action Planning.* Alexandria, VA: Association for Supervision and Curriculum Development.

DARLING-HAMMOND, L. 1991. "The Implications of Testing Policy for Educational Quality and Equality." *Phi Delta Kappan* 73, no. 3: 220–25.

FALK, B. 2000. *The Heart of the Matter: Using Standards and Assessment to Learn.* Portsmouth, NH: Heinemann.

HUGHES, J. 2001. "The Benefits of Benchmarks." *Education Update* 43, no. 1: 6.

KOHN, A. 2000. *The Case Against Standardized Testing: Raising the Scores, Ruining the Schools.* Portsmouth, NH: Heinemann.

———. 2001. "Fighting the Tests: A Practical Guide to Rescuing Our Schools." *Phi Delta Kappan* 82, no. 5: 348–357.

LEWIS, A. C. 1999. *Figuring It Out: Standards-Based Reforms in Urban Middle Grades.* New York: Edna McConnell Clark Foundation.

MADAUS, G. F., M. M. WEST, M. C. HARMON, R. G. LOMAX, AND K. A. VIATOR. 1992. *The Influence of Testing on Teaching Math and Science in Grades 4–12.* Boston: Center for the Study of Testing, Evaluation, and Educational Policy.

MCNEIL, L. M. 2000. "Creating New Inequalities: Contradictions of Reform." *Phi Delta Kappan* 81, no. 10: 728–734.

OHANIAN, S. 1999. *One Size Fits Few: The Folly of Educational Standards.* Portsmouth, NH: Heinemann.

ROSCHEWSKI, P., C. GALLAGHER, AND J. ISERNHAGEN. 2001. "Nebraskans Reach for The STARS." *Phi Delta Kappan* 82, no. 8: 611–615.

ROSE, L. C., AND A. M. GALLUP. 2000. "The 32nd Annual Phi Delta Kappa/Gallup Poll of the Public's Attitudes Toward the Public Schools." *Phi Delta Kappan* 82, no. 1: 41–48, 53–66.

STOSKOPF, A. 2000. "Clio's Lament." *Education Week* 20, (2 Feb): 38, 41.

WASLEY, P. 2001. "Standards from the Students' Perspective." *Education Update* 43, no. 1: 7.

TEN

Garnering Support from Colleagues, Caregivers, and Administrators

Even if they're not being great parents themselves, they still want to know what's going on with their child.

ANITA, PHILADELPHIA MIDDLE SCHOOL TEACHER

I don't feel like I get that much support from anyone here—especially the principal.

LISA, LOS ANGELES ELEMENTARY TEACHER

I think working with parents is one of our key problems. We have not done a very good job of that in education. We need to nurture those relationships.

SUSAN, SAN FRANCISCO ELEMENTARY TEACHER

Urban teachers want and need assistance as they face seemingly insurmountable responsibilities and objectives. Yet, the expectation among many fellow teachers and administrators is that novice teachers should face and conquer those challenges alone. That message is never explicitly stated, but some colleagues' actions send a clear message to rookie teachers: "If you think you're cut out for the business of teaching, you had better prove it by working alone." Displays of empathy from fellow teachers can be rare during your first couple of years of teaching. Some novice teachers are greeted with open arms and abundant help; however, from the stories I have heard, I suspect that is not as common as being ignored by colleagues.

You will want and need the support of fellow teachers, as well as from parents and caregivers, as you attempt to meet the needs of their children and adolescents. Research clearly supports the role of parental involvement as an essential ingredient to students' and teachers' successes. Teachers and parents complain about how each prevents the other from meeting their desired outcomes for students—perhaps needlessly. You must discover and use creative strategies to receive the support you need to maintain a comfortable working relationship with colleagues, caregivers, and administrators.

Support from Colleagues

The greatest support for the daily experiences you encounter should come from your fellow teachers. Perhaps the primary type of support you receive should be for your emotional state of mind. Odell (1986) reported in a study of eighty-six first-year elementary teachers that emotional support was one of their top needs. What can you expect though, from teachers who may be struggling with a number of issues themselves—especially in urban environments where at least half of the teachers are in their first year or two of teaching also?

Shanika, from Philadelphia, speaks about working with her colleagues: "I really regret not being able to get more help from more senior teachers. I was paired with a mentor last year, and that was a terrible experience! Last year as a first-year teacher, I felt like a failure. I felt like the mistakes I was making I shouldn't have been making, and I definitely didn't feel supported."

Diane has taught for thirty-three years and describes her views on support from other teachers: "The best experiences I've had have been in those places where I received support from colleagues who realized my good ideas. I realized though that those teachers usually didn't accept what you said the first time you spoke to them. Now that I'm near the end of my career, I share my expertise with beginning teachers to help them."

Like any new job, becoming a member of a social group at work can take some time. Becoming friends with fellow teachers may take even more time because socializing with other adults is so difficult during a busy day of teaching. No other friend, family member, or significant other can provide you with the support that your fellow teachers can. Colleagues encounter the same conditions, administrators, parents, and students that you do each day; therefore, they are your best source of assistance and advice each day. Kronowitz (1999) suggested steering clear of teacher cliques or colleagues who are constant "[W]hiners, complainers, or gossips, but remain friendly just the same" (137–138).

You need to initiate social interactions with fellow teachers although you may not be comfortable in that role. For a first-year teacher in an urban school, experienced teachers are an invaluable source of information. Kronowitz recommended discovering which teachers are

- experts in various curriculum areas
- adept at computer-based instruction
- resourceful at securing materials for science and art projects
- musically inclined when you want to include this in your lesson. (138)

There are a few other situations in which it is wise to enlist the aid of fellow teachers. I suggest finding a teacher who is

- aware of how to best work with the principal when you have a need
- savvy about union matters
- knowledgeable about how to obtain the cooperation and help from secretaries and custodians
- aware of which caregivers will help you with their children when problems arise
- able to warn you about potentially irate parents

234

- able to obtain additional supplies at no personal cost
- likely to share their effective strategies for teaching challenging students
- willing to share lunch or recess duty with you the first few times you are responsible for those activities.

I have discovered that teaching is a highly social activity. We are working with humans who are unpredictable in many circumstances. You'll need help in negotiating those challenging interactions.

Lortie (1975) identified a crucial factor influencing the high percentage of novice as well as experienced teachers who leave the profession: *isolation*. Find a way to establish regular and meaningful social interactions with fellow teachers each day despite the doors that close and separate you and your students from the rest of the world.

Involving Parents and Caregivers

Nothing is quite as contentious in the minds of urban teachers as the relationships they form or fail to develop with their students' parents and caregivers. Yet, despite teachers' reluctant attitudes toward improving those relationships, greater collaboration with parents can improve student performance. Research conducted on the value of parental support overwhelmingly provides a picture of success for students when parents and caregivers are actively involved in the school lives of their children (Reyes, Scribner, and Scribner 1999; Hoover-Dempsey and Sandler 1997; Henderson and Berla 1994; Epstein 1992). The stories told about how urban caregivers support their children and teachers are usually quite negative. Lewis and Henderson (1997) mentioned several barriers that exist to prevent teachers and caregivers from meeting each others' needs to help students:

- Teachers are poorly prepared and trained to work with caregivers.
- Parents are unaware of what schools should be doing to help their children.

- Interactions with parents are based on traditional practices that are, at best, minimal-intervention strategies.
- Class and cultural differences keep schools and families apart, and not the least of these is racist attitudes and practice. (x)

Other reasons exist for the failure of both teachers and parents to work cooperatively to insure student success. The insecurity of both groups to approach one another for assistance may be the primary basis of the problem. Teachers and administrators believe that caregivers in urban areas are unable and unwilling to help their children due to a perception that they have poor educational backgrounds (Lewis and Henderson 1997). Research indicates that parents in low-income communities are not involved for three reasons:

- They believe they are not expected to be involved due to traditional patterns of isolation from schools in their neighborhoods.
- Parents are not often comfortable becoming involved.
- Parents perceive negative signals from school personnel toward their involvement in school matters (Hoover-Dempsey and Sandler 1997).

Pete, from a Philadelphia high school, provides fuel to this thinking process: "One of our biggest frustrations is getting parents to come into schools because it's not part of the thing that they do. Parents believe that once their children are in school, they are the teachers' responsibility." Lisa, from Los Angeles, describes what she believes to be the problem: "I don't think most parents know how to help their children." Unfortunately, these beliefs create an even greater divide between schools and homes as both parties are misinformed about each others' desires. Diane, from San Francisco, provides her views on parental attitudes: "Parents are afraid to come to school—too intimidated. They don't speak the language. It's too easy for teachers to say, 'They [parents] don't care because they don't come to school.'"

Lewis and Henderson (1997) related this communication between parents and teachers at one urban school:

> [T]he staff asked parents why they were not coming to school and why so many left the school. "Because we feel that you only have bad things to say about our kids," they said. "You always talk about what we need to do different for our kids to be successful in school. You act all-knowing. You talk down to us and don't take time to listen." (27)

These responses from both groups help explain the challenge of changing the culture of interactions between parents and teachers. The negative attitudes among teachers create a greater divide between the groups and discourage each from crossing the line to develop a more collaborative relationship.

Lois Weiner (2001) added another explanation why parents are unlikely to become involved in school issues when she stated that urban public schools are like fortresses. For instance, every door into the school is locked except the one furthest from the parking area; parents aren't able to speak to the teacher because the teacher isn't near a telephone and isn't readily available; and parents do not have time to call teachers because of their work schedules.

Colette, from Philadelphia, speaks of the challenge of reaching the caregivers of her high school students: "I have little parental involvement. When I call home, the phones are blocked, so you can't get through. The kids probably do it—they block the school's phone number. When I send interim notes home, I never get a call from parents. There's really very little parental involvement in this school. We had a shooting in October. You would think the school would have been swarming with parents—it wasn't!"

Kathleen, from a Chicago elementary school, speaks of the challenges she faces with parental assistance: "The majority of parents are involved, but some can't help with homework due to language problems. Last year we had open house and only three parents showed up among all of the six classes in third grade. This year only five parents showed up."

Despite these frustrations, teachers must initiate communication with caregivers to improve relationships between home and school. If your initial call is merely to introduce yourself or to find out more about their child, caregivers may not understand the reason for your call. These positive interventions may be confusing to parents, so they react negatively at first. Be patient in explaining the positive intent of your call and your interest in future contacts. Caregivers should be partners because they know more about their children than teachers can possibly learn in any one year. Adrienne, from Los Angeles, explains the role of teachers in reaching out to caregivers: "If we want parents as partners, then we need to treat them as partners. Maybe the hours aren't conducive. We've been doing the same open houses for years now. When are we going to get it?"

Positive Parental and Caregiver Interactions

Positive interactions do occur, however, in urban schools if specific actions are devised by classroom teachers to initiate collaborative activities. Tim, from Minneapolis, states that increased family involvement is one of the school's improvement goals for the year. He provides a view of urban parents: "A small body count [at open house] doesn't necessarily mean you don't have parental support. They may not show up for conferences or open house; but when you call them at home, most are always happy to hear from you!"

Because Anita grew up in the Philadelphia neighborhood where she teaches, she is quite comfortable speaking to parents and believes strongly that parents want to know how their children are doing in school. "I've had a lot of contact as the years have gone on because now I'm having children of mothers and fathers I taught. I usually try to contact parents immediately if there is an issue or a problem so parents know. You know that's all they want—to know what's going on— and *not at the last minute.* I've always had a positive relationship with parents." Anita explains that frequently she interacts with her students' siblings as much as with their parents. Siblings often care for their younger brothers and sisters and inquire about how they can help Anita.

Pete describes the families and lives of students outside of school: "I've found that for the most part, these parents are not very well educated. This creates a tremendous divide between parents and their children. We have parents who drive their sons and daughters to school; watch them go in the front door; only to discover a month later that their child was absent every day. We have lots of Asian parents coming to school in tears saying, 'Please help us; help us get to court to send our child someplace safe because they won't listen to us— they're out of control.'" You can understand from hearing Pete's comments how crucial it is for teachers to reach out to caregivers.

Adrienne suggests a more involved role for schools: "We used to do things like literacy nights for parents. School became a community center." Diane, from San Francisco, describes similar positive roles: "Family math nights and literacy nights have been effective. We have given things to parents to take home to help them understand what we do here." Jackie, who taught in New York City and now teaches in Philadelphia, adds some valuable ideas for meeting with parents: "If we're asking parents to be a part of who we are, then we also have to go out into the community. For instance, we just started doing home visits for all new kindergarten students each summer. We visit the homes and read the children a book the teachers wrote that has pictures of our school. We show them pictures of the outside of the school, their classroom, and the lunchroom. We're doing this in hopes of building a real strong home/community, school relationship."

Weiner (2001) cautioned that forcing parents to meet on the teachers' turf at school may not be the best way to encourage parents to help with the schooling process. She suggested that teachers invite parents to meet them at community centers, churches, local libraries, or even restaurants. Churches are a focal point of community relations for many ethnicities. Anita, from Philadelphia, explains how she frequently meets parents or just her students at church on Sundays.

Lewis and Henderson (1997) offered other suggestions for improving relationships with caregivers:

- Recognize and invite contributions local families can provide through their traditions, culture, language, and knowledge of their community.

239

- Address the effects of race, class, and cultural differences on relationships between schools and parents.
- Adopt a specific outcome and timeline for strategies to improve parental relationships.
- Consider student academic success to be everyone's responsibility—no blame, no excuses.
- Involve families in establishing policies and focusing on school priorities. (39)

Lewis and Henderson (1997) provide additional critical information: "In many low-income schools . . . the most formidable barrier to parent involvement is racism" (22). The attitudes and beliefs of urban teachers must be explicitly addressed by faculty to insure that educators at all levels develop appropriate and healthy expectations for all children and adolescents.

Several strategies exist for implementing healthy and valuable parent-teacher and caregiver-teacher relationships:

- Establish early and frequent contacts with parents.
- Explain your expectations for students' behaviors and responsibilities for completing assignments to parents.
- Develop a flyer for parents that explains classroom policies and expectations.
- Identify and use appropriate interpreters to assist in speaking to caregivers who are second language learners.
- Develop and pass out a handbook for students that is shared with parents.
- Establish and publish a homework policy based on parental input and review.
- Publicize your role for helping students during the year and parental responsibilities for helping their own children grow.
- Initiate social gatherings among other grade level teachers and invite parents to participate.

- Send frequent positive notes to caregivers about their children.
- Establish conference times that are flexible enough to meet the needs of all caregivers.
- Invite immigrant parents to bring other family members to interpret for them during conferences.
- Encourage children and parents to share personal stories, histories, and cultural norms with the rest of the class.
- Invite caregivers to volunteer, share skills, knowledge, and expertise when needed (some of these items are summarized from Kronowitz 1999).

These are a few strategies for improving relationships with parents and caregivers and further insuring their assistance and support for what you do with their children. I suggest that you and fellow faculty brainstorm other strategies for getting parents more involved in the lives of their children. High school and middle school teachers will need to be even more proactive because the research clearly demonstrates less parental involvement as students progress in school (Lewis and Henderson 1997).

Teachers must never underestimate the impact of parental involvement on the improvement of student performance and effort. Lewis and Henderson (1997) explained this quite clearly in these statements: "[T]he income and social status of a child do not determine how well he or she will do in school, or in life. More important is whether family members create a home environment for learning, express high expectations for their children and become involved in their children's education" (47). Another critical piece of information is that Henderson and Berla (1994) discovered that students who are performing most poorly make the greatest gains when parents become more involved in their school lives. Furthermore, efforts by teachers have the greatest influence on the degree of parental involvement and cooperation (Epstein 1992). Don't wait for caregivers to contact you. Make caregiver contacts an essential component of your weekly teaching processes.

Gaining Assistance from Administrators

Administrators have many responsibilities within schools. Principals are your first line of defense in many situations that arise each week of teaching. Often you will need the professional and personal support of your principal. It is imperative that you establish a comfortable working relationship with the principal. You should develop an open communication pattern with him or her that is based on mutual respect, honesty, and professionalism. Susan, an experienced urban teacher from San Francisco, indicates that, "All people need is support and respect, and our school will work! Administrators should help rebuild morale and give us our freedom to teach."

Relationships between teachers and principals are obviously not always positive as these urban teachers profess. Kathleen shares the frustration she experiences in communicating with her principal: "Much of what our administrator gives us is negative. She tells us to always say something positive to parents; but we never hear anything positive from her. She blames the teachers for student problems saying, 'You're not doing your jobs.' Her vision is for all students to make a year's gain [on test scores]; but she never tells us how to do that—never."

Adrienne, from a Los Angeles high school, has these thoughts about administrators: "I have worked with the most incompetent administrators in Los Angeles. A good administrator says, 'How can I help you do your job better?'; but I've never heard it."

Administrators can be highly effective, and when they are, their actions have a positive impact on faculty and students. Tim spoke of his middle school principal in Minneapolis: "The principal has been fairly supportive. She's always talking about what's best for the kids—she's very passionate about those things." After over twenty years of teaching in several Philadelphia public high schools and middle schools, Pete summarizes how he interacts with administrators: "You have to walk a fine line between being a pain in the ass and being a buffer between issues." Pete has accomplished a great deal for students in designing a program for high school second language learners. In that process, he gained support and materials from administrators to accomplish his outcomes. He has succeeded, and with experience re-alizes his responsibility to students often requires cajoling administra-tors to get students' needs met.

The relationship between teachers and principals can be quite complex. As Pete describes, both you and the principal must give and take when the time is appropriate. Principals are more likely to be supportive if they have a clear understanding of your plans and needs prior to any actions that occur. You should establish frequent meet-ings with the principal, both formal and informal, to maintain the re-quired communications to get your needs met. Most principals do not enjoy surprises—especially when they involve parental interactions. It is wise and professional to keep the principal informed about chal-lenging and controversial events as soon as possible.

You are primarily responsible for handling controversial issues be-tween you and your students. When reason is lost and your patience is lost with it, the principal should be called on to provide some pro-fessional advice and assistance. Don't confuse a principal's role with your role to handle student disruptions, as I mentioned in Chapter 4. Principal intervention is needed on occasion. When that time comes, be clear about what you expect the principal to do to assist you. For instance, I once had reached the end of my rope with a highly un-cooperative and aggressive sixth grader. After two periods of attempt-ing to gain his cooperation, I was on the edge of complete irritation. I convinced the student to walk to the office with me where I informed the principal that in order for me to continue to teach this student and allow him into my classroom, I needed a conference with his parents and him. I didn't want the principal to intercede except to understand my level of frustration and helplessness at that point. The principal knew me well enough to understand my level of concern. He called the parents for me and arranged a conference. His actions were more than I expected, due in part, I'm sure, to our frequent communication during the year.

Weiner (1999) provided an explanation for why principals in urban schools are often unsupportive. She explained that the huge bureaucracy associated with urban schools lends itself to a top-down

243

management system that is frequently rigid in its policies to insure what appears to be an equitable system of policies, procedures, punishments, and rewards. This "administrator talk" does nothing to help you in many circumstances, leading to disagreements with principals once you clearly understand what students need and how the administrative system often works. Rules and policies established by distant school boards and central office personnel are often evenly applied to schools that have entirely different student populations. Teachers are caught in the middle of an unwieldy system.

Effective curricula, instructional activities, collaborative teaching strategies, and special programs for students are often jettisoned in the name of uniformity and due to differences of opinion with each change in administration, on what is best for students. What's a teacher to do? Weiner (1999) provides some advice for the struggling new teacher:

> [A]dministrators are under great pressure to attend to superficial details that make the school seem to operate efficiently. The school bureaucracy's greatest concern is the appearance of sound educational practice, not the reality. If you're using a brilliant teaching strategy, no one will see or ask, so your effort won't be acknowledged. However, if you knowingly or unknowingly violate a regulation and the violation is noticed, the issue will receive immediate attention. Because your adhesion to school rules will receive more attention from most school administrators than your teaching ability, you need to rely on your colleagues for help in your classroom. (44–45)

You can see how important your teaching partners are in providing assistance when needed and acknowledging your strengths. Urban teachers ultimately realize that administrators have differing personalities, levels of professionalism, and degrees of support for the faculty within the school. Effective educators study each new administrator that enters the building and develop interaction strategies that support what they need to do to provide a meaningful learning environment for their students. Being proactive for your students often requires administrative support. When the support is unlikely to appear, brave teachers use a bit of creative insubordination to get their needs met

244

despite the minor risks involved in acting without administrative support or knowledge. Wise urban educators know when to take a stand with administrators and use their assertiveness appropriately to garner resources for their students. They must also realize when it is imperative to back down and wait to try to get needs met later.

Gaining Additional Assistance

Teaching should never be an isolated practice—especially in urban schools. Developing meaningful relationships with fellow teachers, administrators, and parents and caregivers is crucial to insure a satisfying professional life. There are others, however, who you will need.

Teachers obviously cannot resolve every problem they encounter. You will frequently encounter circumstances that require the assistance of other professionals. School counselors, psychologists, reading and speech specialists, and special needs teachers are invaluable resources when you encounter students who need their services. Novice teachers frequently believe that they can solve all the problems that arise with students. Nothing could be further from fact! I urge you to be cognizant of the emotional, physical, social, and cognitive situations that your students experience that require professional expertise that you do not possess. Parents and caregivers expect you to act in a professional manner to help their children get the services they need, even if you believe that you are qualified to respond to students' emergencies.

You may be the first adult to recognize a serious problem exists for a child or adolescent. Begin asking questions about service providers prior to your first day with students. Ask fellow teachers about how to refer students to counselors, the school nurse, or the instructional support team for possible resource room assistance. Policies exist in each state for how to refer students for special services. Learn about the policies early in the academic year so that you will be prepared to help students as part of early intervention techniques. Seek the assistance of psychologists immediately when dangerous situations arise with students.

The message I hope you will understand is that you don't have to solve problems alone, and you shouldn't. Public schools historically have been expected to solve the social, emotional, and economic problems that exist for American children. Your influence on the lives of students does have a limit, as much as you might want to believe that you will be able to resolve their personal problems. Being an advocate for students is expected; however, that role doesn't mean taking on responsibilities that are beyond your capabilities, knowledge base, or training.

Securing Instructional Materials

Urban teachers are the first to admit that they lack the instructional materials that students need to learn at an appropriate developmental level. Urban school budgets rarely provide enough, if any, money for teachers to purchase art supplies, glue, pencils, paper, construction paper, tape, and many of the other supplies required to maintain a creative classroom. The job is left up to you to find the resources needed to expand on your teaching. Urban teachers often speak of the hundreds of dollars of their own money they spend to purchase supplies and instructional materials.

Despite this discouraging message, supplies are available from many resources. Kronowitz (1999) suggested several possible sources for obtaining materials:

- district media or resource centers
- local state educational agencies that may stock supplies
- public and university libraries
- local city museums
- seasoned colleagues who may have a stockpile of resources
- your own recyclable items from home such as coffee cans, milk and juice containers, cardboard boxes, margarine containers, styrofoam, clothing scraps, and other items you might normally discard

- caregivers to whom you may send a note home to request resources
- old textbooks and library books from homes and other schools about to discard them
- local businesses that are willing to donate materials or supplies (adapted from pages 31–45).

In her book, *Your First Year of Teaching and Beyond*, Ellen Kronowitz (1999) provided a list of several organizations that provide free instructional materials that you may want to access before spending all of your additional monies on supplies.

It is certainly no secret that humans are social beings. School is the place where thousands of social and emotional interactions occur each week for every teacher. Gaining support from others is a critical strategy for insuring your survival and success as an urban teacher. Use every resource available from people to materials to maintain a comfortable and healthy professional demeanor.

References

EPSTEIN, J. L. 1992. "School and Family Partnerships," Report No. 6. Baltimore, MD: Johns Hopkins University, Center on Families, Communities, Schools, and Children's Learning.

HENDERSON, A. T., AND N. BERLA. 1994. *A New Generation of Evidence: The Family Is Critical to Student Achievement.* Washington, DC: Center for Law and Education.

HOOVER-DEMPSEY, K., AND H. M. SANDLER. 1997. "Why Do Parents Become Involved in Their Children's Education?" *Review of Educational Research*, 67, no. 1: 3–42.

KRONOWITZ, E. L. 1999. *Your First Year of Teaching and Beyond.* 3rd ed. New York: Longman.

LEWIS, A. C., AND A. T. HENDERSON. 1997. *Urgent Message: Families Crucial to School Reform.* Washington, DC: Center for Law and Education.

LORTIE, D. 1975. *School Teacher: A Sociological Study*. Chicago: University of Chicago Press.

ODELL, S. J. 1986. "Induction Support of New Teachers: A Functional Approach." *Journal of Teacher Education* 37, no. 1: 26–29.

REYES, P., J. D. SCRIBNER, AND A. P. SCRIBNER, EDS. 1999. *Lessons from High-Performing Hispanic Schools: Creating Learning Communities*. New York: Teachers College Press.

WEINER, L. 1999. *Urban Teaching: The Essentials*. New York: Teachers College Press.

———. "Improving Relationships with Parents in Urban School Districts." Speech presented at the 100 Years of Urban Education Symposium, 17–19 May, at Buffalo State University, Buffalo, New York.

Is This the Right Teaching Job for You?

In an urban setting, you mean something more than what you mean to kids in a suburban school.

JEFF, WICHITA HIGH SCHOOL TEACHER

Don't judge the rest of your career on your first year.

KATHLEEN, CHICAGO ELEMENTARY TEACHER

This job has taught me a lot about myself, and the lessons have been invaluable.

SHANIKA, PHILADELPHIA MIDDLE SCHOOL TEACHER

I have discovered through hours of interviews with thirteen urban teachers that they are dedicated professionals who possess great pride in their responsibilities as teachers in America's city schools. Jeff, who teaches in a Wichita high school, shares his views after three years of experience in this urban school: "I don't think I'd want to teach in any other type of school. The successes are exciting." Kathleen speaks of her pride in teaching third grade in Chicago with this story: "My daughter grew up in the suburbs. When she was school age, I brought her to my school and she said, 'Look at this playground, it's not very nice!' I told her that what I do on the inside of the building is just as good as what goes on in her school."

249

As I listen to people at workshops, I find that most teachers who practice their profession outside of city schools are highly ignorant of the real stories that unfold in urban classrooms every day. Other adults who are not educators are even more unaware of the exciting events occurring in urban classrooms. It's seems easy for the general public to dismiss urban schools; but in so doing, they devalue the lives of thousands of children and adolescents whose hopes are as genuine and significant as their own children's and grandchildren's.

Urban schools are safe havens for youth where opportunities for reaching their dreams can be discovered and developed for future success. Bartoli (2001) reminded us that not so long ago most European Americans' ancestors were clawing their way out of low-income situations and urban neighborhoods to obtain what they believed to be a more satisfying life. It's no secret and most Americans believe that receiving an appropriate and equitable education is the most powerful means for gaining greater opportunities, better health, and a more satisfying life. Almost all adults realize this, even if they weren't able to receive a quality education themselves.

There are many reasons to teach in urban schools; perhaps many more than to teach in the suburbs. One of the primary reasons that people enter the teaching profession is to make a difference in the lives of children and adolescents. As Jeff clearly states in the opening line of this chapter, he believes that urban teachers have a much greater impact on students' lives than those who teach in other settings. It is difficult to ascertain whether Jeff's contention is actually founded. It is clear to me though, having been involved in teaching in rural, suburban, and city environments, that urban teachers experience a much higher degree of challenge. Teachers who choose to teach in urban settings may come away with greater rewards for their successes with students, perhaps because of the depth of the challenges they face.

Peter Jennings (2001) recently reported that the New York City public school system hired eight thousand teachers for the fall of 2001 to meet their classroom demands. Ladson-Billings (2001) reported that the Chicago public schools hire between a thousand and two thousand new teachers every year, and the Los Angeles School District hires

250

approximately five thousand new teachers a year. Who will fill these teaching positions? Many teachers will refuse to enter urban schools despite the fact that in some suburban school districts it is not uncommon to have a thousand applicants for every one teaching position that opens each year. I suspect many preservice teachers avoid applying for urban teaching positions due to unfounded fears about children, adolescents, and the families that live in cities. Prospective urban teachers must determine whether they have the characteristics it takes to enter urban schools and succeed there. These suggestions from urban teachers of all ages and years of experience will hopefully alleviate some of the ignorance and fear associated with becoming a professional educator in an urban school.

Advice from Effective Urban Teachers

Fears associated with teaching are often based on the premise that one might make some mistakes with the lives of children. Novice teachers, no matter how effective, make many mistakes; just as do new doctors, plumbers, attorneys, and taxi cab drivers. Beyond the first-year teacher mistakes, however, is a noble and exciting profession with daily rewards that last a lifetime. As you read these explanations of characteristics for urban teachers, think about how your personality and integrity match the qualities of these successful urban teachers.

Diane, who has taught in San Francisco urban schools for over thirty years, suggests the following required characteristics for an urban teacher: "[C]aring, commitment, resiliency, and the ability to find humor in a situation." Pete, from Philadelphia, agrees with Diane about having a sense of humor and adds, "You must have a genuine concern for students; and, you can't be afraid. Kids pick up on your fear." Anita has been in the same Philadelphia middle school for over twenty-five years. Here are her astute words of advice about being assertive: "You've got to be tough; not wishy-washy. If you have that fear, you can't do it. These kids will challenge you. They don't have a problem saying what they think. You have to be firm. You have to be strong because you'll get all kinds of challenges from parents and kids."

Polly, from a Chicago high school, describes what her colleagues are like: "These teachers are very self-confident. They consider teaching here a challenge. They like teenagers and they like this type of kid." It's clear that these teachers recommend you leave your fears behind when you enter the classroom. Like sharks, children sense your fear and feed off of your own lack of self-confidence as you stand in front of them. Fear can be paralyzing and prevent you from succeeding in reaching the lives of children and adolescents.

Colette believes that teachers must possess a desire and energy for personal and professional growth: "You must have a commitment to excellence; the desire to keep learning and doing well while always searching for better ways to do things. You must build partnerships with other teachers, collaborating with them on what does and doesn't work while you continue sharing ideas."

Shanika speaks of the value of professional knowledge, pedagogy, creativity, and persistence: "If people want to teach in urban schools, they really need to know how to be prepared for the worst-case scenarios. They need to know how to teach special education students when they don't have any support; that they won't have any prep time; and, that they may not have any textbooks. Basically, new teachers must learn how to be creative with very little materials." Anita speaks about curriculum and how teachers must be able to adjust to students' needs: "You must know how to handle social studies and science when you're going to get a seventh-grade book and kids are reading on the second grade level."

Jackie, who taught in Harlem in New York City, speaks of the importance of possessing creative problem-solving skills: "I think urban teachers need to think fast and make their own decisions—not say, 'Let me see what the book says about that.' If you're the kind of person who needs to rely on all the prepackaged programs, it's going to be very hard for you."

City children and adolescents need leaders, and that's what urban teachers must be for their students. Urban teachers must also be caregivers, role models, nagging adults, flexible problem solvers, creative thinkers, independent actors, and possess and demonstrate high-efficacy personalities. The persistence needed to be an influential teacher in the lives of urban children and adolescents may rival that previously required for any of your life experiences and successes. You have to bring your best game to the ballpark every day to have an impact on the lives of city students.

The following recommendations from the teachers may help you to determine whether urban schools are the right place for you to seek professional employment. Colette mentions something that several other teachers suggested: "Spend some time in an urban setting before you actually make a commitment to do it. People have these idealistic views that they're going to change the world. It doesn't work like that! Check it out first. Do some substituting." Tim states a problem that many teachers experience quite succinctly: "So many teachers who don't understand these families come in from white, middle-class neighborhoods and try to teach here. You must visit these schools; hang out here for a few days. You're not going to get it by hearing about it from a professor." Lisa, from Los Angeles, adds, "I just don't want people to think that the progressive ideas they learn are what really helps them. Often in teacher training there's too much of a focus on things to do instead of learning how to deal with people and the kids."

Kathleen explains the value of persistence: "There's no magic involved in teaching here [Chicago]. It takes a lot of hard work. It takes three years to build a program, and each year you must focus on one thing. You can't do it all in one year." Jackie adds, "If you can stick it out for the first five years, your whole life changes and your perspective on teaching, especially if you're there for your students." Isn't that the reason we choose to teach: to be there for our students?

Several of the teachers I spoke to mentioned that when they started their jobs, they believed they were destined to save the lives of urban students. Jeff provides these cautions to that erroneous belief: "You come out of college being upset you couldn't save all two hundred students you have. Understand that you're going to choke. You've got to expect you're not going to get to every student." Adrienne from Los Angeles suggests that teachers, "Find a cadre of colleagues who are upbeat and want to continue learning so they challenge you. Find teachers who will question you about what you do."

You may discover after reading these comments that you already possess these personal and professional attributes. If that's the case, then perhaps you're ready to apply for an urban teaching position. Urban schools need quality teachers: people who possess a broad range of personal qualities and professional attributes that combine in a way to have an immediate impact on the lives of urban children and adolescents.

I have provided a list of questions in the next section for you to respond to if you have a genuine interest in becoming a successful urban teacher. I suggest that after you respond to these questions, you reflect on your belief systems and personality before you determine your possible effectiveness as a future urban teacher. I also suggest that you visit urban classrooms and begin asking questions of effective teachers to discover how they establish a successful learning environment.

Assessing Personal Qualities

Prior to walking into an urban classroom, consider how you respond to the following questions:

1. Identify your personal, family, and neighborhood cultural beliefs (e.g., How do friends interact with one another? How do you spend money? How hard should people work and for what purposes? How have European values affected your personality and preferences?).
2. What injustices exist for cultural groups in America?
3. What does it mean to be biased, and what evidence of bias have you heard of or seen?
4. How willing are you to accept that your own cultural experiences and beliefs may be inappropriate for many Americans?
5. What influences affect how you act, perceive others, view families, or perceive your role in American society?
6. How have other cultural and ethnic groups in America

been afforded fewer opportunities than you and your family members?

7. Which cultural characteristics from other groups do you value more than your own?
8. How interested are you in becoming acquainted with the lives of your students and their families?
9. How comfortable are you with the idea of visiting the homes of urban children and adolescents that you will teach?
10. What are some of the ways that people learn that are different from how you learn?
11. How do ethnicity and culture influence learning preferences of children?
12. What does it mean to be assertive? How important is assertiveness to your culture and to other cultures?
13. What role should the culture of your students play in lesson planning, instructional design, curricular content, and assessment practices?
14. How creative are you when you develop lesson plans, present lessons, or design assessment activities?
15. How comfortable are you with changing lesson plans or teaching strategies in the middle of a lesson to meet the needs of your students?
16. Are you willing to establish your own high expectations for student performance and content learning that meets their needs instead of the unrealistic expectations of a large state bureaucracy?
17. Are you able to persist in establishing relationships with co-workers?
18. How persistent are you in helping students despite their resistance to your efforts?
19. Do you enjoy challenges on a daily basis?
20. Is problem solving enjoyable to you?
21. How good are you at negotiating and resolving conflicts?
22. Can you handle uncertainty and unpredictable situations?

23. What do you know about the learning needs of students with cultural backgrounds that differ from your own?
24. What is the role of teachers in insuring student academic success?
25. How much time are you willing to put into becoming a successful teacher?

Although there will be many more questions you will need to answer, this list is a reasonable beginning to help you identify the characteristics required of an effective urban educator. I don't recommend responding to these questions in one sitting. Take a look at the list over time and discuss the questions with other prospective teachers and current teachers as your philosophy unfolds. Many of your beliefs on these issues will change over time, perhaps due to direct experiences. This is a good sign that you are growing as a professional. May you choose this profession for the right reasons: helping all children see their hopes and dreams become a reality just as yours have!

References

BARTOLI, J. S. 2001. *Celebrating City Teachers: Making a Difference in City Schools*. Portsmouth, NH: Heinemann.

JENNINGS, P. 2001. *National Broadcasting Company 6:00 p.m. Nightly News*. 12 July.

LADSON-BILLINGS, G. 2001. *Crossing Over to Canaan: The Journey of New Teachers in Diverse Classrooms*. San Francisco: Jossey-Bass.

Index

A

administrators: support for teachers, 53, 242–245

Advice from Effective Urban Teachers, 251–254

African American students: instructional communication needs, 166–170; instructional needs, 147–153, 169–170; topic-associative speaking, 179; topic-chaining writing, 179; topic-centered instruction, 179; understanding ethnicity, 25–30; verbal interaction styles, 73–74

Assessing Personal Qualities for becoming an urban teacher, 254–256

assessment: alternatives, 206–207; Components of, 184–185; description of, 185–186, 189; Genuine Assessment Activities, 206–207; questions pertaining to, 186–188; purposes of, 185; student involvement with, 209–211. *See also* Assessing students

Assessing students: Content-Area Knowledge, 199–200; English Language Proficiency, 197–198; IDEA Oral Language Proficiency Test (IPT); Language Assessment Scale, 198; Mathematics Knowledge, 198–199; Reading Ability, 190–195; Writing Skills, 196–197

B

Baseline Data: how to gather, 145–146, 189–200

behavioral expectations: establishment of, 77–80. *See also* classroom rules

benchmarks, 216

Bilingual education, 176–178

Black English Vernacular: acceptance of, 168; description of, 167–168

blame cycle: blaming students, 136; stages of, 36

C

call-response, 73-74, 170. *See* Verbal Interaction Styles and African American students

caring teachers, 67–70

Cary, Stephen, 173, 176, 177, 198

class meetings, 81